ANTICHRIST

THE FULFILLMENT OF GLOBALIZATION

The Ancient Church and the End of History

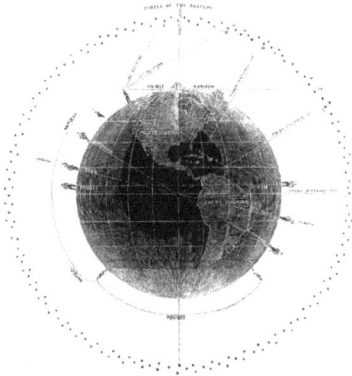

ANTICHRIST

The Fulfillment Of Globalization

The Ancient Church and the End of History

BY G. M. DAVIS, PHD

Uncut Mountain Press

ANTICHRIST: THE FULFILLMENT OF GLOBALIZATION

The Ancient Church and the End of History

uncutmountainpress.com

Scriptural quotations are primarily taken from the New King James Version. The translator has emended some quotations to better reflect the original Greek text.

Library of Congress Cataloging-in-Publication Data
G. M. Davis, PhD, 1975 -

Antichrist: The Fulfillment of Globalization - The Ancient Church and the End of History by G. M. Davis, PhD – 1st ed.
Edited by: Albion Winslow Land

ISBN: 978-1-63941-004-0

Subject entries:
I. Christianity - Eastern Orthodox
II Christian History- Eastern Orthodox
III. Political Science

Dedication

To the memory of Tsar Paul I

Repose, O Lord, the soul of Thy murdered servant, Emperor Paul I, and by his prayers grant us – in these evil and fearful days – wisdom in affairs, meekness in suffering, and Thy salvation for our souls.

Look down, O Lord, upon Thy faithful intercessor for the orphaned, the handicapped, and the destitute, – Emperor Paul, – and by his holy prayers grant, O Lord, quick and true help to those who ask Thee, our God, through him. Amen[1].

And to the memory of my father.

---

[1] "Prayer for the Repose of Tsar-Martyr Paul I." Accessed September 13, 2019. http://www.holy-transfiguration.org/library_en/royal_paul.html.

TABLE OF CONTENTS

Part III: The Age of Confusion

PREFACE

Politics and the study of it once constituted a search for truth in a way that our age no longer understands. Political science, properly conceived, is the study of order and, ultimately, what constitutes a right or good order for society. Bound up with political order is the question of truth and how truth may be represented in history. The pre-Christian Greek philosophers were trying, with the tools available to them, to find the truth and apply it to their world. They regarded the *polis* of their day, the city-state, as the human soul writ large. Just and healthy souls made for a just and healthy *polis* and vice versa. But what is justice? What is the "good" for the individual and for the community? How is the soul properly to relate to larger reality and how may that relationship be articulated in society? Such are the questions that political science was conceived to answer.

The events of history constitute the data of political science. It is natural to ask where we are and how we got here. When we examine the history of our own modern Western Civilization, we are presented with two remarkable, apparently contradictory phenomena: astonishing material and technical advances alongside equally astonishing political disasters, with no real precedent in history. For much of the modern age, Western Civilization has strained its remarkable material resources in efforts seemingly directed at self-annihilation. The World Wars and the rise of totalitarianism in the forms of Communism and National Socialism arguably constitute the most intensively destructive socio-political phenomena ever witnessed on the historical landscape. The obvious question is: what happened? How could the world's leading progressive, enlightened civilization having achieved so much in the material realm, go so terribly wrong? Are we in the twenty-first century safe from similar political calamities? Are Western material progress and political disaster somehow related? If so, how?

In trying to diagnose what happened for anti-Christian movements to have developed in the self-consciously Christian West to such an extent that they nearly destroyed the civilization itself, it becomes apparent that the origins of the disease are not a recent development. While it is easy to imagine that this or that bygone era was a golden one, closer examination belies any such fantasy. Some commentators point to early America as a model society, the "shining city on a hill" to echo a popular sentiment; others venerate the pre-World War I *pax Britannica* or pre-French Revolutionary Western Europe during the Age of Reason; some regard the High Middle Ages before Western Christendom was rent by the Reformation as the ideal. Yet even the great Latin scholar, Thomas Aquinas, as early as the thirteenth century, in his titanic *Summa Theologica*, was involved in a basically conservative enterprise, an attempt to regain a lost harmony, to get back to a more coherent world that had somehow been lost. What is it that has transpired, such that the best and brightest minds of Western Civilization have so consistently failed, over the course of nearly a thousand years, to arrest the progressive disintegration of their culture and society? While many capable and well-intended people have endeavored through the generations to "stand athwart history yelling, Stop. . .",[1] history, it is by now plainly obvious, has kept moving.

---

1   Buckley Jr., William F. *"Our Mission Statement"*, National Review. November 19, 1955. https://www.nationalreview.com/1955/11/our-mission-statement-william-f-buckley-jr/. Accessed September 12, 2019.

But the question arises: moving to and from where exactly? What is this movement of history that some perceive as progress and others as decline? Can a civilization advance and decline at the same time? Will there be an end to the ongoing "march" of history? If so, what does that end look like? In particular, what is the significance of the tremendous political and cultural changes occurring in our own age of "globalization"? These are the questions that weigh on the thoughtful in our time, and they are the questions that this book seeks to answer. To answer them we must penetrate to the very center of the meaning of history and of human existence.

THE NATIONS ARE MAD

JER. 51:7

Introduction
The Spirit of the Times

A new partnership of nations has begun, and we stand today at a unique and extraordinary moment.... Out of these troubled times... a new world order can emerge: a new era—freer from the threat of terror, stronger in the pursuit of justice and more secure in the quest for peace. An era in which the nations of the world, east and west, north and south, can prosper and live in harmony.

US President George H. W. Bush
Sept 11, 1990, Washington, DC[1]

Today we must embrace the inexorable logic of globalization—that everything, from the strength of our economy to the safety of our cities, to the health of our people, depends on events not only within our borders, but half a world away. We must see the opportunities and the dangers of the interdependent world in which we are clearly fated to live.

US President William J. Clinton
February 26, 1999, San Francisco, CA[2]

---

1   https://www.washingtonpost.com/archive/politics/1990/09/12/bush-out-of-these-troubled-times-a-new-world-order/b93b5cf1-e389-4e6a-84b0-85f71bf4c946/?noredirect=on. Accessed September 13, 2019.

2   https://www.mtholyoke.edu/acad/intrel/clintfps.htm. Accessed September 13, 2019.

As some want, we could close our markets—for capital, financial services, trade and for labour—and therefore reduce the risks of globalization. But that would reduce global growth, deny us the benefits of global trade and confine millions to global poverty. Or we could view the threats and challenges we face today as the difficult birth-pangs of a new global order—and our task now as nothing less than making the transition through a new internationalism to the benefits of an expanding global society—not muddling through as pessimists but making the necessary adjustment to a better future and setting the new rules for this new global order.

UK Prime Minister Gordon Brown
January 26, 2009, London, England[3]

It has been said that arguing against globalization is like arguing against the laws of gravity.

UN Secretary-General Kofi Annan
September 3, 2000, New York City[4]

The foregoing are a small sample of numerous statements made by world leaders affirming the most significant historical phenomenon of our time: globalization. From economics to politics to religion, the world's inhabitants increasingly identify and function as members of a single global system with a degree of integration that far exceeds that of any great civilization of the past. Globalization's worldwide reach marks it as one of the most significant developments in human history. Among both its proponents and detractors, there is widespread agreement that,

3   https://www.theguardian.com/politics/2009/jan/26/gordon-brown-economic-policy. Accessed September 13, 2019.
4   https://www.nytimes.com/2000/09/03/world/globalization-tops-3-day-un-agenda-for-world-leaders.html. Accessed September 13, 2019.

whether globalization bodes good or ill, it is unquestionably of tremendous significance.

While globalization is often presented in terms of economic integration and harmonization across international boundaries ("globalization is the process by which markets integrate world-wide"[5]), political forces are also operating to unify it has become evident that social and political forces are also operating to unify hitherto disparate peoples and polities in unprecedented ways. While major cultures have often cross-fertilized one another, it is now possible to discern a global process of "cultural synchroni-zation"[6] in which different cultural systems are being subsumed into a unified culture of global reach. As much as any economic factor, this emerging global monoculture is drawing the peoples of the world into a common consciousness at the social, political, and even religious levels. To treat globalization as merely an economic phenomenon without addressing its social, political, and religious ramifications would be empirically inadequate and theoretically remiss.

At the political level, globalization directly implies the ongoing centralization of power. While some political entities, such as some nation states, undergo disintegration into smaller units, the overwhelming tendency at the political level is the supra-national aggregation of power. The nations of the world are increasingly bound by institutions, treaties, and cultural systems that exceed and transcend the control of their national govern-ments. Nations are no longer independent rational actors in an anarchic environment whose freedom of action is limited only by the raw power they wield. Now nation states, both large and small, find themselves pulled along by global issues as varied as the openness of trade to humanitarian crises to the

---

5   Michael Spence. *"Michael Spence Quotes"* https://www.brainyquote.com/quotes/quotes/m/michaelspe718172.html. Accessed September 18, 2017.

6   Hamelink cited in John Tomlinson, *"Cultural Imperialism"* in The Globalization Reader, Fourth Edition (Chichester, Wiley-Blackwell, 2012), 348.

coordination of fiscal and monetary policy to tackling our age's greatest bogeyman, climate change.

While many lament the Western-driven "cultural imperialism" that threatens to overwhelm regional cultural differences, a consensus is emerging among the world's leaders that globalization is both beneficial and, above all, irresistible. Certainly, a case can readily be made for the latter. At the technological level alone, the transformation has been stupendous: instantaneous communications are now possible over distances that in ages past would have taken months. The "abolition of distance" that is at the heart of globalization shows no signs of stopping and, furthermore, is proving highly democratic in many ways: from air travel to the internet, huge numbers of ordinary people are now active participants in the "global village." Smaller and fewer are the areas of the globe—and the aspects of individual lives—that remain untouched by globalization's apparently relentless advance. More than anything else, ours is the age of globalization; it is the spirit of our time.

But what does globalization ultimately amount to? What is the significance of an increasingly globalized world in which traditional national and cultural boundaries are being erased? Should globalization someday advance to the point of uniting the world, what would be the ultimate significance of the resulting global civilization? The political philosopher Carl Schmitt, writing between the World Wars, foresaw the ultimate question that globalization would present:

> The acute question to pose is upon whom will fall the frightening power implied in a world-embracing economic and technical organization. This question can by no means be dismissed in the belief that everything would then function automatically, that things would administer themselves, and that a government by people over people would be superfluous because human beings would then

be absolutely free. For what would they be free? This can
be answered by optimistic or pessimistic conjectures, all
of which finwally lead to an anthropological profession
of faith.[7]

What does the ever-tightening centralization of global power
imply for human organization and individual freedom? Who or
what will emerge to lead mankind should globalization someday
achieve its goal of uniting the world? How would a unified world
civilization "arrive" onto the stage of history? While various
globetrotting statesmen, financiers, and celebrities, as well as a
host of institutions such as the United Nations, the World Trade
Organization, the International Monetary Fund, the World
Council of Churches, etc., all manifest aspects of globalization, none may be said to lead or represent the phenomenon
itself. For globalization to achieve concrete form, for it to attain
the unity that its logic by nature strives towards, a representative will have to emerge who will be able to unite the various
strands of the globalizing world, someone who will give flesh
and blood to globalization's hitherto disembodied spirit. As the
American Revolution found an effective leader in the person of
General George Washington and became the United States; as
Revolutionary France exalted the military genius Napoleon and
became the French Empire; as Weimar Germany installed the
leader of the National Socialist Workers' Party as chancellor
and president and became the Third Reich—so globalization
will someday need to find a figure who can personify it on the
stage of history or it will eventually cease as a meaningful movement. Should such a leader someday emerge, he would focus the
hearts and minds of the world to an unprecedented degree. And
this remarkable time toward which it seems the whole world is

---

7   Carl Schmitt, *The Concept of the Political*, Expanded Edition (Chicago, The
University of Chicago, 1996, 2007), 57-8.

straining, the fulfillment and apex of globalization and the true end of history, when all the world would be brought together under the guiding hand of a single man has, astonishingly, been precisely foreseen in the most ancient Christian prophecies. It is the reign of Antichrist.

It is in some "profession of faith" as mentioned by Schmitt above that the ultimate meaning of globalization is to be found. If history is defined by its temporality, then the study of history must by nature transcend the temporal and be grounded in the eternal. To study history without reference to eternity is to relegate historical science to a self-referential circle in which theories of history themselves become products of the very history they are trying to explain. Every historical situation invariably gives rise to its own theories about how history works, but every such theory is inherently limited by the very historical circumstances that gave rise to it. But if we must have a reference to eternity, whose version of eternity are we to accept? Which profession of faith is the right one? Contrary to much modern "scientific" thought, this is by no means an arbitrary question. If the science of history is not itself to be an arbitrary and ultimately meaningless undertaking, then our understanding of eternity, which grants perspective to history, must not be either.

The correct profession of faith—in this or any investigatory work—is that which lends the greatest insight into the matter at hand. For us, it is that of the Orthodox Christian Church, not merely because of the author's personal disposition, or because the Orthodox perspective is "interesting" in an academic sense, but because Orthodoxy (literally "correct worship") is capable of rendering theoretical clarity to our topic of study in a way that other perspectives cannot. "It is the (Orthodox) Church that introduces eternity into history and offers history the perspective of eternity."[8]

It is only the Church that can lend the necessary vantage point of eternity on the full sweep of human history, which otherwise continues into the unknown future; it is only the eternal Church, preserved by the Spirit of God without defects through the ages, that can reveal the meaning of temporal history, which otherwise would be left obscure and meaningless. The reader need not be an Orthodox Christian to appreciate the explanatory power of an Orthodox understanding of history even while, should he find the analysis in this work persuasive, there is the hope that he will seek out Orthodoxy in its fulness.

The great minds of the Orthodox Church, from the time of Christ to our present age, describe the end of history in terms of a great "falling away"[9] from the worship of the True God, of a world united by a great lie at the end of time.

> According to these sources, world history will culminate in an almost superhuman "Christian" figure, the false messiah or *Antichrist*. He will be "Christian" in the sense that his whole function and his very being will center on Christ, Whom he will imitate in every respect possible, and he will not be merely the greatest enemy of Christ, but, in order to deceive Christians, will *appear to be Christ*, come to earth for a second time and ruling from the restored Temple in Jerusalem.[10]

---

8   Georgios I. Mantzaridis, *Time and Man* (South Canaan, St. Tikhon's Seminary, 1995), 51.

9   2 Thess. 2:3. Scriptural quotations are, with minor exceptions, taken from the New King James Version, ® Copyright © 1982 by Thomas Nelson. Used by permission. All rights reserved.

10   Blessed Hieromonk Seraphim Rose, *Orthodoxy and the Religion of the Future* (Platina, St. Herman of Alaska Brotherhood, 1997), 174.

During a time of great confusion and tumult, Antichrist will arise as a world leader who alone will seem able to remedy the problems of his age. In their blindness, most of the world will believe that they are beholding the prophesied Messiah come again, a diabolical mimicry of the God-Man Jesus Christ, and will receive the man-god, Antichrist, as their king and savior. Antichrist will crown a process of apostasy that has been gestating through the centuries in a myriad of forms. He will fulfill the world's ancient desire for a unified global civilization and the yearnings of an inner-worldly "Christianity." Far from coming as a hated oppressor, Antichrist will be revered as a savior and his reign as the apotheosis of world history. "The Antichrist will be the logical, just, and natural result of the general moral and spiritual direction of mankind."[11]

The future reign of Antichrist may sound like so much feverish "end times" speculation symptomatic of unbalanced modern sectarianism, but in fact the Orthodox picture of the end of history is very different from contemporary notions popular in the heterodox West. As St. Paul instructs us, "concerning the times and the seasons" we must "watch and be sober";[12] we must not be "tossed to and fro and carried about";[13] we must not lose our heads with "millennial fever." Above all, the Lord commands us, "Fear not, little flock; for it is your Father's good pleasure to give you the kingdom."[14] While we have here linked the eventual coming of Antichrist to the historical process of globalization, this is not to say that globalization is necessarily nearing the culmination of its evolution or that it may not suffer significant reverses. St. John Chrysostom, one of the greatest minds of the Church, who did so much to elucidate the meaning of many

---

11   St. Ignatius Brianchaninov as quoted in Hieromonk Damascene, *Father Seraphim Rose*, Second Edition (Platina, St. Herman of Alaska Brotherhood, 2005), 731.

12   I Thess. 5:1, 6.

13   Eph. 4:14.

14   Luke 12:32.

prophecies, admonishes us: "Do not seek clarity in prophecies, where there are shadows and riddles, just as in lightning you do not seek a constant light, but are satisfied that it flashes only momentarily."[15] We are not here to pontificate on which prophecy has been fulfilled by this or that historical event or to provide a timetable for the end of the world ("of that day and hour no one knows"[16]); rather, it is our purpose to discern the general principles of history, and of history's end, through the lens of Orthodox teaching as expressed in Holy Scripture, the Holy Fathers, and the overarching wisdom of the Orthodox Church as revealed, enunciated, and upheld for twenty centuries.

Drawing on the perennial wisdom of Orthodoxy provides insulation from a common error, which is the tendency to see in one's own time the measure of all things, to imagine that one's local perspective on human events, reflecting the assumptions and prejudices of the era in which one lives, is the right measure with which to assess history generally. Modern man is especially guilty of this tendency. Surrounded by unprecedented material and technical marvels, increasingly insulated from the natural cycles of life and death, he imagines himself superior to his ancestors—poor, benighted souls enslaved to myth and superstition. He never imagines that the myths and superstitions of his own time possess a tyranny over his mind and soul that would astonish and horrify his more "primitive" forebears. Modern man cannot grasp the larger meaning of history because he is too much a product of history itself; he is too caught up in the increasingly confused affairs of his age to be able to understand the meaning of history and of his own, small place, in history's larger sweep.

---

15   Archbishop Averky Taushev and Hieromonk Seraphim Rose, *The Apocalypse in the Teachings of Early Christianity* (Platina, St. Herman of Alaska Brotherhood, 1998), 69.
16   Mark 13:32

Without connection to eternity, to a transcendent reality beyond history, this life and all of human history are rendered meaningless for the simple reason that everything in this world eventually, inevitably, ends. God in His wisdom has enlightened His Church with certain facts about history and history's end for the salvation of her members. If we neglect this knowledge or, to the contrary, demand more from it than it is intended to provide by forcing it into a mold of our own imagining, we err. As we proceed in this study, we must bear in mind that the purpose of the Church's apocalyptic teachings is not to provide a crystal ball into the future but to encourage the faithful in times of adversity to keep their spiritual eyes focused on the world to come.

> The aim of the Apocalypse is to depict [the] battle of the Church and its triumph over all enemies, to show clearly the perdition of the enemies of the Church and the glorification of her faithful children.... This vivid picture of the battle of the dark kingdom of Satan with the Church and the final victory of the Church over the "old serpent" (Rev. 12:9) is necessary for the believers of all times . . . to console and strengthen them in the battle for the truth of the faith of Christ, a battle which they must always wage against the servants of the dark forces of hell, who strive in their blind malice to annihilate the Church.[17]

The countless terrible facts of human history—the wars, genocides, monstrous crimes and injustices—can be hard to look upon; only those hopeful of a better, eternal world to come are able to face historical reality objectively without shrinking.

Conversely, theological or mystical speculation, if it is not connected to the plight of real people living out the drama of history, relegates itself to irrelevance. Knowledge of this

---

17   Taushev in Taushev and Rose, *The Apocalypse*, 49–50.

world and knowledge of the next must be brought together; the science of history and the science of eternity must be made to unite, a task that the Orthodox Church has undertaken for almost two thousand years. The Church is, in the words of the twentieth-century political scientist Eric Voegelin, "the flash of eternity into time,"[18] the Kingdom of God on earth, the presence of transcendent eternity in the here-and-now of human history. It is within her inexhaustible store of wisdom that we will find the answers to our questions.[19]

This book is chiefly a work of synthesis, of trying to bring into focus a variety of apparently disparate facts and concepts into a meaningful big picture. It is not the first work to argue that globalization is anti-Christian. Increasingly, Christian writers of various stripes are recognizing that globalization is spiritually dark. "Globalism is far more than 'geographical' or 'eliminating national borders and boundaries.' It is spiritual and demonic at its core."[20] One prominent Orthodox hierarch went so far as to say that, "Globalization has its main goal of, above all, destroying the Orthodox Church. The tentacles of globalization are trying to penetrate into the Church Body to destroy it."[21] While this book may be the first Orthodox Christian work in English to address globalization specifically at length, what is far more important than any claim to originality is the ultimate cogency of its arguments, which must stand or fall on their own merits. To keep the considerable subject matter manageable, we will often examine

---

18   Eric Voegelin, *The New Science of Politics, An Introduction* (Chicago, The University of Chicago, 1987), 109.

19   While Voegelin appeared to have in mind the early and medieval Roman church, his analysis is even more cogent when applied to the Orthodox Church, which included the Roman See of the first millennium.

20   Dr. Jim Garlow, *"If You're on the Fence About Your Vote,"* *Charisma News*. http://www.charismanews.com/politics/opinion/59206. Accessed August 15, 2017.

21   Patriarch Theophilos of Jerusalem, *"Tentacles of Globalization,"* Orthodox Christianity. https://orthochristian.com/115638.html. Accessed September 12, 2019.

in detail a particular theorist whose work is representative of a broader intellectual current. Also, while we will make reference to books of Scripture, we will not provide detailed interpretations thereof. Several excellent Orthodox interpretations of apocalyptic Scripture now exist in English, including *The Apocalypse in the Teachings of Ancient Christianity* by Archbishop Averky Taushev (+1976) and Hieromonk Seraphim Rose (+1982); as well as the magisterial work of Archimandrite Athanasios Mitilinaios (+2006) recently translated from the Greek. The interested reader is directed to them.[22]

First, we will look to the Orthodox Church's teaching on Antichrist as revealed in Holy Scripture and the Fathers of the Church with an eye to the historical circumstances of Antichrist's advent into history and the characteristics of his reign.

Next, we will examine the phenomenon of globalization with special reference to the biblical precedent of the Tower of Babel and how it ties into the Orthodox teaching on Antichrist and the end of this world. We will then endeavor to understand globalization as a historical process with the aid of the theoretical work of Voegelin. Voegelin will help us to make sense of the revolution that the rise of the Church effected in mankind's understanding of history and how the historical decline of Orthodox Christianity in the second millennium paved the way for the powerfully destructive anti-Christian political movements of the modern age.

We will then provide a more detailed analysis of globalization at the economic, political, and religious levels.

Finally, we will offer cautious speculation as to what the future may hold and counsel as to how we may navigate the times while preserving our souls.

---

22   There is also now available an excellent summary work on the Antichrist by Fr. Andrew J. Anderson, *"The Antichrist: An Orthodox Perspective from the Church Fathers,"* Orthodox Christianity. http://orthochristian.com/106805.html. Accessed September 12, 2019.

As we set out, let us bear in mind the words of one of the greatest interpreters of the Orthodox tradition to the contemporary world, Hieromonk Seraphim Rose of blessed memory:

> Futile and over-literal speculation on apocalyptic events is an only too obvious cause of spiritual harm; and no less so, I think, is the facile way in which many of our contemporaries refer to the "apocalyptic" character of the times.... If a Christian is going to speak of the Apocalypse at all, it is quite clear that—in this as in everything else—his words must be sober, as precise as possible, and fully in accord with the universal teaching of the Church.[23]

Bearing Father Seraphim's admonition in mind, let us proceed.

---

23   Taushev and Rose, *The Apocalypse*, 5.

PART I

THE FULFILLMENT OF GLOBALIZATION

Chapter 1

Who is the Antichrist?

So be warned, my friend. I have given you the signs of the Antichrist. Do not merely store them in your memory. Pass them on to everyone without stint. If you have a child after the flesh, teach them to him forthwith. And if you have become a godparent, forewarn your godchild, lest he should take the false christ for the True. "For the mystery of lawlessness doth already work."[1]

St. Cyril of Jerusalem (+386)
Catechetical Lectures, ch. XV, no. 18[2]

Antichrist is a figure central to the Orthodox understanding of history and of the end of this world. The Orthodox Church identifies Antichrist as the "beast" described by St. John in his Apocalypse:

And I saw a beast rising up out of the sea, having seven heads and ten horns, and on his horns ten crowns, and on his heads a name of blasphemy.... And all the world marveled and followed the beast.... It was granted to him to make war with the saints and to overcome them. And authority was given him over every tribe, tongue, and na-

---

1   2 Thess. 2:7.
2   http://www.newadvent.org/fathers/310115.htm. Accessed September 18, 2019.

tion. All who dwell on the earth will worship him, whose names have not been written in the Book of Life of the Lamb slain from the foundation of the world. If anyone has an ear, let him hear.[3]

"By this 'beast which rises up out of the sea,' almost all interpreters understand Antichrist who comes out of the 'sea of life', that is in the midst of the human race which is agitated like a sea."[4] St. Paul describes Antichrist as "the lawless one" who comes "according to the working of Satan, with all power, signs, and lying wonders, and with all unrighteous deception among those who perish, because they did not receive the love of the truth, that they might be saved."[5] This man, who will appear on the stage of human history shortly before the Second Coming of Christ and the end of the world, will, as St. John tells us, hold "authority … over every tribe, tongue, and nation such that all the world marveled and followed the beast." Antichrist is thus identifiably connected with the historical process of globalization, which is progressively uniting the world's peoples into a unified political society.

The term "antichrist" (with both lower—and upper-case As) like many once-serious concepts, has come to be flung about quite casually and, as a result, has lost its proper significance. Numerous popular works of fiction dramatize about who the Antichrist might be or employ the term Antichrist inaccurately. This debasement of a concept crucial to Orthodox theology desensitizes us to the significance of who Antichrist is and the danger he represents. It is important, therefore, to recover the meaning of the term.

3   Rev. 13:1, 3, 7–9.
4   Taushev and Rose, *The Apocalypse*, 187.
5   2 Thess. 2:9-10.

In Orthodox terminology, "antichrist", while connoting a contradiction of, or opposition to, Christ, primarily means "in place
of," i.e., that which stands in the place of Christ. The English
term "Christ" is an anglicization of the Greek (Χριστός, Christos,
"anointed" and is a translation of the Hebrew מָשִׁיחַ [Mashiah,
"Messiah"). All Orthodox Christians are anointed during the
sacrament of chrismation following baptism, as are Christian
monarchs; in one sense, then, all are "christs." A false Christian
or a pretender to a throne could be considered an "antichrist,"
but such is not what is generally meant by the term. Christ, with
a capital C, refers to Jesus Christ, the Messiah prophesied by
the Old Testament Scriptures, the Word and Son of God, the
Second Person of the Holy Trinity, Who entered human history
as a Man. An antichrist then may rightly be considered anyone
or anything that arrogates to itself the worship and dignity of
Jesus Christ. Worship, practically defined as one's highest allegiance, may be given to almost anything, from statuary idols
to money and power to one's nation, tribe, work, self, or even
to an ideology. Anything, if it usurps the primacy due to God
alone, may be thought of in some way as an antichrist, but the
term especially applies to individuals who set themselves up as
savior figures in the place of the True Savior. Leaders of cults
and modern demagogues are obvious examples of this, some of
whom may explicitly claim to be Christ, or his chosen one, and
others who imply a capacity to "save" their followers in some
way even if they reject all forms of Christianity.

In Holy Scripture, the term antichrist appears only four times,
all in the general epistles of St. John the Apostle (+c. 100). In
those epistles, the Orthodox Church discerns three basic mean-
ings of antichrist. First, is anyone or anything that denies the
incarnation of God as Jesus Christ and its salvific significance.
Any person, institution, or idea that denies that Jesus of Nazareth
is the Christ prophesied by the Old Testament prophets is an
antichrist.

Who is a liar but he who denies that Jesus is the Christ?
He is antichrist who denies the Father and the Son.[6]

For many deceivers have gone out into the world who do
not confess Jesus Christ as coming in the flesh. This is a
deceiver and an antichrist.[7]

The denial of Jesus Christ by any such deceiver and antichrist
is a manifestation of the "spirit of the Antichrist," the second
meaning of the term.

Every spirit that confesses that Jesus Christ has come in
the flesh is of God, and every spirit that does not confess
that Jesus Christ has come in the flesh is not of God. And
this is the spirit of the Antichrist, which you have heard
was coming, and is now already in the world.[8]

This spirit of the Antichrist, which denies the Christhood of
Jesus of Nazareth, has taken concrete form in various personal
antichrists throughout history, from the Pharisees of the Lord's
day to the "new atheists" of our own time. This spirit—a demonic inspiration—varies in intensity in particular places, times,
and persons, as does its broader efficacy throughout larger society. While this spirit finds personification in particular antichrists
in various times and places, it will ultimately achieve a sort of
maximal incarnation, a supreme personification, in a specific
antichrist, which brings us to the third meaning of the term.

---

6   1 John 2:22.
7   2 John 1:7.
8   1 John 4:2-3.

Little children, it is the last hour; and as you have heard that the Antichrist is coming, even now many antichrists have come, by which we know that it is the last hour.[9]

Of all the antichrists who have denied Jesus Christ through history, this particular Antichrist (distinguished by the capital A), here mentioned by St. John, who comes "in the last hour," at the end of history, does so most egregiously: he explicitly stands in the place of Christ by pretending that he himself is Christ and God. This Antichrist will be a man, the last world leader of history, who will appear in the final years before the Second Coming of Christ and will arrogate to himself on a global scale the worship and adoration due to God Himself.

It should be known that the Antichrist is bound to come. Everyone, therefore, who confesses not that the Son of God came in the flesh and is perfect God and became perfect man, after being God, is antichrist. But in a peculiar and special sense he who comes at the consummation of the age is called Antichrist.[10]

[T]he man of sin, the son of perdition, who must first be revealed before the Lord comes,[11] who opposes and exalts

---

9   1 John 2:18.

10   St. John of Damascus (+749), *Exact Exposition of the Orthodox Faith*, bk. IV, ch. 26. http://www.newadvent.org/fathers/33044.htm. Accessed September 12, 2019.

11   Antichrist "must first be revealed before the Lord comes" again. It is not our purpose here to address the numerous errors that abound in heterodox Christianity regarding Christ's Second Coming, but one very persistent and very serious error that we will mention is the doctrine of the "rapture," which claims that the faithful on earth will supposedly be suddenly and miraculously transported to Heaven before the appearance of Antichrist. They will thus be spared the "great tribulation" (Matt. 24:21) of Antichrist's earthly reign. This "error, which has no foundation in Holy Scripture and removes from those who follow it all necessity for watchfulness against the deceit of [A]ntichrist, from which they imagine they will be spared," is widespread in Protestant circles. (Rose, *Orthodoxy and the Religion of the Future*, 181).

himself above all that is called God or that is worshipped; and who is to sit in the temple of God and boast himself as being God... According indeed to our view, he is Antichrist; as it is taught us in both the ancient and the new prophecies, and by the apostle John...[12]

As Christ appeared into history as a man, so too will Antichrist. Antichrist's identity and the time of his appearance have not been revealed, but Orthodox teaching tells us much about his characteristics and those of the era in which he will appear.

SATAN AND ANTICHRIST

There has been an unhealthy fascination with Antichrist in recent years, and much speculation as to who he might be and where and when he will reveal himself. Most of this speculation, occurring outside of an Orthodox context, seems likely to contribute to Antichrist's ultimate success in deceiving the world, given its numerous errors and often feverish tone. On such an important topic, we do not need hysterics, a frenetic seeking after "signs and wonders"[13] in an attempt to predict who Antichrist will be and the date of his advent; instead, we need sober examination that draws on the unchanging wisdom of Christ's eternal Church that does not succumb to the prejudices of the times. As St. Peter admonishes us, "But the end of all things is at hand; therefore be serious and watchful in your prayers."[14] If we are to penetrate the mystery of history and of its end, we must approach the figure of Antichrist with sobriety

---

12   Tertullian (+220), *Against Marcion*, bk. 5, ch. 16.
http://www.newadvent.org/fathers/03125.htm. Accessed September 12, 2019.
13   John 4:48.
14   1 Pet. 4:7.

and clear mindedness, so often lacking in modern variations of heterodox Christianity.

In his excellent short work, *Apostasy and Antichrist*, Archpriest Boris Molchanoff is careful to preface his analysis of Antichrist with a discussion of the Orthodox Church's demonology. It is only by coming to understand the nature of the demons—of Satan and the fallen angels—that Antichrist may be properly understood. The Prophet Isaiah (+ c. 8th century BC), speaking analogically about the prideful King Nebuchadnezzar of Babylon, describes Satan's fall from grace. Lucifer ("bearer of light"), an angel of God, was cast out of Heaven for trying to usurp God's rightful supremacy.

> "How you are fallen from heaven, O Lucifer, son of the morning! How you are cut down to the ground, you who weakened the nations! For you have said in your heart: 'I will ascend into heaven, I will exalt my throne above the stars of God... I will ascend above the heights of the clouds; I will be like the Most High.' "[15]

In a fit of colossal pride, Lucifer insisted on being as God and was cast out of Heaven with his fellow rebel angels. Lucifer thus fell to earth and became Satan, the accuser and enemy of mankind. Satan and the demons now inhabit creation along with man, who opened the door to them through disobedience in the Garden of Eden. The demons' hatred for God and for the crown of His creation—man—drives them to commit all deception in this life that man might share with them their condemnation in Hell, the "everlasting fire, prepared for the devil and his angels,"[16] which will begin at the Last Judgment.

---

15   Isa. 14:12-14.
16   Matt. 25:41.

The Gospel account of the Gadarene swine sheds light on the demons' present relationship with God and man.

> And when (Jesus) stepped out on the land, there met Him a certain man from the city who had demons for a long time. And he wore no clothes, nor did he live in a house but in the tombs. When he saw Jesus, he cried out, fell down before Him, and with a loud voice said, "What have I to do with You, Jesus, Son of the Most High God? I beg You, do not torment me!" For He had commanded the unclean spirit to come out of the man. For it had often seized him, and he was kept under guard, bound with chains and shackles; and he broke the bonds and was driven by the demon into the wilderness.
>
> Jesus asked him, saying, "What is your name?" And he said, "Legion," because many demons had entered him. And they begged Him that He would not command them to go out into the abyss. Now a herd of many swine was feeding there on the mountain. So they begged Him that He would permit them to enter them. And He permitted them. Then the demons went out of the man and entered the swine, and the herd ran violently down the steep place into the lake and drowned.[17]

Legion's plea to Christ not "to torment us before the time"[18] and not to command them to go out into the abyss belies the demons' awareness of their ultimate banishment to Hell. Knowing their fate and blinded by hatred, they labor night and day to destroy as much of God's creation as possible and particularly, man, made in God's image.

---

17   Luke 8:27-33.
18   Matt. 8:29.

One of the greatest errors found in the heterodox West is its persistent treatment of evil as an abstract or disembodied force. The traditional Orthodox rendering of the Lord's Prayer, "and deliver us from the evil *one*," by which is meant Satan, the arch liar and murderer of mankind, reflects the Orthodox identification of evil as personal. Evil, in an abstract or essential form, does not exist; it cannot. God is sole Creator, and He certainly did not create evil. Evil constitutes the rejection of God by a creature with free will; when we speak of evil, we mean disobedience to God's right and beneficent ordering of creation. To imagine that Satan and the demons constitute a vague, abstract negativity of some kind is to misunderstand wildly the danger they pose to man and the nature of spiritual warfare. We are not dealing with a mindless force capable of doing us harm like the weather; rather we are engaged in mortal combat ("unseen warfare"[19]) with a rational intelligence of several millennia's experience who neither sleeps, nor eats, but labors night and day to lead us into deception and eternal destruction. It is this personal intelligence that will assume control of the person of Antichrist and, save for a miracle of God, lead the mass of the world to destruction at the end of time.

While Satan knows that he is ultimately doomed, his unquenchable pride thirsts for the adoration and worship due only to God Himself. God in His mercy does not permit Satan and the demons to destroy or compel worship from mankind, and so Satan must use trickery and fraud—as he used in the Garden of Eden—to deceive man in order to achieve his aims, often appearing in the guise of goodness and wisdom: "Satan himself is transformed into an angel of light."[20] As God came to earth as a man and receives the worship of mankind as Jesus

---

19   See Nicodemus and St. Theophan the Recluse, *Unseen Warfare*, (Crestwood, St., Vladimir's Seminary, 2000).

20   2 Cor. 11:14.

Christ, Satan will control, for a time, a particular man and receive the worship of mankind as Antichrist before his ultimate destruction at the Second Coming.

> Yet you shall be brought down to Sheol, to the lowest depths of the Pit. Those who see you will gaze at you, and consider you, saying: "Is this the man who made the earth tremble, who shook kingdoms, who made the world as a wilderness and destroyed its cities, who did not open the house of his prisoners?"[21]

God's forbearance and the spiritual activity of the Church forestall Antichrist's appearance into history, but, as mankind progressively departs from the laws of God and His Church, as the great "falling away"[22] gathers force, "Satan will be released from his prison and will go out to deceive the nations which are in the four corners of the earth."[23] Antichrist will be the culmination of the great Satanic deception that will occur before the Second Coming of Christ and the Last Judgment, "when there should be time no longer."[24]

ANTICHRISTS IN HISTORY

Antichrist is often thought of as a great villain, a monster tyrant who will bring misery, oppression, and despair to the world; a ruthless dictator and warmonger in the vein of Hitler or Stalin, who will desolate the nations of the earth. While police-state tactics may well figure into Antichrist's regime, it is a mistake to imagine that he will be readily identifiable as a

---

21   Isa. 14:15-17.
22   2 Thess. 2:3.
23   Rev. 20:7-8.
24   Rev. 10:6.

tyrant. While he will bring the most comprehensive tyranny in history, his appearance to the world will be, at least for a time, as a true Christian: loving, forgiving, speaking truth to power, not suffering injustice. Merely being on our guard against a new aspiring despot vastly underestimates the subtlety of the deception that Antichrist will embody. St. Cyril of Jerusalem (+386) explains:

> At first… he will put on a show of mildness (as though he were a learned and discreet person), and of soberness and benevolence: and by the lying signs and wonders of his magical deceit having beguiled the Jews, as though he were the expected Christ, he shall afterwards be characterized by all kinds of crimes of inhumanity and lawlessness, so as to outdo all unrighteous and ungodly men who have gone before him; displaying against all men, but especially against us Christians, a spirit murderous and most cruel, merciless and crafty.[25]

It is worth recalling that many of history's most destructive personalities, particularly those who have appeared in modern circumstances such as Napoleon, Lenin, and Hitler managed to depict themselves as champions of the people. We must not think that we are immune to the charms, tricks, and threats of such political opportunists who aspire to supreme power. The demagogues of the modern era are harbingers of the coming of the ultimate demagogue. Antichrist's arrival will be the crowning of a process of heresy, apostasy, and sin that has been at work throughout the course of human history, and which has gained special momentum in our own time.

---

25   St. Cyril of Jerusalem (+386), *Catechetical Lectures*, ch. XV, no. 12. http://www. newadvent.org/fathers/310115.htm. Accessed September 12, 2019.

Many historical figures have prefigured Antichrist, and some have been confused for Antichrist himself. One of the most egregious examples was the Seleucid emperor Antiochus IV Epiphanes (r. 175-164 BC), who assumed divine epithets including *Theos Epiphanes*, "God Manifest." Following a rebellion led by the deposed Israelite high priest, Jason, Antiochus successfully besieged Jerusalem and committed numerous outrages including wholesale massacre and setting up an idol of Zeus in the Israelite temple.[26] Another example, Emperor Nero (r. AD 54–68), instigated the first systematic persecution of Christians in the Roman Empire. Nero was a clear prefigurement of Antichrist as were numerous subsequent emperors who also warned against the Church. Significantly, the Neronian persecution lasted almost exactly three-and-a-half years, the same length of time as the future persecution of Antichrist as related in the Apocalypse of St. John.[27] Emperor Julian the Apostate (r. AD 360-3) persecuted his former religious brethren and attempted to reconstruct the Old Testament temple (unsuccessfully) in an effort to controvert the New Testament; he perished in battle against the Persians. Indeed, many of the writings of the Holy Fathers on Antichrist occurred in the wake of persecutions under the pagan Roman Empire or under renegade emperors following the empire's Christianization in the fourth century. It was no doubt easy to imagine that the final Antichrist could come as an especially ruthless and destructive emperor. Modern heralds of Antichrist— from Oliver Cromwell to Jim Jones—are frighteningly plentiful, a sign that the time of Antichrist approaches.

By any secular standard, Antichrist will prove himself the greatest statesman in world history. He will achieve the mastery of the world and the adoration of its peoples that the greatest imperialists, from Cyrus to Alexander to Genghis Khan to

---

26   See 1 Macc. 1:20-8; 2 Macc. 5:11-17.
27   See below.

Napoleon, failed to attain. Antichrist will unite in himself all of the material and heterodox religious impulses of the mass of the world such that it will seem that no earthly power can resist him: "authority was given him over every tribe, tongue, and nation," and "all the world marveled and followed the beast … and they worshipped the beast, saying, Who is like unto the beast? Who is able to make war with him?"[28] Mimicking Jesus Christ, Antichrist will come as a priest, prophet, and king to the peoples of the world, who, in their blindness, will receive him in place of the True Christ.

> Finally, just as the Lord revealed Himself to the world and accomplished His work as Prophet, King and High Priest, so also will Antichrist concentrate this threefold authority in his own hands and accomplish his pernicious work as the teacher of all mankind, as the monarch of a universal monarchy and as the supreme high priest of all religions, demanding worship of himself as god.[29]

CHARACTERISTICS OF ANTICHRIST AND HIS REIGN

Slowly, year by year, generation by generation, the preparations for Antichrist are taking shape around us. Whereas Christ came to earth to establish His Church, the imposter church of Antichrist, as a product of human history rather than of divine inspiration, must be constructed for the latter's arrival. Whereas Christ is "the stone which the builders rejected" and "is become the head of the corner,"[30] Antichrist will be the capstone of the builders' choice that will complete the worldly,

---

28   Rev. 13:3-4, 7.
29   Archpriest Boris Molchanoff, *Apostasy and Antichrist*, (Jordanville, Holy Trinity Monastery, 1992), 27.
30   Mark 12:10.

hellish edifice they are busily constructing. The establishment of Christ's Church was a truly miraculous event, a breaking into time by the transcendent God, which permanently reshaped the course of history; in contrast, because Antichrist will have no power or authority from Heaven, he will only be able to avail himself of the instruments of men and of the aid of the fallen sprits. Like an elaborate piece of technology designed to produce a dazzling effect, Antichrist's appearance on the stage of history requires tremendous foundational labors to pull off its desired result.

The Holy Fathers of the Orthodox Church have isolated a number of characteristics of Antichrist and of his coming reign:

1 ANTICHRIST WILL BE A MAN. Like all men, Antichrist will bear the image of God, yet he will, by free choice, be given over entirely to the power of Satan. Antichrist will not be Satan himself. "The devil … does not become man in the way that the Lord was made man. God forbid!"[31] Rather, Satan will inhabit and control the personality of the man Antichrist to the fullest possible extent and will use him as a proxy to receive the worship of mankind.

2 ANTICHRIST WILL BE AN ETHNIC HEBREW FROM THE tribe of Dan. As Christ sprang forth from the Hebrew people, so will Antichrist. But whereas Christ was born of the kingly tribe of Judah, Antichrist will be born from the tribe of Dan, one of the ten "lost" tribes that were scattered during the Assyrian invasion (c. 722 BC).

---

31   St. John of Damascus, *Exact Exposition,* bk. IV, ch. 26. http://www.newadvent. org/fathers/33044.htm. Accessed September 12, 2019.

[W]e find it written regarding Antichrist... "Dan is a lion's whelp, and he shall leap from Bashan."[32] And in naming the tribe of Dan, he declared clearly the tribe from which Antichrist is destined to spring. For as Christ springs from the tribe of Judah, so Antichrist is to spring from the tribe of Dan. And that the case stands thus, we also see from the words of Jacob: "Let Dan be a serpent, lying upon the ground, biting the horse's heel."[33] What then is meant by the serpent but Antichrist, that deceiver who is mentioned in Genesis, who deceived Eve and supplanted Adam? .... That it is in reality out of the tribe of Dan, then, that tyrant and king, that dread judge, that son of the devil, is destined to spring and arise.[34]

3   ANTICHRIST MAY BE A HOMOSEXUAL. In a vision granted to the Prophet Daniel "in the third year of Cyrus King of Persia . . . whose message was true but whose appointed time was long,"[35] Daniel beheld prophecies concerning the Empires of Persia and Greece, in particular wars between the "King of the South"[36] and the "King of the North."[37]

Then the king [of the North] shall do according to his own will: he shall exalt and magnify himself above every god, shall speak blasphemies against the God of gods, and shall prosper till the wrath has been accomplished; for what has been determined shall be done. He shall regard neither the God of his fathers nor the desire of

---

32   Deut. 33:22.
33   Gen. 49:17.
34   St. Hippolytus of Rome (+236), *Treatise on Christ and Antichrist*, ch. 15. Accessed September 13, 2019. http://www.newadvent.org/fathers/0516.htm.
35   Dan. 10:1.
36   Dan. 11:5.
37   Dan. 11:6.

women, nor regard any god; for he shall exalt himself above them all.[38]

While there is no explicit mention of Antichrist in Daniel's prophecy, that this king "shall exalt and magnify himself above every god" and "speak blasphemies against the God of gods" marks him as an antichrist *par excellence*, if not the Antichrist himself. That he shall not regard the "desire of women" seems to imply his possible homosexuality, an especially grievous sin that was the cause of the Lord's destruction of Sodom and Gomorrah.[39] In our time, homosexuality is increasingly accepted as normal even among public figures and politicians.

4   The first of three stages in Antichrist's life will be spent in obscurity. During his youth, Antichrist will be "nurtured in secret."[40] As Christ did not begin His ministry until roughly thirty years of age and remained unknown to the world before then, so Antichrist will similarly reveal himself at around the same age. The world will not watch Antichrist come to his majority or gradually advance his public career during his early years.

5   From the time of his advent into public life, Antichrist's rise to global power, the second phase of his life, will take place over roughly three-and-a-half years ("forty-two months"),[41] roughly the same length of time as Christ's earthly ministry. During this time, Antichrist will appear to the world as a great and benevolent public figure, bestowing peace and justice, solving hitherto insoluble problems. "[I] n the

---

38   Dan. 11:36-7.
39   See Gen. 6:16 -7:29.
40   St. John of Damascus, *Exact Exposition*, bk. IV, ch. 26. http://www.newadvent.org/fathers/33044.htm. Accessed September 12, 2019.
41   Rev. 13:5.

beginning of his rule, or rather tyranny, he assumes the role of sanctity."[42] Through his apparent goodness and unparalleled abilities, he will gain the world's confidence and acquire supreme power. Antichrist's appearance onto the world stage will be sudden and likely in the midst of great turmoil, perhaps during a world war or economic crisis, when the "sea" of humanity will be greatly disturbed, "the sea and the waves roaring."[43]

6   It appears that the seat of Antichrist's political power will come from among the nations of the old Roman Empire, namely, Europe and the Mediterranean Basin. In a visionary dream, the prophet Daniel (c. 600–530 BC) foresaw the rise of four kingdoms in the form of four great beasts, the fourth of which was "different from all the beasts before it, one dreadful and terrible, exceedingly strong with huge iron teeth that had ten horns. The fourth beast shall be a fourth kingdom on earth, which shall be different from all other kingdoms, and shall devour the whole earth, trample it and break it in pieces." It is from among this fourth kingdom, which commentators believe to be the Roman Empire, and its "ten horns" who "are ten kings," from which "another shall rise after them who shall be different from the first ones," who many regard as indicating Antichrist.[44]

> But this aforesaid Antichrist is to come when the times of the Roman empire shall have been fulfilled, and the end of the world is now drawing near. There shall rise up together ten kings of the Romans, reigning in different parts perhaps, but all about the same time; and after these an eleventh, the Antichrist, who by his magical craft shall

---

42   St. John of Damascus, *Exact Exposition,* bk. IV, ch. 26. http://www.newadvent.org/fathers/33044.htm. Accessed September 12, 2019.

43   Luke 21:25.

44   Dan. 7:3, 7, 23-4.

seize upon the Roman power; and of the kings who reigned before him, "three he shall humble", and the remaining seven he shall keep in subjection to himself.[45]

That the fourth beast corresponds to the Roman Empire is also made evident in the dream of Daniel's captor, the Persian King Nebuchadnezzar, which Daniel famously interpreted.[46]

7 THE THIRD AND FINAL STAGE OF ANTICHRIST'S LIFE WILL also last roughly three-and-a-half years ("a time and times and half a time"[47]—one year plus two plus one-half), during which he will exercise supreme authority over the world, with Jerusalem as his capital. During this, the final period of human history, Satan, through his chief human representative, Antichrist, and the global regime that he will head, will unleash an unprecedented persecution against any who withhold their loyalty—especially against the remnant of true Christians— "displaying against all men, but especially against us Christians, a spirit murderous and most cruel, merciless and crafty."[48] This persecution would ultimately prove successful in expunging the Church from the earth had the Lord not promised to shorten those days: "For then there will be great tribulation, such as has not been since the beginning of the world until this time, no, nor ever shall be. And unless those days were shortened, no flesh would be saved; but for the elect's sake those days will be shortened."[49] Antichrist's apparent triumph, however, will presage his eternal destruction and the destruction of Satan

---

45   St. Cyril of Jerusalem, *Catechetical Lectures*, no. XV, part 12. http://www.newadvent.org/fathers/310115.htm. Accessed September 13, 2019.

46   See Dan. 2 and below.

47   Dan. 7:25.

48   St. Cyril of Jerusalem, *Catechetical Lectures*, no. XV, part 12. http://www.newadvent.org/fathers/310115.htm. Accessed September 13, 2019.

49   Matt. 24: 21-2.

himself. "And the devil that deceived them was cast into the lake of fire and brimstone, where the beast and the false prophet are, and shall be tormented day and night for ever and ever."[50]

> But when this Antichrist shall have devastated all things in this world, he will reign for three years and six months and will sit in the temple at Jerusalem; and then the Lord will come from heaven in the clouds, in the glory of the Father, sending this man and those who follow him into the lake of fire.[51]

8 HAVING ACQUIRED SUPREME POWER, ANTICHRIST WILL not suffer the continuation of other representations of the divine. In this sense, he may seem to mimic Christ and the Church in "cleansing" the world of idolatry.

> [Antichrist] being an apostate and a robber is anxious to be adored as God, and that although a mere slave, he wishes to be proclaimed as king. For he, being endued with all the power of the devil, shall not come as a righteous king nor as a legitimate king in subjection to God, but as an impious, unjust, and lawless one… setting aside idols to persuade [men] that he himself is God, raising himself up as the only idol.[52]

In "setting aside idols," it seems possible that Antichrist will attack the Orthodox tradition of icons, decisively upheld at the Seventh Ecumenical Council in 787. Antichrist's possible iconoclasm may prove part of his attraction for heterodox Western Christians, many of whom reject icons as idolatrous.

---

50   Rev. 20:10.

51   St. Irenaeus of Lyons (+202), *Against Heresies,* bk. 5, ch. 25, no. 4. http://www.newadvent.org/fathers/0103525.htm. Accessed September 13, 2019.

52   Ibid. bk. 5, ch. 25, nos. 1–2.

9 AT SOME POINT IN HIS CAREER, ANTICHRIST WILL PER-
FORM, OR appear to perform, extraordinary miracles. In his effort to appear as Christ to the world, and especially to those nominal Christians who will mistakenly imagine that they are seeing Christ in His second advent, Antichrist will mimic the miraculous works that the Lord wrought during His earthly ministry, such as healing the sick and raising the dead. He will perform these "miracles" through a combination of technical and demonic power that will have nothing to do with divine grace. One of Antichrist's greatest tricks will be to appear to return to life after having received a deadly wound, or to appear to resurrect one of his followers, thus aping Christ's Resurrection and His resurrection of Lazarus.[53]

> Now the beast which I saw was like a leopard, his feet were like the feet of a bear, and his mouth like the mouth of a lion. The dragon gave him his power, his throne, and great authority. And I saw one of his heads as if it had been mortally wounded, and his deadly wound was healed. And all the world marveled and followed the beast.[54]

Antichrist's depiction as a beast, with the attributes of carnivorous animals indicates his strength, cunning, and rapaciousness. In the same vein, as Satan took the form of a serpent in the Garden of Eden to entice Adam and Eve, so is he here depicted as a dragon, a great and ravenous serpent.

10 AS ANTICHRIST WILL MIMIC CHRIST, SO A FALSE PROPHET will arise to mimic the Forerunner of Christ, St. John the Baptist ("the voice of one crying in the wilderness: 'Prepare

---

53   See John 11; also Taushev and Rose, *The Apocalypse*, 188. After his resurrection by the Lord, St. Lazarus (+1st century), eventually became the first bishop of Kittium (Kition), now Larnaca, on the island of Cyprus.
54   Rev. 13:2-3.

the way of the LORD; make His paths straight,' "[55]), and instruct the world in the acceptance of Antichrist. "To him, it says, will be given the power so that he makes signs and wonders, going before the Antichrist, preparing for him 'the way which leads to perdition.' "[56, 57]

> Then I saw another beast coming up out of the earth, and he had two horns like a lamb and spoke like a dragon. And he exercises all the authority of the first beast in his presence and causes the earth and those who dwell in it to worship the first beast, whose deadly wound was healed. He performs great signs, so that he even makes fire come down from heaven on the earth in the sight of men. And he deceives those who dwell on the earth by those signs which he was granted to do in the sight of the beast, telling those who dwell on the earth to make an image to the beast who was wounded by the sword and lived. He was granted power to give breath to the image of the beast, that the image of the beast should both speak and cause as many as would not worship the image of the beast to be killed.[58]

As the Prophet Elijah called fire down from Heaven to impress the Israelites that the Lord is God and there is no other, so the False Prophet will endeavor to demonstrate the messiahship of Antichrist through a spectacular feat of sorcery that will imitate St. Elijah's miracle.[59] The Lord Himself specifically admonishes

---

55   Matt. 3:3.
56   Matt. 7:13.
57   St. Andrew of Caesarea (+7th century), *Interpretation of the Apocalypse of St. John the Apostle, translated by Eugenia Scarvelis Constantinou* (Quebec City, Université Laval, 2008), sect. 13, ch. 37, 143.
58   Rev. 13:11-14.
59   1 Kings 18:36; see also 2 Kings 1:9-15.

us about the false miracles of Antichrist and the False Prophet, to wit: "there shall arise false Christs, and false prophets, and shall show great signs and wonders; insomuch that, if it were possible, they shall deceive the very elect."[60] Similarly, St. Paul warns of "him, whose coming is after the working of Satan with all power and signs and lying wonders."[61] The Lord in His earthly ministry refused to put on the sort of show demanded by His adversaries — "an evil and adulterous generation seeks after a sign"[62]—whereas Antichrist and the False Prophet will freely light up the skies with what will be the ultimate conjuring trick. Only a generation that has lost the substance of true Christianity—even if it retains its name—would seek spectacular signs and wonders to "prove" the legitimacy of a supposed man of God.

To facilitate the global worship of Antichrist, the False Prophet will produce an image of Antichrist that will speak[63] in a satanic perversion of Orthodox iconography, which reverently depicts God, Christ, and the saints in holy images. A speaking image would have seemed perversely unnatural in pre-modern times, but, in our electronic age, when many non-Orthodox churches employ television as a commonplace, it seems almost unremarkable. It is easy to imagine Antichrist's image and voice being broadcast electronically into every home, public venue, and even house of "worship."

11   DURING ANTICHRIST'S REIGN, HE WILL SIT IN THE Old Testament temple in Jerusalem, which will be rebuilt for him, and be worshipped as God, "so that he sits as God in the temple of God, showing himself that he is God."[64]

---

60   Matt. 24:24.
61   2 Thess. 2:10.
62   Matt. 12:39.
63   Rev. 13:15.
64   2 Thess. 2:4.

Moreover [St. Paul] has also pointed out this which I have shown in many ways: that the temple in Jerusalem was made by the direction of the true God. For the apostle himself, speaking in his own person, distinctly called it the temple of God. . . in which the enemy shall sit, endeavoring to show himself as Christ.[65]

12 During Antichrist's reign, the False Prophet will cause the inhabitants of the world to receive a mark that will be necessary for them to conduct exchange in the world economic system. "He causes all, both small and great, rich and poor, free and slave, to receive a mark on their right hand or on their foreheads, and that no one may buy or sell except one who has the mark or the name of the beast, or the number of his name."[66] Whereas the sign or mark of the Orthodox is the cross, so Antichrist and the False Prophet will give to their followers a mark, which will permit them to engage in worldly commerce. The Orthodox sign of the cross is made with the first three fingers of the right hand first brought up to the forehead; Antichrist's mark, given on the right hand or on the forehead, will be a Satanic perversion of the sign of the cross. As to whether the mark will be outwardly physical or not, a clue may be offered by the Orthodox "sealing" with holy chrism on various parts of the body following baptism, including the forehead and the hands, which represents the sealing of the mind and heart to God. In the Apocalypse of St. John, when the angels of the Lord are sent forth to wreak punishment upon the earth among the followers of Antichrist, they are commanded to spare those with the "seal of God. And it was commanded them that they should not hurt the grass of

---

65   St. Irenaeus of Lyons, *Against Heresies*, bk. 5 ch. 25, nos. 1-2. http://www.newadvent.org/fathers/0103525.htm. Accessed September 13, 2019.
66   Rev. 13:16-17.

the earth, neither any green thing, neither any tree; but only those men which have not the seal of God in their foreheads."[67] Some have argued that the "mark" of Antichrist may represent the state of soul and mind of Antichrist's followers and not necessarily be outwardly visible.

> Like [other marks mentioned in the Apocalypse], it would seem that this mark or brand of the beast finds its fulfill-ment in a *spiritual* mark, not a literal one. There is no reason for thinking the godless will receive a literal tattoo of sorts, any more than for thinking that Christians will literally have the Name of Christ, His Father, the new Jerusalem, and Christ's new Name written on *their* fore-heads.[68]

However, the mark, given to man as a psycho-somatic being, would seem likely to be both physical and spiritual. By giving the mark to their followers, Antichrist and the False Prophet would seem to harness all of the spiritual and material powers of darkness in order to ensnare the inhabitants of their global empire. Even now, contemporary technology is approaching the point where it can produce implants in the human body that would permit the user to buy or sell in much the same way as a credit card already does. It is not impossible to imagine a future world in which, following some gigantic economic upheaval or war, a movement arises to "mark" the inhabitants of the earth for the sake of social and economic order. Some contemporary Fathers have affirmed that no Orthodox Christian should accept any implant, tattoo, or mark of any kind lest it has a connection to the mark of Antichrist.

---

67   Rev. 9:4.
68   Fr. Lawrence R. Farley, *The Apocalypse of St. John, A Revelation of Love and Power* (Chesterton, Conciliar, 2012), 148.

13 PRESSURE TO RECEIVE ANTICHRIST'S MARK WILL COME by way of being threatened with exclusion from the world economic system. Antichrist will exercise a global monopoly on the means of trade, indicating the provenance of his power from the realm of mammon. The money-changers whom Christ expelled from the temple during his earthly ministry provided special, ritually clean temple money to be used to purchase animals for sacrifice.[69] Just as they monopolized exchange in the temple grounds of their day, Antichrist, the ultimate money-changer, reigning from the rebuilt temple in Jerusalem, will monopolize exchange worldwide until he, like his predecessors, is driven out by the Lord's return. "Here is wisdom. Let him who has understanding calculate the number of the beast, for it is the number of a man: His number is 666."[70] The mark will be Antichrist's name, or a numerical transposition thereof, which will add up to six hundred sixty-six. This number consists of three consecutive sixes: six, representing incompleteness, is one short of the numerically perfect seven and mystically encapsulates all of the evil manifested in human history.

And there is therefore in this beast, when he comes, a recapitulation made of all sorts of iniquity and of every deceit, in order that all apostate power, flowing into and being shut up in him, may be sent into the furnace of fire. Fittingly, therefore, shall his name possess the number six hundred and sixty-six, since he sums up in his own person all the commixture of wickedness which took place previous to the deluge, due to the apostasy of the angels. For Noah was six hundred years old when the deluge came upon the earth, sweeping away the rebellious world, for the sake of that most infamous generation

69   See John 2:15.
70   Rev. 13:18.

which lived in the times of Noah. And [Antichrist] also sums up every error of devised idols since the flood, together with the slaying of the prophets and the cutting off of the just. For that image which was set up by Nebuchadnezzar had indeed a height of sixty cubits, while the breadth was six cubits; on account of which Ananias, Azarias, and Misael, when they did not worship it, were cast into a furnace of fire, pointing out prophetically, by what happened to them, the wrath against the righteous which shall arise towards the [time of the] end. For that image, taken as a whole, was a prefiguring of this man's coming, decreeing that he should undoubtedly himself alone be worshipped by all men.[71]

Furthermore, six hundred sixty-six talents was the annual revenue in weight of gold of the Kingdom of Israel during the reign of King Solomon.[72] As Solomon was renowned throughout the world for his wisdom and the glory of his reign, yet later became ensnared in idolatry, so Antichrist will appear to the world as incomparably wise and glorious.

14 During the reign of Antichrist, the faithful remnant of the Church will withdraw from secular society to save themselves. This final ordeal of Christ's Church on earth is dramatically depicted in the Apocalypse of St. John. Here the Church, the bride of Christ, is depicted as a woman in labor struggling to give birth to a man-child just as the Church struggles to give birth to Christ in each of her members. A multi-headed, multi-horned great, fiery-red dragon, Satan, desires to devour the man-child and persecutes the woman.

---

71   St. Irenaeus of Lyons, *Against Heresies*, bk. 5, ch. 29, no. 2. http://www.newadvent.org/fathers/0103529.htm. Accessed September 13, 2019.
72   1 Kgs. 10:14. More than two tons.

Now a great sign appeared in heaven: a woman clothed with the sun, with the moon under her feet, and on her head a garland of twelve stars. Then being with child, she cried out in labor and in pain to give birth. And another sign appeared in heaven: behold, a great, fiery-red dragon having seven heads and ten horns, and seven diadems on his heads. His tail drew a third of the stars of heaven and threw them to the earth. And the dragon stood before the woman who was ready to give birth, to devour her Child as soon as it was born. She bore a male Child who was to rule all nations with a rod of iron. And her Child was caught up to God and His throne .... Now when the dragon saw that he had been cast to the earth, he persecuted the woman who gave birth to the male Child. But the woman was given two wings of a great eagle, that she might fly into the wilderness to her place, where she is nourished for a time and times and half a time, from the presence of the serpent. So the serpent spewed water out of his mouth like a flood after the woman, that he might cause her to be carried away by the flood. But the earth helped the woman, and the earth opened its mouth and swallowed up the flood which the dragon had spewed out of his mouth. And the dragon was enraged with the woman, and he went to make war with the rest of her offspring, who keep the commandments of God and have the testimony of Jesus Christ.[73]

The flood of water the dragon spews forth to drown the woman may be thought of as the sea of humanity given over to Satan and Antichrist who will persecute the Church. During the three-and-a-half-year reign of Antichrist, the faithful will flee from the centers of civilization to escape the persecution

---

73   Rev. 12:1-5, 13-17.

of Antichrist. With the world following a man and regime utterly given over to Satan, the faithful's salvation will come only from the Lord's descent from Heaven "with power and great glory."[74]

15 AT THE POINT DURING ANTICHRIST'S REIGN WHEN nearly the whole world has gone after him, God will permit terrible plagues to afflict humanity in a last effort to bring it to its senses. "And men were scorched with great heat, and they blasphemed the name of God who has power over these plagues; and they did not repent and give Him glory."[75]

> But the rest of mankind, who were not killed by these plagues, did not repent of the works of their hands, that they should not worship demons, and idols of gold, silver, brass, stone, and wood, which can neither see nor hear nor walk. And they did not repent of their murders or their sorceries or their sexual immorality or their thefts.[76]

The plagues may be literal in the sense of epidemic disease and catastrophic meteorological events evocative of the scourges sent upon pharaonic Egypt or the destruction of Sodom and Gomorrah, but it seems that they may also be understood as plagues of sinfulness and spiritual blindness, e.g., the "heat of temptations, it says, so that by painful afflictions they will hate sin, the mother of these (attacks)."[77]

> Then the fifth angel poured out his bowl on the throne of the beast, and his kingdom became full of darkness; and they gnawed their tongues because of the pain. They

---

74   Matt. 24:30.

75   Rev. 16:8.

76   Rev. 9:20-1.

77   St. Andrew of Caesarea, *Interpretation of the Apocalypse*, sect. 17 ch. 49, 165.

blasphemed the God of heaven because of their pains and their sores, and did not repent of their deeds.[78]

This reminds one of the ninth plague in Egypt (Exod. 10:21). By this plague one must understand the significant decrease of the greatness and authority of Antichrist whose magnificence up until then had struck people, and at the same time one must understand the stubborn lack of repentance of those who worshipped the Antichrist.[79]

While most of the relevant passages from St. John's Apocalypse tell us that humanity will not repent despite widespread, divinely ordained chastisement, there appears an important exception: "In the same hour there was a great earthquake, and a tenth of the city [Jerusalem] fell. In the earthquake seven thousand people were killed, and the rest were afraid and gave glory to the God of heaven."[80] Even in these last days of human history, when the mass of humankind will have followed the great deceiver, it seems that God's call to repentance will be heeded by some: "When the unbelieving are castigated and the martyrs of Christ are glorified, it says those worthy of salvation will glorify God."[81]

16 ANTICHRIST WILL BE DEFEATED IN BATTLE IN THE HOLY Land near the mount of Megiddo (Armageddon). " 'Armageddon' signifies cutting up or murder. . . This name is taken from the valley of Mageddo, where King Josias fell in battle with Pharaoh Necho (II Chron. 35:22)."[82] It is not clear whether the "battle" will be spiritual and/or literal in nature in

---

78   Rev. 16:10-11.
79   Taushev and Rose, *The Apocalypse*, 218-19.
80   Rev. 11:13.
81   St. Andrew of Caesarea, *Interpretation of the Apocalypse*, sect. 11 ch. 31, 124.
82   Taushev and Rose, *The Apocalypse*, 220.

the sense of a military clash; it may refer to the Second Coming of Christ Itself: "And then the lawless one will be revealed, whom the Lord will consume with the breath of His mouth and destroy with the brightness of His coming."[83]

> And I saw the beast, the kings of the earth, and their armies, gathered together to make war against Him who sat on the horse and against His army. Then the beast was captured, and with him the false prophet who worked signs in his presence, by which he deceived those who received the mark of the beast and those who worshiped his image. These two were cast alive into the lake of fire burning with brimstone. And the rest were killed with the sword which proceeded from the mouth of Him who sat on the horse. And all the birds were filled with their flesh.[84]

17 WITH THE DEFEAT OF ANTICHRIST, THE SIGN OF Christ—the Cross—will appear in the heavens, which will signal Christ's Second Coming, the end of this world, and the imminent Last Judgment.

> Immediately after the tribulation of those days the sun will be darkened, and the moon will not give its light; the stars will fall from heaven, and the powers of the heavens will be shaken. Then the sign of the Son of Man will appear in heaven, and then all the tribes of the earth will mourn, and they will see the Son of Man coming on the clouds of heaven with power and great glory. And He will send His angels with a great sound of a trumpet, and they

---

83   2 Thess. 2:8.
84   Rev.19:19-21. See also Taushev and Rose, *The Apocalypse*, 247.

will gather together His elect from the four winds, from one end of heaven to the other.[85]

That "all the tribes of the earth will mourn" the appearance of the sign of Christ indicates that the great majority of the world will have followed Antichrist and will greet the Second Coming of Christ, not as the return of the rightful King over a usurper, but as the calamitous defeat of their counterfeit champion. With the glorious, supernatural appearance of the Cross in the heavens, the world will realize in a moment that it will have believed a lie—but it will be too late, the world will have made its choice "that they all may be condemned who did not believe the truth but had pleasure in unrighteousness."[86]

Christ's Second Coming, "as the lightning comes from the east and flashes to the west, so also will the coming of the Son of Man be,"[87] will be the end of world history when "there should be time no longer."[88] This cataclysmic event will mark an inconceivable transformation of fallen creation when "the elements will melt with fervent heat; both the earth and the works that are in it will be burned up."[89] All the great willful works of man through the centuries will be consumed with divine fire. Human civilization as we understand it will vanish "in a moment, in the twinkling of an eye."[90] All of those alive on earth, and all of the dead from ages past, whose bodies will be resurrected, will be judged—the Last Judgment—and sent in a moment either to eternal blessedness or eternal perdition from which there will be no appeal.[91]

---

85   Matt. 24:29-31.
86   2 Thess. 2:12.
87   Matt. 24:27.
88   Rev. 10:6.
89   2 Pet. 3:10.
90   1 Cor. 15:52.
91   ". . . His second advent from heaven will not happen secretly as did His coming at first, but will be illustrious and terrible. For He shall descend with the holy angels guarding Him, and in the glory of God the Father, to judge the world in righteousness.

In His former advent, He was wrapped in swaddling clothes in the manger; in His second, He "covereth Himself with light as with a garment."[92] In His first coming, "He endured the Cross, despising shame;"[93] in His second, He comes attended by a host of Angels, receiving glory.[94]

When He comes again on His throne of glory, He will not be unseen by anyone. No one will ask, as did the Magi before His first coming: "Where is the King?" Everyone will see the King and recognize Him as the King. But this vision and recognition will be unto joy for some, and unto fear and terror for others.[95]

THE APE OF CHRIST

Antichrist has been described as the "ape of Christ," an impostor who will trick men into accepting him as their savior. Antichrist is not merely the enemy of Christ but is a pretender to the Prototype. Antichrist will appear as Christ to a world that has come adrift from the authentic sources of Christian inspiration; he will be the messiah that the world can accept, a world leader who will promise, and to an extent deliver, peace, prosperity, and social harmony, an earthly paradise that will in fact be a design of the devil. In short, Antichrist will be an actor,

---

. ." (St. Cyril of Alexandria, *Commentary on the Gospel of Saint Luke*, ch. 21, homily 139. B#42, 555 as quoted in Manley, *The Bible and the Holy Fathers for Orthodox*, [Crestwood: Monastery Books, 1999], 676-7)

92   Ps. 104/105:2.

93   Heb. 12:2.

94   St. Cyril of Jerusalem, *Catechetical Lectures*, XV, 1. http://www.newadvent.org/fathers/310115.htm. Accessed September 13, 2019.

95   St. Nikolai Velimirovic, *The Prologue of Ohrid*, Volume One, translated from the Serbian by Fr. Timothy Tepsić (Alhambra, Serbian Orthodox Diocese of Western America, 2002), March 11, 240)

a pretender, a faker, one whose whole purpose is to give a false impression. And invariably the most convincing performance is given by the actor who has fully convinced himself that he has actually become the character that he has taken on. It is significant in our own time that actors receive widespread adulation for their craft, for making us believe what they are not. Far from serving merely as entertainers, actors often assume significant political roles; their favor is routinely sought by established politicians; they garner huge fees; they attract enormous audiences for their political and cultural pronouncements. Indeed, in the worlds of entertainment and politics, the one sometimes merges completely into the other as in the cases of certain Western politicians and at least one US president who made a career in acting (and another who had his own "reality" TV program). That acting is so closely intertwined with politics, and vice versa, bespeaks the fact that modern politics is itself increasingly a game of acting, of pretending to be something that one is not. Politics has always to some extent been about putting on appearances, but, in our time of electronic mass media, the falseness that politics naturally elicits is amplified exponentially. When Antichrist comes, he will do so as the supreme example of the actor and politician made one.

Christ and Antichrist are polar opposites. One is life, the other death; One leads to salvation, the other damnation; One loves, the other hates; One is pure, the other debased; One reigns eternally, the other temporarily; One gives Himself sacrificially for the world, the other arrogates the world to himself. Antichrist is the antithesis of Christ, but, because he will stand in place of Christ, he will bear outward similarities.

> [T]he deceiver seeks to liken himself in all things to the Son of God. Christ is a lion, so Antichrist is also a lion; Christ is a king, so Antichrist is also a king. The Savior was manifested as a lamb; so he too, in like manner, will

appear as a lamb, though within he is a wolf. The Savior came into the World in the circumcision, and he will come in the same manner. The Lord sent apostles among all the nations, and he in like manner will send false apostles. The Savior gathered together the sheep that were scattered abroad, and he in like manner will bring together a people that are scattered abroad. The Lord gave a seal to those who believed on Him, and he will give one in like manner. The Savior appeared in the form of man, and he too will come in the form of a man. The Savior raised up and showed His holy flesh like a temple, and he will raise a temple of stone in Jerusalem.[96]

Perhaps what is most difficult to accept about Antichrist—and what is most important to remember—is that he will come as "Christ" and therefore his followers will likely consider themselves "Christians" even while they reject everything that is truly Christian and Orthodox. Such "Christians" are those about which the Lord spoke when He warned:

> Not everyone who says to Me, "Lord, Lord," shall enter the kingdom of heaven, but he who does the will of My Father in heaven. Many will say to Me in that day, "Lord, Lord, have we not prophesied in Your name, cast out demons in Your name, and done many wonders in Your name". And then I will declare to them, "I never knew you; depart from Me, you who practice lawlessness!"[97]

The Lord's admonition is not limited to the followers of Antichrist, but they will above all be condemned by it. The

---

96   St. Hippolytus of Rome, *Treatise on Christ and Antichrist*, ch. 6. http://www. newadvent.org/fathers/0516.htm. Accessed September 13, 2019.
97   Matt. 7:21-3.

time of Antichrist is not a time of universal atheism, but of widespread false Christianity. The devil and his proxy, Antichrist, do not merely want to suppress the True Church, they want to build their own perverse imitation of it, a "false Christian Kingdom."[98] Satan's hatred of Christ is largely envy: he desires the worship and adoration that is rightly Christ's alone and so endeavors to engineer his own "church" and "messiah" to fake what he cannot rightly have. "Woe to the inhabitants of the earth and the sea! For the devil has come down to you, having great wrath, because he knows that he has a short time."[99]

One point regarding the timeline of events leading up to Antichrist's reign seems worth mentioning here. Because Antichrist will be seen by many heterodox Christians as Christ come again, it seems at least possible that his reign from the temple in Jerusalem will have to occur after the defeat of a false antichrist. By defeating another who claims to be Christ, Antichrist could more plausibly claim to be fulfilling prophecy as Christ come again. By defeating another antichrist, he could more plausibly claim that he is the true savior whose supposed "thousand-year reign"[100] has now begun. Antichrist may even orchestrate a battle at Armageddon against this other antichrist in order to "fulfill" prophecy more exactly. Of course, there is no end to the possibilities of how Antichrist may try to fulfill prophecy and mimic Jesus Christ but defeating a false antichrist and thus demonstrating his "messianic" power and status could help pave the way for his acceptance as the messiah.

Whatever the events leading up to Antichrist's reign, we must remember that the tyranny that he represents is, first and foremost, a spiritual tyranny, a despotism of souls, that can perdure even in a time of apparent freedom. We should remember that

---

98   Taushev and Rose, *The Apocalypse*, 215.
99   Rev. 12:12.
100   Rev. 20:4.

the slave who imagines himself free is doubly enslaved, some-thing increasingly prevalent in the modern world. Even while Antichrist will emerge as a great historical figure, his appear-ance will ultimately be the consequence of the spiritual state of mankind, of which the outward, visible state is a reflection.

While it is understandable that the prophecies concerning Antichrist's coming should appear worrying, even frightening, a competent examination of Antichrist and his reign and the promise of Christ's Second Coming should provide reassur-ance to the faithful when persecutions and adversity arise. We should not be surprised when evil manifests itself in history in massive and frightening ways, nor should we lose heart when the world belittles, ostracizes, or persecutes those of the True Church: "These things I have spoken to you, that in Me you may have peace. In the world you will have tribulation; but be of good cheer, I have overcome the world."[101] It is important to appreciate that, while Antichrist and his regime represent the ultimate manifestation of evil in history, the danger they embody has been at work throughout the ages. In examining them, we are not only preparing for his arrival (whether that will transpire in our earthly lifetime we do not know) but endeavor-ing to preserve ourselves from the anti-Christianity burgeoning in the world now, which seeks to deceive us and rob us of our salvation, "for the mystery of lawlessness is already at work."[102] Antichrist's attributes as a pretender and imposter, how he feigns love and good intentions; his roles as king, high priest, and savior of a global church and empire; the great falling away from the Church that is to precede his advent; his control over a universal monetary regime; his use of sorcery to deceive the masses—are all currents at work in the world today.

---

101   John 16:33.
102   2 Thess. 2:7.

CHAPTER 2

THE PRINCIPLES OF GLOBALIZATION

That will be the time in which righteousness shall be cast out, and innocence be hated; in which the wicked shall prey upon the good as enemies; neither law, nor order, nor military discipline shall be preserved; no one shall reverence hoary locks, nor recognise the duty of piety, nor pity sex or infancy; all things shall be confounded and mixed together against right, and against the laws of nature.

Lactantius (ca. +320), *Divine Institutes*
Book VII, Ch. 17[1]

In many ways, the Church was the first (and only) successful undertaking of globalization, an enterprise that takes people from all backgrounds, cultures, races, and languages and places them in voluntary submission to the One True God for the purpose of salvation in eternity, "where there is neither Greek nor Jew, circumcised nor uncircumcised, barbarian, Scythian, slave nor free, but Christ is all and in all."[2] Contemporary globalization mimics the spiritual unity of the Church with a

---

1   http://www.newadvent.org/fathers/07017.htm. Accessed September 13, 2019.
2   Col. 3:11.

fraudulent unity that has nothing to do with the genuine life of the Spirit.

Secular globalization's process of drawing the disparate elements of the world ever more tightly together implies a corresponding diminution in the traditional distinctions that have historically ordered and differentiated human society. Those distinctions have chiefly been ethnic, territorial, linguistic, and religious. Peoples have historically organized around their common ancestry, the land they shared, the languages they spoke, and the gods they worshipped. Such distinctions gave definition and meaning to the tribes, empires, and nation-states that rose and fell, dispersed and coalesced, throughout history; they are what made it possible to tell "us" from "them." Globalization involves the displacement of these ancient distinctions by an emerging global consciousness that will eventually engender allegiance to a global authority that will, at least in principle, allow for no distinctions. In a fully globalized world, the individual would, at least in theory, identify only with the global society and not with any particular subset. In such a world, loyalties to nation, clan, and particular religion would wither away (even while they need not disappear entirely – one can easily imagine a federal world polity, perhaps analogous to the United States, in which local distinctions would remain even while a central authority reigned supreme). In a fully globalized world, there would be no "them," only "us"; it would, in the thinking of some political theorists, amount to a post-political world.[3]

It is obvious, however, that, even in the midst of globalization's ongoing process of unification, social, religious, and national differences persist and, in some cases, appear to be intensifying. Indeed, integral to globalization's centripetal process is the apparently paradoxical phenomenon of fragmentation. On the one hand, globalization implies ever greater unification; on

---

3   Schmitt, *The Concept of the Political*, 57.

the other, in order for greater global unity to become possible, old centers of power must be broken up. Resistance to globalization can only come from sub-global alternative centers of power dedicated to their own self-preservation, namely, the old nation-states, which marks them as key targets in the globalists' crusade. It has been at the level of the nation-state that the greatest erosion of power and political legitimacy has occurred in our time. Perhaps more than anything, "nationalism" has come to be considered the greatest political sin. In the modern era, people have tended to identify as members of particular nation-states, which themselves grew out of the old, nominally Christian, empires of the past. The breakdown of the nation-state in our time is essential to global unification. The cases of the old Soviet Union and Yugoslavia illustrate this principle vividly: in both cases, independent nation-states suffered disintegration into their constituent regions, which, weakened and disoriented, were then picked off piecemeal and incorporated into the Western-dominated global system.[4]

Some have argued that, rather than as a force complimenting globalism, fragmentation in fact cuts against it. One commentator went so far as to assert, "Tribalism suddenly seems ascendant over globalism,"[5] but this is to miss the forest for the trees. Strong, self-supporting nation-states are the natural adversaries of globalization because they are not dependent on outside centers of power for their well-being; they are "sovereign" in the classical sense. Nations rent by "tribalism" and similar forces, however, more readily succumb to globalist pressures because they are by nature internally weaker. And tribal forces within a nation

---

4   The important exception appears to be that of Russia, which, after a generation of tremendous struggle and hardship following the breakup of the Soviet Union, has emerged as one of the few true counterweights to the Western-led global order, perhaps history's last Orthodox great power. See Conclusion.

5   Patrick Buchanan, "*Is Tribalism the Future?*" http://buchanan.org/blog/is-tribalism-the-future-4668. Accessed September 9, 2017.

naturally look to international and global centers of power for assistance in their quest to emerge onto the international scene. In sum, tribalism and other fragmenting forces (examples of which include Scotland in the UK, Catalonia in Spain, Tibet in China, Kurdistan across Turkey, Iraq, and Iran, etc.) are helping to put pressure on old nation-states and render them more dependent on the global system.

However, contrary to all accepted understandings of sovereignty and national self-interest, some other, more robust, nation-states, are voluntarily ceding their independence to supranational bodies that are slowly acquiring the trappings of political legitimacy. The most salient example of this principle at work has been the diminution of national authority among the European nation-states and their amalgamation into the European Union, which in turn has become one of the principal building-blocks of the emerging global system. The vote of the United Kingdom to leave the European Union, which some argued spelled the beginning of the end for the bloc, has tended to illustrate its resiliency rather than its brittleness: so far, Britain's departure is proving the exception rather than the rule; there has been no sudden "race for the exit." As negotiations for Britain to leave proceed, it is not clear what the meaningful differences will turn out to be for a non-EU United Kingdom – except that it may precipitate its breakup through a second, this time successful, Scottish referendum for independence. So far, "Brexit" is proving a case of "the more things change the more they stay the same." Despite the "lurch to the right" of the past few years, the centralizing program of the European project continues apace, not the least abetted by the recent influxes of Muslim migrants, who are playing havoc with the traditional European social order and paralyzing independent government. Why so many individual nation-states should voluntarily cede much of their independence is one of the most perplexing questions in modern political science. Power and decision-making have historically been something that nations have guarded jealously rather than permitted to slip away without a fight. The why of it can only be answered by transcending the merely political and discovering the motivations behind the ideology of globalization itself.

It is worth noting that globalization has often made its greatest strides, not in times of peace, when it advances incrementally, but in times when the international order seems most broken and fragmented, namely, during times of war. Globalization is a centuries-long process that has continued to advance even in the face of enormous setbacks. Major war would appear to be a situation when globalization has most spectacularly failed, yet it has been out of wars – such as World War II – that some of the most prominent and lasting institutions for global integration have come forth, the United Nations and the EU being notable examples. Contemporary short-term setbacks to globalization, such as the rise of nationalist parties, while heartening for some anti-globalists, have proven themselves ineffective over the long-term in reversing the march of globalization, which is so clearly a program of "the establishment."[6]

THE AGE OF CONFUSION

The age of globalization is the age of confusion. "Con-fuse" means to perplex or bewilder but also to fuse, or mix, together. The progressive delegitimization of the traditional criteria for ordering human society – ethnicity, religion, territory, language – increasingly leaves humankind in a state of bewilderment. Individually and collectively, man needs palpable distinctions to make sense of his world; without such distinctions, individual man is cast adrift, unable to know who he is, with whom he

---

6   See below and chs. 6 and 7.

should associate, or how he should live. Today, with traditional distinctions fast losing their currency, and especially with the disintegration of traditional Christianity, human society and individual human psyches grow increasingly disordered. The age of confusion entails the disorientation of individuals, the breaking up of old means of associating, and the fusing together into a new, global mass groups and individuals hitherto separate.

As the world grows more confused, individuals look for new forms of identity and order. With each new political/social/economic crisis that erupts onto the world stage and the ensuing response, old forms of order are weakened, and new ones emerge. Whatever the nature of the problem that arises, one can be sure that in our time the solution will involve more globalization. The one answer that cannot be permitted to gain traction, regardless of the question asked, is a reasonable return to greater local independence among the nations of the world and a reviving of traditional forms of identity and order.

To disorient and bewilder someone is to leave him open to the suggestion or solution that one cares to provide. The shocking, disorienting, maddening whirl of the contemporary world keeps us perpetually off balance and makes us prone to whatever is "latest and greatest" that promises to relieve our confusion. Thus are we led, bit by bit, to the denouement, the point at which all roads converge. When the time comes, Antichrist will appear to bring order to a confused and bewildered world, which, in its misplaced gratitude, will revere him as its savior. Whereas Christ came not to "bring peace but a sword,"[7] separating His "sheep from the goats,"[8] the mantra of the age of confusion is "unite." Jesus said:

---

7   Matt. 10:34.
8   Matt. 25:32.

> Do you suppose that I came to give peace on earth? I
> tell you, not at all, but rather division. For from now on
> five in one house will be divided: three against two, and
> two against three. Father will be divided against son and
> son against father, mother against daughter and daughter
> against mother, mother-in-law against her daughter-in-
> law and daughter-in-law against her mother-in-law.[9]

Truth is divisive; it separates the holy from the unholy, the
faithful from the unbelieving, the Orthodox from the heterodox.
Truth is often unpleasant and inconvenient; it makes demands
contrary to our personal desires and beliefs. Whereas Christ
came to bring truth and, thereby, division, Antichrist comes to
bring a fraudulent unity and to drive truth from history.

The bewilderment many people feel when trying to understand the world's ongoing slide into greater confusion results
from a fundamental misconception at the heart of the modern
world. One of the most mistaken and pernicious modern ideas,
championed by, among others, John Stuart Mill (1806-73) and
Oliver Wendell Holmes (1841–1935), is the belief that, over time,
that which is good and true will naturally overcome that which is
evil and false. This is the premise behind Mills' "marketplace of
ideas": as long as ideas are allowed to circulate freely, the truth
will, over time, prevail in society. Mill's argument is effectively
an inversion of the Lord's words, "If you abide in My word,
you are My disciples indeed. And you shall know the truth, and
the truth shall make you free."[10] Contrary to Mill's thinking,
it is truth that grants freedom, not an artificial freedom that
naturally fosters truth.

Mills' and Holmes' notion could never take root in a genuinely Christian society because one of (Orthodox) Christianity's

---

9   Luke 12:51-3.
10   John 8:31-2.

principal tenets is that this world is subject to sin, and, therefore, rather than the triumph of goodness and truth, we should expect exactly the opposite. The examples of Christ and of innumerable martyrs through the centuries testify as to how we can expect goodness and truth to fare in this world. The ultimate triumph of goodness and truth comes not in this world but in the next, not in the realm of history but in eternity. In this world, goodness and truth must be fought and suffered for, against the odds, if they are not to be overwhelmed by darkness. The modern mind, however, expects goodness and truth to be the norm and therefore is perplexed when falsity and evil persist and multiply; even more dangerously, it begins to mistake the one for the other. The modern mind expects "peace and safety"[11] rather than turmoil and insecurity in this life. When the latter reigns, the modern mind is ever looking for that great solution that will end the perplexity and usher in the golden era that it believes is its right. The modern conception of history is inseparable from the related notion of "progress," the idea that, given sufficient time, the world must naturally ascend toward higher degrees of perfection, where mankind will enjoy greater peace, comfort, and justice. However,

> The Christian view of world history is entirely opposed to this kind of evolutionary optimism. What we are taught to expect are disasters in the world of nature, increasingly destructive warfare between men, bewilderment and apostasy among those who call themselves Christians (see especially Matt. 24:3-27). The period of tribulation will culminate with the appearance of the "man of sin" or Antichrist.[12]

---

11   1 Thess. 5:3.

12   Metropolitan Kallistos Ware, *The Orthodox Way* (Crestwood, St., Vladimir's Seminary, 2012), 134.

The world makes far more sense if the modern mindset is discarded. The course of history is far easier to understand if the wars, genocides, revolutions, false teachings, and multiplying social pathologies of the modern age are seen as logical manifestations of a fallen world that increasingly rejects the only sure bulwark against evil, the Church, and a society oriented around her. Orthodox Christian society was premised on the awareness that this life is but temporary and that hardship, death, disease, and suffering are integral aspects of it, something which modern society, premised on the hope of perfecting the world, rather than perfecting individual souls for eternity, rejects. To scratch our heads in bewilderment at the course of modern history is to miss the point: a post-Christian civilization—still thirsting for salvation but having rejected the means of attaining it—will naturally unravel while it seeks solutions in all the wrong places and from all the wrong people.

The age of confusion is doubly bewildering without an awareness of *why* the world grows increasingly confused, disordered, and irrational. Without knowledge of the coming Antichrist, the manifest failure of efforts to arrest the slide into global confusion—efforts led through the years often by capable and well-intentioned people—are incomprehensible. Many perceive the slide, but few there are who correctly apprehend the larger forces at work or where it is all leading. Genuine understanding in an age of confusion is a rare thing indeed. But it is this understanding that we must come to if we are to "hold fast"[13] until the end: "it is very easy to give up the battle if one does not have a picture of the *meaning* of this seeming triumph of evil, and a knowledge of the eventual triumph of good and Christ's Church."[14]

---

13   2 Tim. 1:13.
14   Taushev and Rose, *The Apocalypse*, 33.

Babel, Then and Now

The modern enterprise of globalization has an explicit biblical precedent in the story of the Tower of Babel. United in those days in a common language, mankind sought to construct a temple to its own greatness in the form of a tower that would "reach unto heaven."[15] The tower itself symbolized mankind's unity and its intention not to be disunited and "scattered abroad."

> Now the whole earth had one language and one speech.... And they said, "Come, let us build ourselves a city, and a tower whose top is in the heavens; let us make a name for ourselves, lest we be scattered abroad over the face of the whole earth." But the LORD came down to see the city and the tower which the sons of men had built. And the LORD said, "Indeed the people are one and they all have one language, and this is what they begin to do; now nothing that they propose to do will be withheld from them. Come, let Us go down and there confuse their language, that they may not understand one another's speech." So the LORD scattered them abroad from there over the face of all the earth, and they ceased building the city. Therefore, its name is called Babel, because there the LORD confused the language of all the earth; and from there the LORD scattered them abroad over the face of all the earth.[16]

Babel was mankind's first collective effort to recover the paradise that had been lost through sin in the Garden of Eden and to achieve a unity outside of God's providence. Babel then and

---

15   Gen. 11:4.
16   Gen. 11:1, 4–9.

globalization today seek to undo the divisions among men that have served to check man's prideful dream of regaining paradise through his own knowledge and power. Genuine unity is only achieved in the mystical communion of the Church as the Body of Christ, something that no terrestrial political organization can provide. As mankind endeavored to unite at Babel, to "make a name"[17] in defiance of God, so will the world unite under the banner of Antichrist and will construct for him a temple and throne in Jerusalem.

God's descent to confound the tongues of man at Babel was, like the curse pronounced in Eden, for man's ultimate salvation. It is not for man's benefit to believe a lie, to believe that Satan's counsel bestows life rather than death. Had the Lord not "scattered" the builders of Babel "abroad," it seems possible that Antichrist—or a comparable antichristian figure—may well have then appeared into history with all of its catastrophic consequences. Modern globalization is another attempt to undo the ancient curse, to prove that man, without God, can save himself and "be like God."[18] The builders of the global regime of Antichrist will, for a short time, achieve what the builders of Babel failed to do: they will unite the world in a global imperium and set up their own god, their own christ, in a temple of their own building, in place of the True God and True Christ. God's forbearance will permit them this much, but His love for His faithful will not permit His Church to be driven from the earth entirely. It will, however, be a close-run thing: "When the Son of Man comes, will He find faith on the earth?"[19]

Globalization's promise of world unity mimics the unity of believers in the Church that was, among other times, dramatically played out on the day of Pentecost.[20] Pentecost is the

---

17   Gen. 11:4.
18   Gen. 3:5.
19   Luke 18:8.
20   See Acts 2.

anti-Babel, the miraculous unifying of different tongues in the Church by the Holy Spirit. The Church may be considered the original form of globalization, in which individuals from all nations, languages, and cultures willfully bent their necks to the yoke of Christ and came to look upon one another as fellow heirs of the Divine Kingdom. The oneness of the Church, however, is neither an historical artifact nor a function of terrestrial politics but an expression of the eternal love and oneness of God manifested through grace in the realm of human history.

> The idea of the Church as a new, perfect community as distinct from a community of the state organization is profoundly and beautifully expressed in the kontakion for the feast of the Descent of the Holy Spirit (Pentecost), when the Church recalls and celebrates its beginning. "When the Most High came down and confused the tongues, He divided the nations, but when He distributed the tongues of fire, He called all into unity. Therefore, with one accord we glorify the All-holy Spirit."[21] Here the creation of the Church is placed into opposition to the Tower of Babel and the "confusing of tongues," at which time God, the Most High, came down, confused the tongues and divided the nations.[22]

Globalization's great appeal is its superficial resemblance to the Church and her mission to make all peoples one. Whereas the Church is one in Christ through the love of God, the process of globalization is driven by willful men who reject the Kingdom of God and seek to build in its place a global kingdom of man.[23]

---

21   Kontakion hymn for Holy Pentecost.

22   St. Ilarion Troitsky, *Christianity or the Church?* http://orthodoxinfo.com/inquirers/sthilarion_church.aspx. Accessed September 13, 2019.

23   Significantly, with the rise of English in our time as a (near) global language, once again it seems that "the whole earth had one language and one speech" much as at the time of Babel.

The tendency of so many commentators to be swept up in globalization's currents and to confuse the secular process of global integration with the evangelical Christian mission has reached even to Orthodox circles. One of our time's most distinguished theologians and historians of the Church, His Beatitude Archbishop Anastasios Yannoulatos of Albania, has addressed the topic of globalization directly, and what he says is worth reflecting on. He begins by observing that human disunity began with the Fall, which broke the *koinonia*—the loving community—between man and God and man and man. "Ever since then, human history has been defined by two opposing tendencies: the path toward unity, which is an attribute of our 'divine image,' and the path toward fragmentation, which is a consequence of the fall."[24] His Beatitude affirms that, with the Incarnation of the Word of God, "Humanity, which had once been alienated from its own true nature, could now return to *koinonia* with the Holy Trinity through Christ."[25]

While there is much genuinely Orthodox insight in His Beatitude's words, in his conception of "unity" and "fragmentation" he strikes a false note that bespeaks a subtle but consequential error. While affirming that "*koinonia* with the Holy Trinity" comes "through Christ," he does not elaborate on how "the path toward unity" is properly to come about. An Orthodox answer, however it might be articulated, must put the Church foremost: it is only in the Church, the concrete manifestation of the Kingdom of God on earth, that true unity can exist. While His Beatitude observes that both "[h]istory and Christian hope have been imprinted with a vision of ultimate unity,"[26] those visions of unity are very different, and it is a positive danger to confuse them. That he does confuse them is evinced by his later assertion that "History

---

24   Archbishop Anastasios Yannoulatos, *Facing the World: Orthodox Thoughts on Global Perspectives* (Crestwood, St., Vladimir's Seminary, 2003), 25-6.

25   Yannoulatos, *Facing the World*, 27.

26   Ibid., 30.

is humanity's extraordinary evolution toward its ultimate *koinonia* in God,"[27] which is exactly the sort of misguided secular thinking that conflates the eschatological vision of the Church with that of antichristian globalization. If anything, history has shown itself to be the opposite, namely, a progressive falling away from God's Law and His Church rather than a movement toward them (see chs. 4 and 5). Man's attempts to bring an "ultimate unity" to the world—from Babel to the great pre-Christian empires, to the conquests of Islam, to the French Revolution's "Universal Republic," to Communism's stateless workers' paradise—have proven the bloodiest and most destructive undertakings in history. While the fragmentation of humanity—the discord among nations, the striving of clans and ethnicities, even the simple absence of love between individuals—is indeed a manifestation of the Fall and sin, it does not therefore follow that unity of any sort is a Godly remedy; we have seen as much in the example of Babel.[28] The Church's global mission to "make disciples of all the nations"[29] is the force for true unity in the world, and it cannot be supplanted by any merely historical process or political program. Orthodoxy's "role" in globalization—if it may be said to have one—is to carry on with its ancient mission of witnessing to the Gospel of Jesus Christ and the perduring unity of His Church while refuting the pretense of any secular enterprise to providing an equivalent of Christian salvation.

---

27   Ibid., 41.

28   "For it is possible to do well in separating. Wherefore also He has said, 'I have come not to bring peace upon the earth but a sword' (Matt. 10:34). For there is an evil concord, and there is a good disagreement. So those who built the tower (Gen. 11:4) agreed together to their own hurt, and these same again were separated, though unwillingly, yet for their good. So also Korah and his company agreed together for evil, therefore they were separated for good; and Judas agreed with the Jews for evil. So division may be good, and agreement may be evil." (St. John Chrysostom, *Homily LVII on John* IX, 2. B#58, 206 as quoted in Manley, *The Bible and the Holy Fathers*, 747)

29   Matt. 28:19.

At moments, His Beatitude seems to want to discourage us from taking too optimistic a view of globalization and any tendency to imagine that it is some kind of path to paradise— exactly the sort of worldly optimism that has been the shipwreck of so many utopian projects through history: "The reality of evil, which manifests itself in the various dark forces that operate within human souls and social formations, continually corrupts our purest efforts and aspirations…. There is no room for excessive optimism regarding the future of the world."[30] This is the sort of sober talk that those who imagine that globalization—or any human undertaking—will somehow wreak a fundamental change in human existence would do well to heed. It is just at this moment, however, when His Beatitude reminds us of "the reality of the cross: the reality of the passion, of outward failure, which is a permanent fact of life,"[31] that he affirms:

> But this tragic dimension of the cross, which casts a shadow over our lives, is ceaselessly illuminated by an unswerving eschatological hope… Our final and all-embracing victory—world unity, in the present case—does not belong to the present. It is coming, however. Our foretaste of this victory in the present fills us with peace and fortitude. The reality of Christ transcends history.[32]

Apparently, the faithful's "unswerving eschatological hope," their "final and all-embracing victory," is one and the same as the globalists', namely, "world unity." While the "reality of Christ" indeed "transcends history," expecting His "final and all-embracing victory" to occur within the plane of history— as "world unity" or anything else—is a grievous mistake. "My

---

30   Yannoulatos, *Facing the World*, 41.
31   Ibid., 42.
32   Ibid., 42.

principal aim in the foregoing analysis," His Beatitude writes, "has been to offer a cohesive view of Christianity as found in Orthodox tradition and to point out the potential, the power, and the responsibility that Christians have to further the world's progress toward a global community."[33]

Orthodox Christians, who through the ages have been concerned primarily with repentance, charity, prayer, and the general aim of transforming themselves into citizens fit for the Kingdom of Heaven, are now to take up the cause—not specifically of the salvific community of the Church—but of a vague "global community," His Beatitude seems to be saying. "The true Christian Church is therefore not conceived of as some novel, insular community or as some kind of corporate enterprise that seeks to expand so as to increase its own power; rather, the Church is a symbol, an indication of the desire for worldwide unity."[34]

No, the Church is not "novel" nor "insular", but she is also not, or she is far more than, a mere "symbol" that indicates "the desire for worldwide unity." The Church is the living, breathing Body of Christ, which symbolizes, but also concretely manifests on earth, the eternal Heavenly Realm—a fact that His Beatitude seems to recognize even while he fails to draw the correct conclusions from it.[35] His Beatitude's mistake seems to be one of believing that there is some potential "world unity" that transcends the Eternal Church of Christ—whereas it is the Church herself that by nature transcends any historical "unity" or secular "global community." "The New Jerusalem"[36] that His Beatitude mentions, "Our final end is symbolically portrayed as a gathering of people in a new and different kind of city."[37]

---

33   Ibid., 36.
34   Ibid., 28.
35   Ibid., 28-9.
36   Rev. 3:12.
37   Yannoulatos, *Facing the World*, 30.

"This city 'on high' is a gift that has been offered to the entire
human race, and the gathering of people that takes place there
includes everyone."[38] This "city," however, the eschatological
vision of the Church, is the Church herself triumphant—not
any "city" on the plane of history. The Church has always been
united, universal, and ecumenical, but the only "worldwide
unity" that she seeks is the unity of mankind *in herself*, the Body
of Christ—precisely because unity in Christ is the only true unity
and the only path to salvation; salvation, which is an infinitely
higher goal than any expression of secular unity. It is a tragedy
that an esteemed Orthodox hierarch of our time can mistake
the object of globalization for the true "eschatological hope,"
the eternal Kingdom of God, which is found only in the true
koinonia of Christ's Orthodox Church.[39]

"THE OPEN CONSPIRACY"

If a learned Orthodox hierarch can be derailed in his understanding of globalization to such an extent such that he can
confuse a worldly, modern historical process with the ancient,
sacred mission of the Church, it is worth asking why. What is it
about the promise of global unity that is so compelling? What is
the self-conscious motivation of the "globalists" who champion
global integration as a good, just, and eminently desirable goal?
What is the source of globalization's peculiar charm?

The wars and upheavals of the modern era certainly helped
to pave the way for the notion that a single global order was
both desirable and possible. While no specific date or event

---

38   Ibid., 31.
39   His Beatitude Anastasios Yannoulatos' shortcomings in his analysis of
globalization should not detract from his general body of written work or his pastoral
activity in Africa and the Balkans both before and after the fall of Communism in
1991. We do not indict the man.

may be said to mark the beginning of the modern effort of globalization, it certainly gained tremendous momentum in the twentieth century. In approaching the contemporary literature on globalization, one is confronted by a glut of books, essays, and studies with no ready means of sifting the wheat from the chaff. One significant void in the literature is the absence of compelling treatments of *why* globalization has retained its allure across generations. While there are undoubtedly a myriad of private interests that help spur globalization—gains from increased international trade, for example, about which much has been written—it can be hard to glean much insight into the genuine "globalists" and their motivations.

As is often the case, a voice from the past offers insight. While he never used the term itself, one of globalization's greatest champions was the famous English science-fiction author Herbert George (H. G.) Wells (1866–1946). Writing during the time of the World Wars, Wells enthusiastically made the case for a unified world political organization strong enough to overawe any rival center of power and render conflict between nations effectively impossible. Only by welding the peoples of the world into a common identity with allegiance to a single global authority, he believed, could the specter of war, so vivid during his lifetime, be banished from human history.

Wells was no mere academic or teller of tales. He was a globalizing "true believer" passionately committed to the absolute necessity of building a unified world order. While many treatments of globalization take their approach from the outside in, Wells expresses the aspirations and motivations of an evangelist for the cause. In Wells, we can come to understand why globalization has proven such a powerful idea across generations and why it continues to hypnotize today.

Many of Wells' works of fiction depicted futuristic one-world governments and technological utopias such as *The World Set Free* (1914), *Men Like Gods* (1923), and *The Shape of Things to*

Come (1933). Eventually, Wells translated his ideas about world unification from the realm of fantasy to that of advocacy. His 1931 *What Are We to do with Our Lives?* first published in 1928 as *The Open Conspiracy: Blueprints for a World Revolution*, and his *New World Order* of 1940, afford both a philosophy of globalization as well as a strategy for bringing a new global order about. In these works, Wells develops many of the concepts and terms that would become commonplace in our time.

> We are coming to see more and more plainly that certain established traditions which have made up the frame of human relationships for ages are not merely no longer as convenient as they were, but are positively injurious and dangerous. And yet at present we do not know how to shake off these traditions, these habits of social behaviour which rule us.... For example, the general government of human affairs has hitherto been distributed among a number of sovereign states.... Everyone was taught a history glorifying his own state, and patriotism was chief among the Virtues.... Our political and economic ideas of living are out of date, and we find great difficulty in adjusting them and reconstructing them to meet the huge and strenuous demands of the new times.[40]

Here Wells adumbrates the basic struggle for modernists of all stripes: how to "shake off" and replace traditional mores with some new and improved system that will supposedly allow for a beneficial transformation of human life. Invariably, what is old is "out of date" and must be replaced with that which is new and improved. What Wells and other anti-traditionalists fail to fathom is where their efforts are ultimately leading.

---

40   H. G. Wells, *The Open Conspiracy* (1928), ch. 1. https://www.voltairenet.org/ IMG/pdf/Wells_The_Open_Conspiracy.pdf. Accessed September 13, 2019.

> The fundamental task of the servants of the coming Anti-christ is to destroy the old world with all its former concepts and "prejudices" in order to build in its place a new world suitable for receiving its approaching "new owner," who will take the place of Christ for people and give them on earth that which Christ did not give them.... One must be completely blind spiritually, completely alien to true Christianity not to understand all this![41]

The revolutionary, subversive, and progressive ideologies of the modern era, while often outwardly at odds with one another, have all served the same basic end of denuding the world of its traditional orienting principles, which, however tenuously, retained the vestiges of Christian society. Wells' project is in keeping with other destructive ideologies of his day in its aim to dismantle the old world to make way for a new.

A common theme that often surfaces in discussions of globalization and the move toward a unitary political system is whether such phenomena constitute an organic, if remarkably persistent, aspect of history or whether they are driven by some kind of deliberate program or conspiracy. Conspiracies by nature are occult, or hidden, and so definitive proof of a conspiracy is, by nature, hard to come by. Of course, conspiracies at various levels abound; governments, for example, regularly prosecute crimes of "conspiracy." To determine the existence of an actual conspiracy driving globalization would require an extensive examination of the historical record, which we will not undertake here. In his advocacy for a unified world order, Wells very usefully articulated the idea of a loosely knit "Open Conspiracy" that would work through established channels of power and opinion toward its goal of world unification.

---

41   Archbishop Averky Taushev. *Stand Fast in the Truth*. http://archbishopaverky. blogspot.com/2012/08/stand-fast-in-truth.html. Accessed September 13, 2019.

It amounted to a protest, first mental and then practical, it amounted to a sort of unpremeditated and unorganized conspiracy.... But unlike conspiracies in general this widening protest and conspiracy against established things would, by its very nature, go on in the daylight, and it would be willing to accept participation and help from every quarter. It would, in fact, become an "Open Conspiracy," a necessary, naturally evolved conspiracy, to adjust our dislocated world.[42]

In Wells' vision, this Open Conspiracy would not have an identifiable central command but would be united by a common faith and a common objective. It would comprise a global ideological fraternity transcending traditional social and economic distinctions that would work through established channels to further the globalist program. Wells' identification of an Open Conspiracy, while made in the spirit of partisanship, is in fact a major theoretical contribution to understanding the forces driving globalization. For some reason, however, the idea of a "conspiracy" of any kind—hidden or open—impelling events engenders antipathy from many "mainstream" sources. In days past, any interpretation of historical events required naming names, explicating motivations, discovering organizational mechanisms, etc., much in the way of a forensic investigation. Now, however, it is the fashion to invoke vague and apparently ineluctable "forces" that supposedly drive events: "evolution," "progress," the march of "democracy" and "human rights," etc. The only time that a conspiracy is accepted to have driven a great historical event is when one can pin it on the losers, for example, Germany and Japan in World War II.

---

42   Wells, *The Open Conspiracy*, ch. 2. https://www.voltairenet.org/IMG/pdf/Wells_The_Open_Conspiracy.pdf. Accessed September 13, 2019.

"Forces" of history do certainly exist, and it is the task of the historical scientist to make sense of them, but they are only discernible through careful examination of the personalities and motivations intimately bound up with events themselves. Globalization itself is often portrayed as a "natural" or "inevitable" force or process in which particular political actors are merely swept along and thus bear no responsibility for their actions. By identifying a conspiracy of like-minded persons and organizations, Wells is merely affirming that globalization, like any significant undertaking, requires the efforts of capable people working deliberately toward a common goal. In our own time, the Open Conspiracy seems well-nigh omnipresent: politicians, celebrities, businessmen, even religious figures, all espouse their belief in the promise of globalization.

> [The Open Conspirators] will do all they can to spread and perfect this conception of a new world order, which they will regard as the only working frame for their activities, while at the same time they will set themselves to discover and associate with themselves, everyone, everywhere, who is intellectually able to grasp the same broad ideas and morally disposed to realize them.[43]

The Open Conspiracy "must carve out a Society of its own from Society,"[44] which will grow and perpetuate itself in order to command the highest ranks of human life. This global elite, not bound by allegiance to any traditional country or nation-state, will serve as the shepherd class of the New World Order.[45] Indeed, supporting, or at least not gainsaying, globalization

---

43   Wells, *The New World Order* (1940), ch. 8. https://www.voltairenet.org/IMG/pdf/Wells_New_World_Order.pdf. Accessed September 13, 2019.
44   Wells, *The Open Conspiracy*, ch. 11. https://www.voltairenet.org/IMG/pdf/Wells_The_Open_Conspiracy.pdf. Accessed September 13, 2019.
45   Ibid., ch. 17.

increasingly seems a litmus test for ascendancy in any field. To express a desire to halt global integration or for a return to greater local and national independence routinely draws accusations of "isolationism," "nationalism," "turning the clock back," and other progressive bromides. Wells' Open Conspiracy has advanced very far, indeed.

The expansion of central state power and a broad socialist agenda is an integral theme to Wells' program, which indeed became a hallmark of the post-World War II age.

> The establishment of a progressive world socialism … is the plain, rational objective before us now. Only the effective realization of this objective can establish peace on earth and arrest the present march of human affairs to misery and destruction.[46]

"Great Britain, like America, may become a Socialist system with a definitive Revolution, protesting all the time that it is doing nothing of the sort."[47] The course of the last century has borne out many of Wells' aspirations. If we had to summarize what the last hundred years have wrought, "progressive world socialism" pretty well hits the nail on the head. The great nations of the world, both those that underwent a Communist phase and those that did not, have now wound up largely socialized: their economies, educational systems, health services, etc. are, if not officially, then effectively, centralized under their respective governments, which in turn are coordinated by the ascendant Open Conspiracy on trajectories of global convergence.

Writing some hundred years before Wells, one of the greatest modern political theorists and observers of American democracy,

---

46   Wells, *The New World Order,* ch. 9. https://www.voltairenet.org/IMG/pdf/Wells_New_World_Order.pdf. Accessed September 13, 2019.
47   Ibid., ch. 8.

Alexis de Tocqueville (1805-59), foresaw the slow but seemingly inexorable process by which the central state would expand control over its subjects even in ostensibly democratic circumstances. De Tocqueville spelled out with remarkable prescience the process through which "progressive world socialism" would, contrary to the desires and interests of the public, slowly but ineluctably take hold.

> [The modern state] covers the surface of society with a network of small complicated rules, minute and uniform, through which the most original minds and the most energetic characters cannot penetrate, to rise above the crowd. The will of man is not shattered, but softened, bent, and guided; men are seldom forced by it to act, but they are constantly restrained from acting. Such a power does not destroy, but it prevents existence; it does not tyrannize, but it compresses, enervates, extinguishes, and stupefies a people, till each nation is reduced to nothing better than a flock of timid and industrious animals, of which the government is the shepherd. I have always thought that servitude of the regular, quiet, and gentle kind which I have just described might be combined more easily than is commonly believed with some of the outward forms of freedom, and that it might even establish itself under the wing of the sovereignty of the people.[48]

The socialization and unification of the West is a process that has happened by degrees, "progressively," even while the great capitalist nations such as the United States continue to protest "that it is doing nothing of the sort." The slide was summed

---

48   Alexis de Tocqueville, *Democracy in America*, v. 2 (1840) part 4, ch. 6. https://oll.libertyfund.org/titles/democracy-in-america-english-edition-vol-2. Accessed September 13, 2019.

up quite neatly during the 1948 US presidential campaign by the Socialist Party Candidate, Norman Thomas (1884–1986), who allegedly remarked in an interview: "The American people will never knowingly adopt Socialism. But under the name of 'liberalism' [and other benign-sounding phrases] they will adopt every fragment of the Socialist program, until one day America will be a Socialist nation, without knowing how it happened."[49] Instead of socialism, one might choose a different term, perhaps corporatism or oligarchy, the better to reflect the dominating interests of the megacorporations and the very rich, but the substance—a powerful, central state tightly enmeshed with all sectors of society—education, medicine, banking, the factors of production—remains the same (see ch. 6). The socialized nations, then, already having centralized power in themselves and effectively "extinguished and stupefied" their peoples, are all the readier to be amalgamated into a unified world system led by the Open Conspiracy.

While globalization is often thought of as primarily an economic or political phenomenon, Wells candidly affirms that it constitutes nothing less than a religious movement. The great faith shown by many globalists that a future united world will somehow transform the structure of history from a place of want and injustice to one of righteousness and plenty is indeed a religious sentiment. Wells and others like him evince that persistent assumption of modern thinkers, echoed throughout the ranks of the Open Conspiracy that religion is not properly an end in itself but is instrumental to achieving higher, worldly ends. While religion has traditionally defined what the ultimate ends of individual and collective existence are—what constitutes moral action, how one finds salvation, what is the ultimate

---

49   This quote is often attributed to Thomas, many argue incorrectly. For our purposes it is less important whether Thomas actually said it; the uncomfortable fact is that it rings true.

end and purpose of life—Wells affirms that the ultimate end of human endeavor is globalization itself, and he proceeds to reason that religion, like everything else, must serve that end.

> It seems unavoidable that if religion is to develop unifying and directive power in the present confusion of human affairs it must adapt itself to this forward-looking, in-dividuality-analyzing turn of mind; it must divest itself of its sacred histories, its gross preoccupations, its posthu-mous prolongation of personal ends.[50]

Wells thus envisions a global religion purged of everything that once defined religion—the sacramental, the mystical, the ritual, the eternal ("posthumous prolongation of personal ends")—in short, religion, hitherto defined by its otherworldliness, is to be stripped, to become entirely this-worldly, so as to serve the highest good of the Open Conspiracy. "Other-worldliness has become unnecessary."[51] The desacralizing of religion, in par-ticular of traditional forms of Christianity, is a process that was well underway in Wells' time and continues apace in our own. In the New World Order, traditional religion will no longer properly be considered religion at all, as a set of absolute or ultimate truth claims; rather, it will become merely functional to the "religion of the future" that will define the new ultimate ends of human existence.

> The modernization of the religious impulse leads us straight to this effort for the establishment of the world state as a duty, and the close consideration of the necessary organization of that effort will bring the reader to the

---

50   Wells, *The Open Conspiracy*, ch. 5. https://www.voltairenet.org/IMG/pdf/Wells_The_Open_Conspiracy.pdf. Accessed September 13, 2019.
51   Ibid., ch. 6.

conclusion that a movement aiming at the establishment of a world directorate [is necessary]... or admit from the outset the futility, the spare-time amateurishness, of its gestures.[52]

The Church of Christ, which exists in both this world and the next, is to make way for an entirely inner-worldly church—the world state—with a new priesthood—a world directorate. As in the case of Babel, this world state is in actuality globalization's eschatological vision, one that has proved compelling even to many who remain self-consciously Christian. Wells, like any good fire-and-brimstone preacher, proposes an absolutist dichotomy: either the adoption of his program and success and salvation or its rejection and failure and damnation; a unified, systematic, heaven-on-earth or "spare-time, amateurish" gestures that end in "futility." We will either believe and strive to reach the promised land of the New World Order or we will perish on the journey from our own lack of conviction. And, lest we imagine that the Open Conspiracy must by nature be tolerant, Wells tells us that the renunciation of force has no place in the furtherance of its goals.

> Non-resistance, the restriction of activities to moral suasion is no part of the programme of the Open Conspiracy.... By its own organizations or through the police and military strength of governments amenable to its ideas, the movement is bound to find itself fighting... The Open Conspiracy rests upon a disrespect for nationality, and there is no reason why it should tolerate noxious or obstructive governments because they hold their own in this or that patch of human territory.... It is fantastic

---

52   Ibid., ch. 7.

pedantry to wait for all the world to accede before all the world is pacified and policed.[53]

Policing and pacifying the world—by force if necessary—is thus explicitly part of the globalizing program, a fact eminently visible in our own time when the haves of the international community regularly employ military and economic coercion against the have-nots to compel their obedience to the new global order. Wells would have the reluctant enter his heaven-on-earth at the barrel of a gun. Notable is the comment of American banker James Paul Warburg: "We shall have world government, whether or not we like it. The question is only whether world government will be achieved by consent or by conquest," captures this non-negotiable quality of the New World Order.[54] "Conquest or consent" implies, of course, that consent is immaterial.

Wells proceeds to promise us "much actual warfare" to snuff out "ancient loyalties and traditions" and "local independence."[55] The historical freedoms and cultural traditions of the great nations are "no better than excuses for brigandage and obstructive action," which hold back their "subject people from the citizenship of the world."[56] There will be few places to hide under the New World Order, a fact we are seeing taking more and more concrete form with each passing day. Here we see Wells' supposedly enlightened system morphing into the shades of totalitarianism so common among modern idealists. But this transformation is only the logical extension of those earlier

53   Ibid., ch. 17.

54   Testimony to the US Senate Committee on Foreign Relations, February 17, 1950. https://www.globalresearch.ca/one-world-governance-and-the-council-on-foreign-relations-we-shall-have-world-government-by-conquest-or-consent/5541363. Accessed September 13, 2019.

55   Wells, *The Open Conspiracy*, ch. 18. https://www.voltairenet.org/IMG/pdf/Wells_The_Open_Conspiracy.pdf. Accessed September 13, 2019.

56   Ibid., ch. 18.

benign-sounding phrases that permeate Wells' argument and so much modern thought.

Wells evinces a zeal, common among his intellectual progeny of today, as sanctimonious and vehement as any self-appointed evangelist or witch-finder, precisely the sort of people he claims to despise. In our time, the Open Conspiracy, the society of the "economically-functional,"[57] the "social elite,"[58] labors to bring about a global order, cleansed of all genuine religion and patriotic feeling, which treats its enemies as a "cancer"[59] to be eradicated. Here, in the words of one of its greatest champions and prophets, we see in no uncertain terms the true colors of the New World Order unfolding around us.

Wells was certainly not the architect of globalization, but he was one of its leading prophets. Better perhaps than anyone did he articulate the major strains of modern globalization, its assumptions, goals, and logic. He also typifies that peculiarly modern type of personality: the antichristian zealot. The two are closely related. The globalizing utopians are in fact on a spiritual mission whether they know it or not: nothing less than to save mankind from its existential plight without God and without His Church. This inner-worldly act of self-salvation, which somehow will lead to a paradise on earth that cannot be specifically described, amounts to a feat of modern sorcery, of magic or alchemy, as much a function of deluded superstition as the chants and spells of the ancient pagan world. While Wells and other utopians are forever insisting on the "scientific" or "rational" basis of their programs, in fact, they evince the most profound superstition. In their minds, the arrival of the New World Order will transform not only the political landscape but the inner being of man as well.

---

57   Ibid., ch. 11.
58   Ibid., ch. 17.
59   Ibid., ch. 13.

> And not only from natural evils will man be largely free. He will not be left with his soul tangled, haunted by monstrous and irrational fears and a prey to malicious impulses. From his birth he will breathe sweetness and generosity and use his mind and hands cleanly and exactly. He will feel better, will better, think better, see, taste, and hear better than men do now. His under-soul will no longer be a mutinous cavern of ill-treated suppressions and of impulses repressed without understanding.[60]

In short, Wells' holds out the promise of "men like gods."[61] The promise of globalization, while usually not explicitly stated lest it seem to overreach, is effectively an earthly paradise not unlike the promises made by the ideologies of National Socialism and Communism of Wells' day. Like those ideologies, the globalizing program cannot ultimately deliver on the promise of paradise-in-history, but it nonetheless possesses all of their sirenic charm; and, like them, it will ultimately bring misery and death to those it seduces.

> Like the Christian vision of the universal Kingdom of God, the religion of secular globalism claims universality, but is an earthly minded substitute for the Church universal. The Christian vision sees the Church as God's Kingdom ruling the earth. The religion of globalism sees an earthly, utopian world order in which all men pay allegiance to priests who rule over a World City without national borders.[62]

---

60   Ibid., ch. 19.

61   H. G. Wells, *Men Like Gods* (1923). http://gutenberg.net.au/ebooks02/0200221h. html#book1. Accessed September 13, 2019.

62   Fay Voshell, "*Globalism: The Religion of Empire,*" in *The American Thinker.* September 4, 2016. http://www.americanthinker.com/articles/2016/09/globalism_the_religion_of_empire_.html. Accessed September 13, 2019.

In contrast to the Church whose founder and builder is God, it is Man—stirred by demonic inspiration—who is the great architect of the New World Order. While Wells has ably described the operative principles of globalization, he, like the rest of the globalizing elite, is unable to penetrate to the transcendent significance of the historical phenomena around him. While Wells was not an atheist like many modern intellectuals, he nonetheless categorically denied Christian revelation and its view of man and of history. He therefore lacked a perspective beyond history and could not fathom where his New World Order ultimately ends. Globalization, and history itself, do one day come to an end; the process does not go on forever. The true father of globalization is Satan, the same father of the primordial sin, the Tower of Babel, and the countless antichristian movements and ideologies that have risen and fallen throughout history. And there will be a day when the New World Order finds definitive fulfillment: the day when Antichrist ascends his unholy throne in Jerusalem and receives the adoration of the world. In order to understand the significance of the rise of global antichristianity and the historical eclipse of the Church, we must come to understand the tremendous transformation that the Church wrought upon the ancient pagan world in her first centuries of existence and how that transformation came to be distorted and turned back.

PART II

HISTORY AND THE CHURCH

CHAPTER 3

THE CHRISTIAN REVOLUTION

I was watching in the night visions, and behold, One like the Son of Man, coming with the clouds of heaven. He came to the Ancient of Days, and they brought Him near before Him. Then to Him was given dominion and glory and a kingdom, that all peoples, nations, and languages should serve Him. His dominion is an everlasting dominion, which shall not pass away, and His kingdom the one which shall not be destroyed.

Daniel 7:13-14

In our time, we are accustomed to think of history in essentially linear terms. Events succeed one another along a "timeline" on which the future becomes the present which becomes the past. Any given event in history occurs at a unique moment and may be placed only before, after, or coterminously with any other event. In his highly popular *A Brief History of Time*, physicist Stephen Hawking talked about "the arrow of time," a phrase coined by astronomer Arthur Eddington. Widely held modern ideas about "progress" and the "march of history" reflect this linear conception of time and of history. Indeed, one of the leading concepts in modern thinking, "evolution," first applied to the political realm before its application to biology, is inextricably linked with a progressive understanding of history in which stages of lesser development are succeeded by ones greater.

Yet, while it is rarely acknowledged, this linear or progressive view of history so prevalent in modern thinking has a Christian basis. It was not modern science or philosophy that originated this idea but rather the Church. The pre-Christian pagan world generally adhered to a repetitive, cyclical view of history, in which nations and empires rose and fell, people were born and died, political societies coalesced and dissolved in a repetitive, circular fashion.[1] The persistent belief of eastern pagan religions in reincarnation is perhaps the clearest example of this circular view of existence. The Christian understanding, however, affirms a definitive beginning and end to this world. While the cyclical rise and fall of political societies and the birth and death of individuals perdures, it is the overarching movement of history from a beginning to an end that distinguishes the realm of history, that of men, from the realm of eternity, that of God.

In the Biblical dispensation, the axis of history, its meaningful core, is the plight of individuals and societies that have oriented themselves toward transcendent reality, toward God. In the Old Testament, the people of God were the faithful among the tribes of Israel; in the New, they are the Church, the New Israel, the faithful throughout the world. Under the Old Testament dispensation, the revelation of God remained localized to the tribes of Israel, whereas the evangelical mission of the Church brought the exceptionally powerful Biblical understanding of history to the world.

> While for Israel, interest centered on the saving revelations of time and history, in the Church, time and history are oriented towards eternity. Christ is the fulfillment of the Law and the Prophets. In his person are fulfilled God's promises to his chosen people. And this fulfillment lays the foundation for the final promise of eternal life. In

---

1   See Mantzaridis, *Time and Man*, 1–2.

his life and his teaching, in his Death and Resurrection,
Christ gave to man the prospect of eternity. It is this new
perspective that imbues the New Testament and the
whole of the Church's tradition.[2]

In contrast to the never-ending cycles of paganism, the
Church affirms that, through God's revelation to man, the full
sweep of history is rendered meaningful. Man, a creature of
finite historical existence, is simultaneously a creature of eternity.
History began with the separation of man from God through
sin and unfolds in the saga of man's redemption through divine
grace. Man's plight in this world is rendered meaningful because
it has an ultimate purpose and end: salvation in eternity. The
Church is the presence of eternity in history and is the vehicle
by which man takes leave of this world of sin and death and
begins the journey to God and eternal life.[3]

The Christian understanding of human existence is thus
teleological, which is to say that it moves purposefully toward
an ultimate end. Salvation is the ultimate end or goal, the *telos*
(τέλος), or *eschaton* (ἔσχατον), of the individual and of the collective Church. While the Church as the Kingdom of God on
earth moves toward her goal of salvation in eternity, secular or
profane history, which is to say the collective existence of man

---

2   Ibid., 5.

3   "O. Cullman has dealt with the biblical concept or theology of time in his well-
known book *Christ and Time.* In it he very clearly presents the fundamental distinction
between the linear Hebrew understanding of time and the cyclical Hellenistic
concept... Time itself can be described as eschatological in the sense that in it those
events develop and happen by means of which time is given its meaning, which makes
it a process or history, and which directs it towards an *eschaton* [or *telos*]... towards its
consummation in a final event revealing its whole meaning: *eschaton* is therefore not
simply an ending, but the fulfillment of that which has developed in time... Time in
this sense is defined by its movement towards the fulfillment of God's plan or design
for the world... by its movement in the direction of the 'Lord's Day.' " (Protopresbyter
Alexander Schmemann, *Introduction to Liturgical Theology.* B#72A, 34-5 as quoted in
Manley, *The Bible and the Holy Fathers,* 143)

outside the Church, does not move toward the same teleological fulfillment. While the Lord's "words will by no means pass away"[4] and "the gates of Hades shall not prevail" against his Church,[5] at the end of time "the earth and the works that are in it will be burned up."[6] The Church, the Body of Christ in history, and her members will endure beyond death and the end of this world, while the rest of historical existence will be consumed with divine fire. While historical cycles perdure—individuals are born and die, nations rise and fall—they do not go on endlessly; there is ultimate meaning to human existence: eternal salvation or eternal perdition. Salvation in eternity is the *telos* of Christ's Church, whereas the fate of historical existence outside the Church is oblivion.

As a theory of history capable of capturing the hearts and minds of men, teleological Christianity showed itself vastly superior to its pagan competitors. The rise and triumph of the early Church in the face of persecution at the hands of the world's pre-eminent pagan civilization, Rome, marked the ultimate revolution in history. Since the time of the Christianizing of the Roman Empire in the first centuries after Christ, any serious competitor to Orthodox Christianity has had to develop a comparable teleological theory of human existence or it simply cannot compete for hearts and minds in a serious way. The questions raised by the Church—questions of salvation and damnation, eternity, paradise, what is the ultimate end and meaning of existence—are questions that any serious ideology, religious or secular, must at least implicitly answer. The rise of the Church forever dispensed with the possibility of leaving history as an endless and ultimately meaningless circle.

---

4   Matt. 24:35.
5   Matt. 16:18.
6   2 Pet. 3:10.

[T]he triumph of Christianity . . . can be called in the fullest sense a "revolution": a truly massive and epochal revision of humanity's prevailing vision of reality, so pervasive in its influence and so vast in its consequences as actually to have created a new conception of the world, of history, of human nature, of time, and of moral good.[7]

THE RISE OF THE CHURCH

In contrast to modern societies that reflexively (and often unthinkingly) differentiate between the religious and the secular realms of existence, the political order of the pre-Christian pagan empires and city-states was generally understood to be an unbroken continuation of the divine order of the cosmos. In the old pagan empires, all elements of the society, from statesman to soldier to priest to slave, served the undifferentiated religious-political order. Modern distinctions between "public" and "private," "religious" and "secular," "spiritual" and "worldly" would have been unintelligible; all was subsumed by the holistic "cosmological truth"[8] embodied by the empire. The realm of the divine was understood to be manifested in the power structure of the empire itself, a fact evident, for example, in the prevalent belief that the ruling figures themselves were in some way divine (what Professor Carroll Quigley aptly referred to as "providential monarchies"). The state power organization derived legitimacy from its being the material manifestation of the realm of the gods on earth.

All the early empires, Near Eastern as well as Far Eastern, understood themselves as representatives of a transcen-

---

7   David Bentley Hart, *Atheist Delusions* (New Haven, Yale, 2009), xi.
8   Voegelin, *The New Science of Politics*, 76.

dent order, of the order of the cosmos; and some of them even understood this order as a "truth."... The empire is a cosmic analogue, a little world reflecting the order of the great, comprehensive world. Rulership becomes the task of securing the order of society in harmony with cosmic order... the ruler himself represents the society, because on earth he represents the transcendent power which maintains cosmic order.[9]

In such societies, to reject the official cult constituted an act of political rebellion as much as one of religious dissent. Denying the existence of the officially sanctioned gods implied a rejection of the legitimacy of the political structures that represented those gods; it was, in effect, a form of treason. Perhaps the first recorded case of a society acting against speculation that it perceived as subversive was when Athens put Socrates to death for allegedly bringing into doubt the pantheon of gods.[10] Socrates was no rebel, but his refusal to be content with official theology and to speculate that there was something "beyond" the pantheon—a supreme principle or being greater than even the known gods—unbalanced the closed theo-political system of the Greek *polis* (πόλις). The rise of Greek speculative philosophy posed a potential danger to the Athenian city-state whose legitimacy was integrally bound up with the gods it claimed to represent.

It is times of upheaval that prompt men to ask the great questions, and it was the aftermath of the hugely destructive Peloponnesian War (431-404 BC) and the end of Athenian pre-eminence in Greece that set the stage for the rise of Platonic and Aristotelian philosophy. Socrates and the Greek philosophers of his time were trying to make sense of a world that had come unstuck; they were trying to penetrate the turmoil

---

9   Ibid., 54.
10   See Daniel and the three youths in Babylon, Dan. 3, 6.

around them to make contact with the unchanging essence of reality that alone could guide them through the chaos. In Plato appears the first use of a term referring to "the beyond," as in that which is beyond perceptible reality, that which transcends the world of man and even the immortal tenants of Olympus.[11] The Greek philosophers were looking for the *logos,* the supreme ordering principle of reality, which, unaided by revelation, they could only vaguely define. Their search would come to fruition generations later when St. Paul would preach the Incarnation of God as Christ in the Areopagus.

> Then Paul stood in the midst of the Areopagus and said, "Men of Athens, I perceive that in all things you are very religious; for as I was passing through and considering the objects of your worship, I even found an altar with this inscription: TO THE UNKNOWN GOD. There-fore, the One whom you worship without knowing, Him I proclaim to you.[12]

A problem analogous to the rise of Greek speculative phi-losophy occurred with the rise of Israel in pharaonic Egypt under the leadership of Moses.[13] The God of Israel, Yahweh, called Moses to lead His people out of Egyptian captivity in defiance of the Egyptian power structure and the gods it rep-resented. Here again was a new truth arising in conflict with the established theo-political order. This time, however, it was not human speculation that sought out "the beyond," but the Beyond that sought out man. Yahweh's call to Moses threat-ened to disrupt the order of the Egyptian "cosmion"[14] that had

---

11   See *Voegelin in Toronto,* DVD, 1978. The Eric Voegelin Institute, Baton Rouge, LA.

12   Acts 17:20-23.

13   See Exod. 3–12.

14   Which is to say the Egyptian self-understanding as the terrestrial embodiment of cosmic order.

enslaved the tribes of Israel and not simply because of the loss of manpower. The ancient pagan world into which the God of Israel suddenly intruded understood the military and political strength of empires and city-states to reflect the power of the gods they represented. A mighty god was manifested on earth by a mighty state and a strong political organization reflected a god great among his cosmic peers. When Moses conveyed Yahweh's command to Pharaoh to let the tribes of Israel go, He was represented by no earthly power organization of any kind. Pharaoh refused; his calculation was simple: Yahweh was not to be feared because there was no earthly power structure to represent Him; if He was as strong as Moses claimed, where were His armies?

Pharaoh's recalcitrance, his "hardened heart,"[15] gave opportunity for Yahweh to demonstrate that His was a peculiar power—and an awesome one. Yahweh had no need of armies to fight for Him or power institutions to represent Him because He was no mere "god" among gods, one member among others of the cosmic household. Rather He was transcendence Itself, the superinfinite Author of reality, Whose dominion transcended earthly politics and its cosmic patrons. Yahweh acted not through conventional political and military channels but through forces of nature and supernaturally. While Egypt and the other pagan empires "trust in chariots, and some in horses," Israel "will remember the name of the LORD our God,"[16] the sovereign Master of the universe.

While Israel in time developed into a kingdom like others, such was not Yahweh's original intention. His rule from the time of Moses was through His judges, whose authority rested exclusively on His inspiration of their prophetic office. It was only after Israel's unfaithful rejection of Yahweh's judges, of

---

15   Exod. 8:15.
16   Ps. 19/20:7.

whom the Prophet Samuel was the last, that He consented to grant them an earthly king.

> Then all the elders of Israel gathered together and came to Samuel at Ramah, and said to him, "Look, you are old, and your sons do not walk in your ways. Now make us a king to judge us like all the nations." But the thing displeased Samuel when they said, "Give us a king to judge us." So Samuel prayed to the LORD. And the LORD said to Samuel, "Heed the voice of the people in all that they say to you; for they have not rejected you, but they have rejected Me, that I should not reign over them. According to all the works which they have done since the day that I brought them up out of Egypt, even to this day—with which they have forsaken Me and served other gods—so they are doing to you also. Now therefore, heed their voice."[17]

In requesting an earthly king, the Israelites rejected the kingship of Yahweh and opted instead for a terrestrial representative in the vein of the gentile empires. But from the beginning it was not God's plan to endow any earthly government with the right to act in His name, a key fact that would later find fulfillment in the Christian differentiation between Church and state: "Render to Caesar the things that are Caesar's, and to God the things that are God's."[18]

The type of problem that occurred locally in the Greek city-states with the rise of philosophy and in Egypt with Israel occurred massively with the irruption of the Church into the ancient Mediterranean world. Prior to the Christian era, the old pagan systems had remained intact even if from time to time

---

17   1 Sam. 8:4-9.
18   Mark 12:17.

they had to silence with hemlock a pesky philosopher who asked too many questions, while Israel remained a localized phenomenon whose political existence waxed and waned no differently, it seemed, than any of her neighbors. Through limited human reason, Greek philosophy had cracked an opening in the ceiling of the official cults, but man alone was unable to reach it. The philosophers were groping toward what lay "beyond," toward the transcendent, but, whatever transcendence was, it remained hidden and beyond reach. The Church changed all that in a cosmic revolution ably described by the political scientist Eric Voegelin. In the Church, it was not individual men who sought out God, but God Who sought out mankind.

> The Christian bending of God in grace toward the soul does not come within the range of these [philosophical] experiences.... The experience of mutuality in the relation with God ... of the grace which imposes a supernatural form on the nature of man, is the specific difference of Christian truth. The revelation of this grace in history, through the incarnation of the Logos in Christ, intelligibly fulfilled the adventitious movement of the spirit in the mystic philosophers.[19]

God's revelation in the Church may be thought of, on one level, as a divine response to the quest of the philosophers. In philosophy, men had begun searching for the nature of the ultimate order of reality, the *logos*, that transcended the official pagan cults, but they had received no answering response from the beyond. Israel alone had made contact with the transcendent "I AM," but Yahweh had purposed to keep Israel distinct from other nations until He fulfilled His promise to "make a

---

19   Voegelin, *The New Science of Politics*, 78.

new covenant with the house of Israel"[20] such that "all peoples, nations, and languages should serve Him,"[21] a promise that would find fulfillment in the Church. Just as Yahweh had called His people out from Egypt in order to worship Him alone, so now in the Church did the incarnate God call out from all nations those who would serve Him. "The Christian bending of God in grace toward the soul," God's condescension to the thirsty souls of men, closed a gigantic circuit through which poured previously unfathomable revelations.

With the rise of the Church, "transcendence" was no longer the remote abstraction that resisted man's attempts to reach it; now it revealed itself as transcendence *incarnate*, the superinfinite God Who entered history as the Man Jesus Christ. The *logos* sought by the philosophers now revealed itself as the *Logos*, the "Word" of God made flesh. The trickle that philosophy had started turned into a torrent. A new, exceptionally powerful type of truth burst upon the old pagan empires, the "soteriological" (from Greek: σωτηρία, *sotiria* – "salvation"), the distinctly Christian truth of salvation. The hitherto hidden and transcendent God, known only locally and inchoately to the tribes of Israel, manifested Himself in history to save lost and suffering humanity. This divine condescension, the experience of divine grace, the answering call of a loving God, has no parallel in history or religion, and it forever shattered the closed cosmological-imperial systems and inundated the tentative gropings of pre-Christian philosophy. "Truly, these times of ignorance God overlooked, but now commands all men everywhere to repent, because He has appointed a day on which He will judge the world in righteousness by the Man whom He has ordained."[22]

---

20   Jer. 31:31.
21   Dan. 7:14.
22   Acts 17:30-1.

That the God of Israel, Yahweh, would become the God of the nations, the Lord Christ, and would build a Kingdom that would supersede the ancient pagan empires—the Universal Church—was dramatically prefigured by the Prophet Daniel. A Hebrew servant at the court of the Babylonian King during the Hebrew captivity, Daniel distinguished himself through his famous interpretation of King Nebuchadnezzar's dream. On the verge of the slaughter of the king's "wise men," who were incapable of revealing the king's dream, Daniel, inspired by God, rose to the occasion. He famously told the king of his dream of "a great image [whose] head was of fine gold, its chest and arms of silver, its belly and thighs of bronze, its legs of iron, its feet partly of iron and partly of clay;"[23] then of the "stone cut out without hands, which struck the image on its feet of iron and clay, and broke them in pieces" and which "became a great mountain and filled the whole earth."[24]

> This is the dream. Now we will tell the interpretation of it before the king. You, O king, are a king of kings … you are this head of gold. But after you shall arise another kingdom inferior to yours; then another, a third kingdom of bronze, which shall rule over all the earth. And the fourth kingdom shall be as strong as iron, inasmuch as iron breaks in pieces and shatters everything; and like iron that crushes, that kingdom will break in pieces and crush all the others. Whereas you saw the feet and toes, partly of potter's clay and partly of iron, the kingdom shall be divided; yet the strength of the iron shall be in it, just as you saw the iron mixed with ceramic clay. And as

---

23   Dan. 2:32-3.
24   Dan. 2:34-5.

the toes of the feet were partly of iron and partly of clay, so the kingdom shall be partly strong and partly fragile.[25]

And in the days of these kings the God of heaven will set up a kingdom which shall never be destroyed; and the kingdom shall not be left to other people; it shall break in pieces and consume all these kingdoms, and it shall stand forever. Inasmuch as you saw that the stone was cut out of the mountain without hands, and that it broke in pieces the iron, the bronze, the clay, the silver, and the gold—the great God has made known to the king what will come to pass after this. The dream is certain, and its interpretation is sure.[26]

Thus did Daniel foretell the decline of the Babylonian empire (the "head of gold"), the rise and decline of Persia ("chest and arms of silver"), its conquest by the Greco-Macedonian kingdom of Alexander the Great ("belly and thighs of bronze"), the rise of pagan Rome ("as strong as iron [that] will break in pieces and crush all the others") and its division into the Western and Eastern empires (the two "legs [with] feet of iron and clay"); and the advent of the "uncut stone," Christ, and the rise of the "kingdom which shall never be destroyed," the Church, which would "break in pieces and consume all these kingdoms." Voegelin convincingly describes the revolutionary nature of Christian soteriological truth and that such a revelation would have tremendous historical implications. "With the appearance of Jesus, God himself entered into the eternal present of history,"[27] and the world would never be the same.

---

25   Dan. 2:36-42.
26   Dan. 2:44-45.
27   Voegelin, *Order and History*, v.1, 345 as quoted in Webb, *Eric Voegelin: Philosopher of History* (Seattle, University of Washington, 1981), 231.

THE CHRISTIAN REVOLUTION

From the view of the pagan empires, in particular, of Rome, early Christianity was unintelligible. Like the philosophers, the Christians claimed knowledge of an alternative truth to the official cults, but, unlike philosophy, this was no mere private truth that could in principle remain confined to personal life; rather, the Church entirely rejected the truth that Rome and her pantheon of gods claimed to represent. At the same time, however, the Christians did not seek to establish a parallel power structure that would threaten Roman political hegemony.[28] The Christians were peculiar. They were not revolutionaries in that they did not seek the overthrow of the terrestrial political order, yet they decisively rejected the truth on which that order was based; they were willing to honor the earthly power structure of Rome, yet they claimed allegiance to a King whose "kingdom [βασιλεία, vasileía] is not of this world."[29] As with the rise of Israel in Egypt under Moses, none of this made any sense to the extant political-religious power structure, which accused the Christians of both treason and atheism.

While the Christians worshipped a God outside the Roman pantheon, the real problem for Rome was that they refused to reverence the civic gods alongside their own. Had the early Christians showed themselves more "open-minded" or "tolerant," one can imagine the Cross being incorporated into the Roman pantheon for the sake of civil concord. The Christians,

---

28   "He [St. Paul] makes much of this subject in other epistles also: setting subjects under their rulers as household servants are under their masters. And he does this to show that it was not for the subversion of the commonwealth that Christ introduced his laws, but for the better ordering of it, and to teach men not to be taking up unnecessary and unprofitable wars." (St. John Chrysostom, *Homily XXIII on Romans XIII*. B#55, p. 511 as quoted in Manley, *The Bible and the Holy Fathers*, 257)

29   John 18:36

however, preferred torture and death by the thousands than to acknowledge the divinity of any other claimant, "a refusal which was tantamount to civil disloyalty."[30]

With the legalization of Christianity by Emperor St. Constantine I (r. 324-37), and the elevation of Orthodoxy as the official religion of the Empire by Emperor St. Theodosius I (r. 378-92), the victory of "the Crucified One" over the Roman pantheon was, in a political sense, complete even while discord, occasionally bloody, would continue in the struggle to maintain Orthodoxy. It was during this "struggle for representation"[31] during the first four centuries of the Church's historical existence that St. Ambrose of Milan (+397) offered a Christian theory of politics that outlined the relationship of the power organization of the Empire and the soteriological truth of the Church. Because Christ was a King Who commanded ultimate and total allegiance from His subjects, the question arose as to how the terrestrial power structure—in this case, the Roman Empire—could justify its legitimacy.

> The formulation of St. Ambrose does not justify the imperial monarchy by pointing to the monarchical rule of God... It does not speak of any rule at all but of service. The subjects serve the prince on earth as their existential representative... Above this temporal sphere of service on the part of the subjects... rises the emperor, who serves only God. The appeal of St. Ambrose does not go to the imperial ruler but to the Christian who happens to be the incumbent of the office... The truth of Christ cannot be represented by the *imperium mundi* but only by the service of God.[32]

---

30   John Meyendorff, *Imperial Unity and Christian Divisions* (Crestwood, St., Vladimir's Seminary, 2011), 28.

31   Voegelin, *The New Science of Politics*, 76.

32   Ibid., 85.

In short, St. Ambrose, expressing the Orthodox position, turned upside down the way of viewing things of the pagan empires. In a Christian context, in sharp contrast to the pagan empires, neither the Empire nor any terrestrial political order enjoys legitimacy by virtue of having a special claim on representing the divine order of the cosmos; rather, its legitimacy stems from the service owed to God by all of its subjects, including the Emperor. Whereas the Emperor's kingdom is terrestrial, Christ's Kingdom is eternal; one is immanent, the other transcendent. Yet the transcendence of Christ is not the unillumined, inaccessible transcendence identified by philosophy. Christ's transcendence can be experienced here, on earth, in this life, by all who would. How? In the Church. The Church is Christ's Kingdom on earth, His *vasileía*, that bridges the temporal and the eternal. "Therefore the Church even now is the kingdom of Christ, and the kingdom of heaven. Accordingly, even now His saints reign with Him, though otherwise than as they shall reign hereafter."[33]

> The coming of Christ brought the kingdom of God into the world, and the place where the kingdom of God is made manifest is the Church…. The kingdom of God is not simply awaited as something that is to come; it is also perceptible as something now present…. It is the period during which God and his kingdom are made manifest in history.[34]

Only the Church, of which Christ is the head, represents the divine order of the cosmos, not the Empire nor any terrestrial political organization. With the rise of the Church, "Political society in historical existence begins to show the hue of temporality

---

33   St. Augustine, *City of God*, bk. XX ch. 8. http://www.newadvent.org/fathers/120120.htm. Accessed September 13, 2019.
34   Mantzaridis, *Time and* Man, 51-2.

as distinguished from spiritual order."[35] The Church displaced the Empire as the representative of eternal order and thereby relegated the latter to a decidedly secondary status. The Church rendered unto Caesar his due, but that wasn't much.[36]

St. Augustine of Hippo (+430) powerfully expressed the Orthodox understanding of the relationship between the Church and the Empire in his *City of God* with the distinction of the two worlds—the city of God and the city of man—reflected in two forms of history, the sacred and the profane.[37] St. Augustine was writing in defense of the Church following the traumatic sack of Rome by Alaric in 410, which the Church's detractors argued was a sign of displeasure by the Roman gods, whose cult the Church had displaced. The Empire, while no longer the manifestation of the divine order on earth, was nonetheless recognized by the Church as playing a providential unifying role in her rise among the nations.

> When Augustus ruled alone upon the earth, the many kingdoms of men came to an end, and when You were made man of the pure Virgin, the many gods of idolatry were destroyed. The cities of the world passed under one single rule, and the nations came to believe in one sovereign Godhead.
>
> The people were enrolled by the decree of Caesar, and we, the faithful, were enroled in the Name of the

---

35   Voegelin, *The New Science of Politics*, 85.

36   Matt. 22:21.

37   We here refer to "Saint" rather than to "Blessed" Augustine to emphasize the vital contribution this man of God made to the life of the Church and to the Orthodox understanding of history. St. Augustine is a fully received saint of the Orthodox Church (commemorated June 15) even while some of his writings have been identified by the Church as in error. See Hieromonk Seraphim Rose's *Place of Blessed Augustine in the Orthodox Church* (Platina, St. Herman, 2007).

Godhead, when You, Our God, were made man. Great is Your mercy! O Lord, glory to You![38]

Echoing this sentiment, numerous Holy Fathers affirmed that it was possible to discern the hand of God in the *pax Romana* that had facilitated the spread of the Gospel,[39] yet it would nevertheless be a serious error to see the Empire as the Kingdom of God on earth even after its acceptance of Christianity. Christ indeed is a King, but His "kingdom is not of this world"[40]— even if an earthly power structure such as Rome had come to profess Christianity. The Roman Emperor is also a king, but his kingdom—even when he is a Christian of good standing—is of *this* world. The two are by no means identical. Whereas the Church will last forever in the age to come, this world and the political power structures thereof, including Rome, will pass away. Christians are citizens of the heavenly kingdom, of the Church, and their King is Christ. On this earth, Christians honor the earthly power structure—they give Caesar his due—but their first allegiance is to Christ their True King. St. Augustine's radical reformulation of imperial authority, which relegated the Empire to a parallel, subordinate historical existence alongside the eternal Church,

> is the end of political theology in orthodox Christianity. The spiritual destiny of man in the Christian sense cannot be represented on earth by the power organization of a political society; it can be represented only by the church. The sphere of power is radically de-divinized; it has become temporal.[41]

---

38   Orthodox hymn on the Nativity of Christ.
39   See Meyendorff, *Imperial Unity and Christian Divisions*, 29-30.
40   John 18:36.
41   Voegelin, *The New Science of Politics*, 106.

It is difficult to do justice to the magnitude of the revolution that the Church effected upon the old pagan world. Contrary to her modern detractors, the Church helped take religion out of politics. The Church, while by no means indifferent to the form that earthly government takes, is her own Kingdom with her own reason for existence which she pursues independently of the terrestrial political situation. Indeed, the Church survives to this day having enjoyed the protection of Orthodox governments as well as the depredations of pagan, heretical, Islamic, and Communist ones. Through the independence that her self-conscious existence in eternity affords, the Church has been able through the centuries to apply moderating pressure on unjust and tyrannical regimes. The Church introduced into history the idea of "limited" government: the principle that there were some aspects of human existence that were not properly the domain of the state; in particular, it was no longer the state that mediated man's relationship to God and that thus commanded the individual's highest allegiance but the Church. Furthermore, the state could only legitimately command civic loyalty when it did not violate God's laws as expressed by the Church, which has served to check the abuse of government power through the ages.

A Word on "Caesaropapism"

In availing ourselves of Voegelin's usually perceptive analysis, we must state our disagreement with him on a key point. Like many Western scholars, Voegelin wrongly ascribes to Eastern Orthodox civilization the error of "caesaropapism," the idea that, with the official adoption of Orthodox Christianity, the Roman-Byzantine Empire reduced the Church to a department of state. Voegelin incorrectly believes that, "Only in the West was the Augustinian conception of the church historically effective to the point that it resulted in the clear double representation of society through the spiritual and temporal powers."[42] In fact, Orthodox Christendom effectively differentiated the spiritual and temporal dimensions of historical existence, which in the first millennium included both East and West.

Constantine I's transfer of the imperial capital from Rome to Byzantium (Constantinople) on the shores of the Bosphorus c. 325 signaled the decline of imperial influence over the Western territories that would formally end in 476 with the barbarian deposition of the last Western Roman Emperor, Romulus Augustulus. The decline of imperial power in the West permitted the Western sees, pre-eminently Rome, greater independence from imperial influence. Oftentimes, this would prove highly beneficial in the struggle to maintain Orthodoxy when heretical forces in the East threatened to impose erroneous doctrinal innovations. On numerous occasions, Orthodox Roman popes were able to lead resistance to heretical imperial policies and steer the Empire back onto the rails of Orthodoxy. In both Orthodox East and West, the Church maintained her self-conscious existence as the Kingdom of God on earth: she was independent of, if naturally entwined with, the Empire, even if it was practically more difficult for the Eastern sees, closer to the imperial center, to remain politically independent. As the first millennium wore on, the pendulum would swing very much in the other direction with the rise of Lombard and Frankish power in the West, as we will see in later pages.

Voegelin's claim that, "In the East developed the Byzantine form of Caesaropapism, in direct continuity with the position of the emperor in pagan Rome,"[43] is not supportable. "It is often said that . . . the West had a greater sense of the Church's independence from the Empire. In fact, in addressing emperors,

---

42   Ibid., 114.
43   Ibid., 114.

Western councils used a language identical with that of the Eastern [Ecumenical] council of 381."[44] In 379, Emperor Theodosius I had become the first emperor to be baptized from the beginning of his reign, but he assumed no position in the Church comparable to the old title of *pontifex maximus* in the old pantheon, which his co-emperor in the West, Gratian, formally renounced in 381.[45] On the contrary, "There are many occasions showing that Constantine and his successors stepped in with great reluctance into the role of interpreters of Christian theology and church discipline, and that Christians themselves called on them to assume that role,"[46] and, "Except in the imperial capital, Constantinople, 'it is remarkable how little the imperial government interfered in episcopal elections.' "[47] Thus, "the concept of caesaropapism does not match the reality of the early Christian imperial system."[48] Among Western scholars, Voegelin's tendency to dismiss the subtleties of Byzantine Christianity as caeseropapist is hardly unique, however seriously mistaken, and reflects a prejudice at least as old as Edward Gibbon (1737-94) and his *History of the Decline and Fall of the Roman Empire.*[49]

---

44   Meyendorff, *Imperial Unity and Christian Divisions*, 37.

45   Ibid., 7.

46   Ibid., 34. A concrete example of the Church demonstrating her independence was the "famous incident of 390 when, in a polite and diplomatic letter, [St.] Ambrose [+397] refused communion to Theodosius I, demanding public penance for the slaying of 7,000 members of the rebellious population of Thessalonica." (Meyendorff, *Imperial Unity and Christian Divisions*, 37) "Similar involvement in social issues, e.g., intercession for an over-taxed citizenry, are characteristic of men like the great [St.] John Chrysostom, archbishop of Constantinople (398-404), or St. John the Almoner, Chalcedonian patriarch of Alexandria (611-619), or, in the West, St. Martin of Tours (371-397)." (Meyendorff, *Imperial Unity and Christian Divisions*, 19)

47   Jones, *Roman Empire*, II, 919 as quoted in Meyendorff, *Imperial Unity and Christian Divisions*, 44.

48   Meyendorff, *Imperial Unity and Christian Divisions*, 35.

49   Significantly, it seems that one of the few gaps in Voegelin's truly impressive body of learning was Orthodox Christianity, and one wonders whether he might have been personally drawn to Orthodoxy had he got around to engaging it professionally.

Having addressed Voegelin's error concerning caesaropapism, we may continue with his valuable theoretical insights:

> The clash between the various types of truth in the Roman Empire ended with the victory of Christianity. The fateful result of this victory was the de-divinization of the temporal sphere of power … the specifically modern problems of [political] representation would have something to do with a re-divinization of man and society.[50]

Whatever earthly politicians would continue to squabble over, as long the Church remained effective in society, they could not contest her exclusive claim to represent divine order on earth. The Church had successfully de-divinized politics by becoming the terrestrial manifestation of divine order; she had overthrown the old theo-political systems of the great empires and become the sole manifestation of the Kingdom of God on earth. The great political misadventures of the second millennium would result from the reversal of this achievement, i.e., from the abandonment of the Church as the embodiment of eternal order and her replacement by terrestrial political forms as the means by which man and society were to fulfill their ultimate destinies. While such efforts early on remained ostensibly Christian, in the later centuries of the second millennium, they grew ever more self-consciously antichristian. While later examples, such as Communism, would utterly renounce Christianity and all explicit ideas of transcendence, they would nonetheless seek to build on earth a mimicry of the heavenly kingdom "which

---

"Voegelin has not discussed Eastern Orthodox theology, but in many ways he would probably find it more congenial than the Western tradition with which he has been in tension, especially since the Eastern Church has preserved more of the tradition of Plato than has the Western on the whole and has always put more emphasis on the mystical side of Christianity." (Webb, *Eric Voegelin*, 227)

50   Voegelin, *The New Science of Politics*, 107.

shall not pass away,"[51] a replaying in modern context of the Tower of Babel. The pursuit of misconceived heavens-on-earth, and the concomitant renunciation of the Church's claim to embody eternal order, would lead to the greatest disasters in world history with body counts in the tens of millions.[52] It is those disasters that have set the stage for our own age of globalization, a time when there is the promise of a global civilization that will instantiate mankind's longing for a worldly paradise that will last indefinitely. We will now turn to the historical process leading up to modern-day globalization, which coincided with the breakdown of Orthodoxy in the West and its replacement with various antichristian thought-systems and the error that lies at their heart: the heresy of Gnosticism.

---

51   Dan. 7:14.
52   Namely, the wars and genocides of the twentieth century. See ch. 5.

CHAPTER 4

GNOSTICISM AND THE
RISE OF THE WEST

Then the LORD God took the man and put him in the garden of Eden to tend and keep it. And the LORD God commanded the man, saying, "Of every tree of the garden you may freely eat; but of the tree of the knowledge of good and evil you shall not eat, for in the day that you eat of it you shall surely die."

Genesis 2:15-17

In Christianized lands of the first millennium, state power lost its claim to represent the divine order on earth. God was now represented exclusively in His Church. The existential representative of the earthly Empire, the Emperor, held legitimacy as a servant of the Church and could lose that legitimacy if he transgressed the Church's laws. The Church, furthermore, as "the flash of eternity into time,"[1] transposed the Israelite expectation of a coming messianic reign from the realm of history to that of eternity.

Ideas about the coming of a heavenly kingdom on earth were widespread among the Hebrews during the time of Christ's earthly ministry, who longed to throw off Roman rule in the

---

1   Voegelin, *The New Science of Politics*, 109.

Holy Land. Much Judaic thought, then and now, anticipated an earthly savior, a second King David, who would crush the enemies of Jewry and re-establish the kingdom of Israel on earth first among the nations. Jesus Himself had to fend off speculation during His ministry that He had come in such a capacity. "Therefore, when Jesus perceived that they were about to come and take Him by force to make Him king, He departed again to the mountain by Himself alone."[2] The problem did not disappear even after the Lord's Crucifixion and Resurrection.

> Therefore, when the disciples had come together, they asked Him, saying, "Lord, will You at this time restore the kingdom to Israel?" And He said to them, "It is not for you to know times or seasons which the Father has put in His own authority. But you shall receive power when the Holy Spirit has come upon you; and you shall be witnesses to Me in Jerusalem, and in all Judea and Samaria, and to the end of the earth."[3]

> But Jesus called them to Himself and said, "You know that the rulers of the Gentiles lord it over them, and those who are great exercise authority over them. Yet it shall not be so among you; but whoever desires to become great among you, let him be your servant. And whoever desires to be first among you, let him be your slave—just as the Son of Man did not come to be served, but to serve, and to give His life a ransom for many."[4]

---

2   John 6:15.
3   Acts 1:6-8.
4   Matt. 20:25-8.

The disciples' mission was to spread the Gospel—not to construct an earthly empire.[5] But *millennialism* or *chiliasm* (Greek χίλιοι, *khilioi*, "thousand") in reference to Christ's reign, figuratively for "a thousand years"[6]), the idea that God would someday set up a terrestrial "kingdom" of which "there will be no end,"[7] would not go away. While human societies would rise and fall, a powerful heretical idea arose that a terrestrial polity could assume the eternal attributes of the Church and escape the cycle of history.

It has been a great and persistent temptation to believe that any human civilization—from the great empires of the ancient world to the nation-states of modern times—is permanent and an exception to the historical reality that all human political constructions ultimately pass away. The temptation has been especially great in recent centuries when heterodox Christian notions mixed with the burgeoning material and technical power of the modern age, a highly powerful combination that drove the utopian thought of men like H. G. Wells and the hugely destructive ideologies of Communism and National Socialism.

> Even the most fervently secular man of our day never ceases to desire something higher and more permanent. He does not cease to hang on at least to the shell of the eschatological view of time, which the Christian tradition shaped over the centuries. In the final analysis, he does

---

5   "Christ said, 'The Kingdom of Heaven is at hand.' He did not say, 'Help me build a Kingdom.' He did not say, 'Let's work towards the advancing of the Kingdom.' The Kingdom of God is a reality that was in-breaking in the coming of Jesus Christ. Everywhere He went, the Kingdom was at hand. Everything He did was the advent of the Kingdom of God. This remains the nature of the Kingdom." (Fr. Stephen Freeman, "Brief Notes on the Kingdom—You Are Not Advancing It." https://blogs.ancientfaith.com/glory2godforallthings/2015/12/08/brief-notes-on-the-kingdom-you-are-not-advancing-it/) Accessed December 8, 2015.

6   Rev. 20:2-7.

7   Luke 1:33.

not deny the *eschaton* [Greek: "end"] that religion professes— it is just that this too he wants here and now. He wants it both "of this world" and easily accessible.[8]

The idea of an earthly reign by the transcendent God, or, more generally, of any kind of paradise-on-earth, whether God- or man-made, that would be immune from the historical cycle of rise and fall, has proven one of the most powerful ideas in history. It is what lent such destructive energy to the totalitarian movements of the modern age, and it will serve as the primary article of faith during the reign of Antichrist.

CHILIASM

In essence, [chiliasm] teaches that not long before the end of the world, Christ the Saviour will come again to earth, defeat Antichrist, resurrect the righteous, and make a new kingdom on earth. As a reward for their struggles and sufferings, the righteous will reign together with Christ for the course of a thousand years and will enjoy all the good things of temporal life.[9]

In the first centuries of the Church's history, Christian eschatology remained a point of sometimes intense disagreement. Many Christians anticipated the imminent return of the Lord and the establishment of a terrestrial kingdom of God. The Apostle Peter, shortly before his martyrdom in Rome, wrote his second catholic epistle to reassure the faithful that the Lord will indeed return but not in accordance with the breathless historical anticipation of some. Rather, "the day of the Lord

---

8   Mantzaridis, *Time and Man*, 34.
9   Taushev and Rose, *The Apocalypse*, 256.

will come as a thief in the night, in which the heavens will pass away with a great noise, and the elements will melt with fervent heat; both the earth and the works that are in it will be burned up."[10] The Lord's timetable is not ours, and His return will not be in the vein of the triumph of one terrestrial political society over another. The earth and human history as we understand it will instantly come to an end with the Second Coming; there will be no earthly Kingdom of God beyond the present life of the Church; but "we, according to His promise, look for new heavens and a new earth in which righteousness dwells."[11] "The holy city, New Jerusalem, comes down out of heaven from God"[12] and is not a product of history.

Chiliasm was condemned by the Second and Third Ecumenical Councils as a heresy, but chiliastic expectation would persist at the fringes of Christendom, often heightened during times of persecution and upheaval. It was in response to pagan attacks against the Church following the sack of Rome by the Visigoths in 410 that St. Augustine composed his masterful refutation of chiliasm in his *City of God*.

> On the theoretical level, the problem [of chiliasm] could be solved only by the tour de force of interpretation which St. Augustine performed in the *Civitas Dei*. There he roundly dismissed the literal belief in the millennium as "ridiculous fables" and then boldly declared the realm of the thousand years to be the reign of Christ in his church in the present saeculum that would continue until the Last Judgment and the advent of the eternal realm in the beyond.[13]

---

10   2 Peter 3:10.
11   2 Peter 3:13.
12   Rev. 21:2.
13   Voegelin, *The New Science of Politics*, 109.

Echoing the Lord's admonition that "the kingdom of God does not come with observation,"[14] St. Augustine affirmed the Orthodox teaching that the "thousand years" of Christ's reign with his saints[15] is *now* in the Church and does in no way correspond to a literal "thousand years" or any specific earthly period of time.

> The thousand-year Kingdom of Christ on earth is to be understood as the victory of Christianity over paganism and the establishment on earth of the Church of Christ. The definite number one thousand is used here in place of an indefinite number, signifying the long period of time until the Second Coming of Christ.[16]

The Church is the Kingdom of God on earth (which will be assumed into Heaven at the Second Coming), an essential doctrine articulated by the early Councils and Church Fathers such as St. Augustine.

> The revolutionary expectation of a Second Coming that would transfigure the structure of history on earth was ruled out [by St. Augustine] as "ridiculous." The Logos had become flesh in Christ; the grace of redemption has been bestowed on man; there would be no divinization of society beyond the pneumatic presence of Christ in his church.... This left the church as the universal spiritual organization of saints and sinners who professed faith in Christ, as the representative of the *civitas Dei* in history, as the flash of eternity into time.... The one Christian society was articulated into its spiritual and temporal

---

14   Luke 17:20.
15   See Rev. 20:4-6.
16   Taushev and Rose, *The Apocalypse*, 253-4.

orders. In its temporal articulation, it accepted the *conditio humana* without chiliastic fancies, while it heightened natural existence by the representation of spiritual destiny through the church.[17]

The foregoing quote from Voegelin is as capable a summary of the Orthodox understanding of the different realms of eternity and of history as one is likely to find. The Church and the Empire, while not separate in the modern understanding of the "separation of church and state," were always distinct by virtue of man's dual existence as both a creature fallen from grace and one redeemed by the incarnation and sacrifice of Christ. In this life, the realms of the sacred and the profane must always remain distinct, and human efforts to fuse the two spheres of history—to turn this world into an eternal paradise—must always end in failure. The reality is that there can never be in this life an end to the tension between the ideal, heavenly realm represented on earth by the Church and the fallen realm of history.

The proper aim of politics in Christian lands—and what Orthodox empires sought, however imperfectly, to accomplish—is to bring into alignment as closely as possible earthly society with the heavenly, but there are intrinsic limits as to how far this can go. Disaster lies in both directions: the confusion of the spiritual and the temporal, a collapse into theocracy, in which the Church becomes overwhelmingly politicized, or, conversely, the separation of Church and state in which the former is systematically excluded from any venue in which it has contact with the latter. Either the Church loses her independence and becomes a worldly polity (as in the case of the Roman Papacy—more anon) or she is driven out of public life, which results in the de facto deification of the state and of political leaders, which has been the tendency during the modern age. The successful

---

17   Voegelin, *The New Science of Politics*, 109.

Christian society is the one that "manages" the tension between the two realms of human existence, but this can never be a truly systematic enterprise and is fraught with perils; it is a perennial "muddling through." The only society capable of muddling through in the long term is the virtuous society, one possessed of the humbling knowledge that no earthly political organization will last forever; the society whose people and leaders possess the faith and patience to "endure great struggle with sufferings"[18] without succumbing to chiliastic fantasies. "Now when He was asked by the Pharisees when the kingdom of God would come, He answered them and said, 'The kingdom of God does not come with observation; nor will they say, "See here!" or "See there!" For indeed, the kingdom of God is within you.' "[19] Looking for the kingdom of God to come in outward political form is a fundamental error and one that the Pharisees of Christ's day, anticipating a conquering messiah who would install them atop a new earthly power structure, were prone to committing. All who lack faith that "the kingdom of God has come upon" them[20] in Christ and the Church, and who cannot find the "kingdom of God within" them, are prone to the error of seeking to regain paradise through fallen human means. Chiliasm thus blends into *Gnosticism*, the idea that, through the apprehension of some special knowledge or *gnosis*, man can escape the broken world or remake it into a paradisal realm that will "rise" but never "fall." While chiliasm and Gnosticism were originally adversaries during the time of the early Church, their differences proved largely cosmetic. Gnosticism lies at the heart of the process of re-divinization identified by Voegelin that has become the defining aspect of the modern West and of our own age of globalization.

---

18   Heb. 10:32.
19   Luke 17:20-1.
20   Matt. 12:28.

Gnosticism

The Greek term *gnosis* translates as "knowledge" and thus "Gnosticism" amounts to a system of thought based on the primacy of knowledge. Since any system of thought involves knowledge in some form, this simple definition is of itself of little theoretical utility. Indeed, Gnostic thought can vary widely while traces of it may be identified in a host of philosophical and religious traditions. A powerful Gnostic strain is evident, however, in pre-Christian Greek philosophy, which appears to have served as the origin for the wider efficacy of Gnostic thought in the early Christian era. While we have mentioned the philosophy of Plato as an important preliminary of Christianity, like any human system, it is prone to error and is at best incomplete. In the early Christian era, Gnostic systems resisted the message of the Gospel with its universal call to repentance; instead they developed the idea that wisdom and salvation came by way of a select few who had achieved gnosis apart from the Universal Church. At a conference held in 1966 in Messina, Italy, an attempt was made to define the phenomenon of Gnosticism formally.

> In the concluding document of Messina the proposal was... to designate "a particular group of systems of the second century after Christ" as "Gnosticism", and to use "gnosis" to define a conception of knowledge transcending the times which was described as "knowledge of divine mysteries for an élite".[21]

Unlike the Orthodox Church where the "mysteries" of Christ—literally holy communion—are universally accessible,

---

21   Christoph Markschies, *Gnosis: An Introduction, translated by John Bowden* (New York, T&T Clark, 2003), 13.

Gnostic systems confine true knowledge to a select few who, by virtue of their possession of gnosis itself, transcend the limits of pedestrian existence. The gnosis possessed by this elite provides an escape from the reality that confines the unenlightened and bestows on them the capacity to perceive the world—even to change the world—in special ways.

While in Orthodox Christianity the key to apprehending reality is faith, in Gnostic systems it is knowledge. The distinction is capital.[22] Certainly, in some sense they are complementary: faith grants knowledge of reality (of man, creation, God), while knowledge cultivates faith. ("The fear of the Lord is the beginning of knowledge."[23]) In the Gnostic sense, however, "knowledge" implies a capacity to overrule or circumvent the normal limits of fallen human ability, to liberate man from the encumbrances of the flesh and of reliance on the unfathomable mercy of God. While both the Christian and the Gnostic perceive the world as broken or fallen, the Gnostic searches out knowledge according to his own will, while the Church in contrast directs the individual to a humble submission before the order of being and of its Author, God. In the Church, humility is not only a moral virtue but a positive necessity to the correct understanding ("standing under") of the order of reality. The "enlightened" Gnostic, in contrast, stands above the reality that he inhabits by virtue of his private gnosis. While the variations on Gnosticism were myriad in the first centuries after Christ, their common thread was the rejection of the need for faith in the correct apprehension of reality and its replacement with "certain" knowledge.[24]

---

22   "Knowledge puffs up, but love edifies. And if anyone thinks that he knows anything, he knows nothing yet as he ought to know." (I Cor 8:2-3)

23   Prov. 1:7.

24   An early example of a Gnostic heresy that afflicted the Church, which claimed that Christ only appeared to possess a material body rather than actually being fully human in the corporeal sense, was Docetism. A tendency in Gnostic heresies is the

In direct contrast to Orthodox Christianity, the brokenness that the Gnostic perceives to infect this world he never extends to his own capacity to diagnose and rectify through *gnosis*. In Gnosticism,

> The instrument of salvation is gnosis itself—knowledge. Since according to the Gnostic ontology entanglement with the world is brought about by *agnoia*, ignorance, the soul will be able to disentangle itself through knowledge of its true life and alienness in this world. As the knowledge of falling captive to the world, gnosis is at the same time the means of escaping it.[25]

Whereas in the Church, sin and death are overcome by the free sacrifice of Christ on the Cross and the salvific life of the Church, Gnosticism sets up man as his own savior through acquisition of the salvific *gnosis*. In his famous conversation with Nicholas Motovilov, St. Seraphim of Sarov [+1833] explains that the supreme goal of the Christian life is the acquisition of the Holy Spirit.[26] While the Holy Spirit may be "attracted" by faith and good works, He comes to the soul ultimately according to God's inscrutable will. There is no formula through which man can tame the Spirit of God; He "bloweth where He listeth."[27] "For us [Orthodox] both the truth and the way to the truth have been defined once and for all. We possess the truth, and all our

---

rejection of the reality of the material realm or the condemnation of the material as inherently evil, rather than as inherently good, created by God, but which has, along with spiritual existence, fallen into sinfulness.

25   Eric Voegelin, *Science, Politics, and Gnosticism* (Washington, Regnery Gateway, 1968), 11-12.

26   See "St. Seraphim's of Sarov Conversation with Nicholas Motovilov, A Wonderful Revelation to the World." http://orthodoxinfo.com/praxis/wonderful. aspx. Accessed September 18, 2019.

27   John 3:8.

efforts are directed toward its assimilation, not its discovery."[28] The Orthodox Christian seeks knowledge but a "knowledge born of spiritual struggle."[29] In the Church, there is no "secret" to be discovered that will provide a shortcut to salvation or an easy life; no resurrection without Golgotha. Whereas the Gnostic believes that he has found sure knowledge, the Orthodox knows himself to be easily deceived by his own senses and reason and in constant need of humility and repentance. "We are all in deception. The knowledge of this is the greatest preventative against deception. It is the greatest deception to acknowledge oneself to be free of deception."[30]

Whereas the true Christian perceives himself as the greatest sinner, the most broken, and the least capable of saving himself, the Gnostic projects his own brokenness onto reality and the Creator thereof, God. Rejecting the soteriological truth of the Church, the Gnostic regards himself to possess the means of his own salvation. Gnosticism thus amounts to a rebellion against God, a rejection of one's own sinfulness, a rejection of faith, and an undertaking of self-salvation. The creed of Gnosticism (now quite popular) may be summed up by the dictum, "knowledge is power." Through the acquisition of special knowledge, the Gnostic achieves a change of consciousness ("building awareness") and grasps the means of his salvation. Gnostic suppositions lie at the heart of enterprises such as occult magic and modern technical science whose raisons d'etre are the acquisition of power over nature. Whereas Orthodoxy seeks salvation through faith and divine grace, Gnosticism seeks it

---

28   St. Theophan the Recluse, *On Orthodoxy with Warnings about Errors Against It*, 7 as quoted in Archbishop Averky Taushev, *Stand Fast in the Truth*. http://archbishopaverky.blogspot.com/2012/08/stand-fast-in-truth.html. Accessed September 13, 2019.

29   Damascene, *Father Seraphim Rose*, 1054.

30   St. Ignatius Brianchaninov (+1867) as quoted in Rose, *Orthodoxy and the Religion of the Future*, 150.

through knowledge and the power over nature that it bestows. Gnostic creeds amount to magic formulas that promise a short-cut to salvation without the need for genuine repentance and the mercy of the sovereign, almighty God.

In the history of the Church, Gnosticism proved one of the first and most persistent dangers to Orthodoxy. It threatened to entice the faithful away by proposing that there was occult wisdom beyond the purview of the Church that would allow the individual to escape from the Orthodox saga of fall and redemption, of sin and repentance, of persistent struggle in the way of the Cross. As the Church grew beyond her early Israelite roots and expanded into the Greco-Roman world,

> The Church first had to protect itself from all attempts to reconcile Christianity too easily with the spirit of the times and reinterpret it smoothly in Hellenistic patterns. If the Church had remained only in Jewish molds, it would not have conquered the world; but if it had simply adapted these molds to those of Hellenistic thought, the world would have conquered Christianity. Gnosticism, the first enemy with which it came into conflict, was in fact inspired by the idea of reinterpretation and reconciliation.[31]

"The history of early Christianity ... is a history not of rap-prochement between Athens and Jerusalem, but rather of a struggle through which there took place a gradual 'churching' of Hellenism which was to fertilize Christian thought forever after."[32] The spread of the Gospel into the Hellenized Mediterranean world in the first centuries AD fostered a powerful synthesis between Greek rationality and Biblical revelation that found

---

31   Alexander Schmemann, *The Historical Road of Eastern Orthodoxy* (Crestwood, St. Vladimir's Seminary, 1992), 39.
32   Ibid., 39.

expression in the great councils of the Church and the writings of early Church Fathers such as Sts. John Chrysostom (+407), Basil the Great (+379), and Gregory the Theologian (+389). This was the Orthodox synthesis, the rational understanding of God's revelation to man in Jesus Christ manifested in the Church. It was providential that Greek philosophy had developed an advanced philosophical vocabulary that the Church was able to employ to give rational expression to her theology. As Voegelin has observed, "The revelation of this grace in history, through the incarnation of the Logos in Christ, intelligibly fulfilled the adventitious movement of the spirit in the mystic philosophers."[33] While it had not been possible for the philosophers to find the *logos* without divine revelation, the revelation of the *Logos* in Jesus Christ answered the most profound philosophical yearnings.

"It was not a matter of Christian wisdom simply overthrowing the pagan, however; here was the first acceptance of Hellenistic values by Christianity in order to convert them to the service of Christ."[34] Contrary to much modern analysis, whatever the "clash of ideas" represented by the rise of the Church into the pagan and philosophical world, the Church's mission has never been primarily intellective: the Church is not a scientific society nor can Orthodoxy be reduced to a mere collection of propositions. While she has fought to maintain the purity of her doctrines, the Church is firstly a living, organic unity, a "divine-human organism,"[35] the Body of Christ on earth, a mystical brotherhood of sinners and saints, visibly expressed by the faithful congregating under the authority of a bishop, into which all persons, slave and free, male and female, and all cultures and systems of ideas are called to participate in and submit to.

---

33   Voegelin, *The New Science of Politics*, 78.

34   Schmemann, *The Historical Road of Eastern Orthodoxy*, 53.

35   St. Justin Popovic, *The Supreme Value and Infallible Criterion*, B#80A, v 4, 124-5 as quoted in Manley, *The Bible and the Holy Fathers*, 383.

> St. Irenaeus of Lyons [+202], chief fighter against
> Gnosticism ... opposed Gnosticism—the seduction of
> schism and partial interpretation of Christianity—not by
> another interpretation but by the very fact of the Church
> as a visible, palpable unity which alone preserves and
> transmits to its members the whole truth and fulness of
> the Gospel.[36]

Insofar as one's behavior and beliefs conflict with the Church's
precepts, they must be reformed, but the idea that there exists
a fundamental tension between Greek rational philosophy
and the revelation of the Logos in Jesus Christ, which ecclesial
power forced into a false unity only to break apart centuries later,
denies the social efficacy of the first millennium Church and her
"catholic consciousness" that remains effective to this day.[37] To
rely on human rationality at the expense of the wisdom of the
Church, however, is to commit the error of Gnosticism. In the
first centuries AD, Gnostic thought, while found both within
and apart from Christian communities, increasingly came to
reject Christianity. More and more, Gnostics defined themselves
in contrast to the Church and claimed a "direct, immediate
apprehension or vision of truth"[38] outside her received wisdom.
While many Gnostics maintained a regard for Christian truths,
they used them as a means of reaching a supposed "higher"
order of knowledge that could take the place of the "patience

---

36   Schmemann, *The Historical Road of Eastern Orthodoxy*, 44-5.
37   Ibid., 46. A common error found throughout the history of the post-schism West.
The tension and ultimate incompatibility between Christian revelation and rational
philosophy ("faith" and "reason" or, during the Reformation and Counterreformation,
"faith" and "works") in the Western mind arose subsequent to the West's divergence
from Orthodoxy in the early second millennium rather than as a weakness of the
Orthodox synthesis itself. It finally resolved itself in the modern era with the utter
rejection of revealed truth and a disastrous collapse into materialism and other
inner-worldly ideologies. See ch. 5.
38   Webb, *Eric Voegelin*, 282.

and the faith of the saints."[39] "The Nicolaitans," for example,
mentioned in the Apocalypse of St. John, "whose deeds and
doctrine the Lord hates,"[40] were a Gnostic sect known for their
indulgence in all forms of immorality.[41] While knowledge can
be found throughout creation, Orthodoxy sublimates all to the
received wisdom of the Church, which alone through divine
inspiration is capable of distinguishing truth from error.

> As in our own time, men were groping for a syncretic
> religion, in which elements of truth from all doctrines,
> philosophies, and religions might, as it were, be one. It
> was this effort to combine and reinterpret all religions
> in its own way that rendered Gnosticism a danger to the
> Church. It was far from hostile to Christianity—on the
> contrary, tried to include it within its own fold.... As the
> Church was taking its very first steps, we see beside it and
> sometimes even within it seeds of Christian Gnosticism,
> attempts to interpret the Gospels, avoiding what seemed
> unacceptable or incomprehensible in them—primarily, of
> course, the very reality of the Incarnation of God and the
> humanity of Christ. We sense uneasiness even in St. Paul:
> "Beware lest any man spoil you through philosophy and
> vain deceit, after the tradition of men, after the rudiments
> of the world, and not after Christ" (Col. 2:8).[42]

In Gnostic interpretations,

> Christianity was transformed into a special mythological
> philosophy: instead of the drama of sin, forgiveness, and
> salvation, a personal encounter between God and man,

---

39   Rev. 13:10.
40   Rev. 2:6, 15.
41   See Taushev and Rose, *The Apocalypse*, 79.
42   Schmemann, *The Historical Road of Eastern Orthodoxy*, 40.

> Gnosticism offered a sort of cosmological scheme according to which the "spiritual elements" in the world were gradually freed from the captivity of matter and evil multiplicity gave way to abstract unity. It was a return in a new Eastern form to ancient Greek idealism.[43]

The phenomenon identified by Voegelin as Gnosticism (whether it travels under that name or some other) not only describes a powerful collection of heresies of the early Church that, importantly, later recrudesced in the modern world in massive political forms (as we shall see), but it captures the essence of the primordial sin that led to the separation of man from God that lies at the heart of all sin.[44] In the Garden of Eden, one will recall, the forbidden fruit grew on the "tree of the knowledge of good and evil,"[45] which God promised would bring death to Adam and Eve should they partake of it. The serpent, which "was more cunning than any beast of the field which the LORD God had made,"[46] animated by Satan, enticed the first humans with the same hope of becoming like God, of usurping the divine kingship that was at the root of Satan's own downfall. "Then the serpent said to the woman, 'You will not surely die. For God knows that in the day you eat of it your eyes will be opened, and you will be like God, knowing good and evil.' "[47] The Gnostic temptation, then and now,

---

43   Ibid., 41.

44   One key attribute to both early and late versions of Gnosticism is a decided impatience. While both the Orthodox Christian and the early Gnostic appreciated the fallenness of this world and the need for turning away from it to seek God, the Gnostic betrayed an insistence on experiencing the divine in an immediate way rather than struggling patiently while waiting for God to act. Similarly, modern Gnostics reject the promises of a heavenly realm to come and insist on building their own vision of paradise in this life.

45   Gen. 2:17.

46   Gen. 3:1.

47   Gen. 3:4.

is to "be like God" ("men like gods" as Wells put it) "knowing good and evil," or, as Nietzsche phrased it, to transcend or be "beyond good and evil." The willful pursuit of knowledge and power is the fundamental rebellion against God and His beneficent ordering of creation. Then and now, Satan, the deceiver, presents himself as "Lucifer," the "bearer of light," bringing the promise of "knowledge" and "enlightenment" that will "empower" man to be "like God." It should not be surprising that Gnostic mythology inverts the Orthodox story of the fall of man. In the Gnostic myth, Lucifer assumes the attributes of the God-Man, Jesus Christ, an uncreated savior sent to liberate imprisoned humanity from the evil creator of this world, a twist on the story of the fall straight from the pen of the Devil himself.

> Gnostic myths relate that Lucifer is the Messenger of the Unknowable God [not the Creator God in the Orthodox tradition]. We had said that this God, the greatest one, unreachable and unknowable, is unable to penetrate this limited universe of impure and satanic matter.[48] But according to these myths, he can send someone, Lucifer…

> According to Gnostic legends and myths, the great Unknowable God sent Lucifer, angel of indescribable fire and light, to show man the light and to help him wake up and see his true origin, the origin of his Spirit, which has been perversely imprisoned in this impure matter called body-soul [by the creator or *demiurge* who is regarded as an evil, "lesser" god, and who is often represented as the Biblical Creator]. He [Lucifer] is an uncreated being, who came to the created world to bring Light: Liberating

---

48   One cannot help but ask, why, if this "God" is "greatest," does it lack the capacity to "penetrate this limited universe" and communicate with man?

Gnosis. The saving knowledge which can wake man up and help him free his imprisoned Spirit.[49]

Thus Lucifer, the Devil, stands in the place of the God-Man, Christ, who "liberates" man from the evil Creator of "impure and satanic matter," not through sacrifice and the way of the Cross but through painless "Liberating Gnosis." In its foundational myth, Gnosticism is set apart as a form of antichristianity *par excellence.*

THE RISE OF THE WEST

Chapter Four of Voegelin's *New Science of Politics* ranks as one of the most profound political science lectures ever given in the English language. In it, Voegelin diagnoses the nature of modern political movements and identifies the inherent error that invariably leads them, and the societies that follow them, to existential failure. This lecture, entitled "Gnosticism— The Nature of Modernity," serves as a critical component in our analysis because it ties the course of modern history into the Orthodox understanding of history and of its ultimate end. Voegelin cogently establishes that modernity—Western Civilization since around 1500—or, indeed, even earlier—is defined by the ascendancy of Gnostic movements. The mass political movements of the modern age bear the same basic structure and symbolism as the early Gnostic and chiliastic heresies that the Church successfully repressed but which broke out with great force in the West following the Latin Schism in the eleventh century and later during the Protestant Reformation.

---

49 "Lucifer, The Liberator." *Primordial Gnosis: The Forbidden Religion.* http://www. theforbiddenreligion.com/index.htm. Accessed September 1, 2017.

Some early forms of Gnosticism led their followers into various, unconventional, largely private, experiences such as stoicism, libertinism, esoteric mysticism, and the like. Some took an ascetic angle, which lent them a superficial resemblance to Orthodox monasticism, which had begun to flourish following the legalization of the Church in the early fourth century. When Gnosticism has assumed a political form, however, it manifests a desire to destroy the extant political order and usher in a new realm that will provide the equivalent of a Christian paradise. The soteriological truth of Christianity, in which salvation is found in the Church and in the realm of eternity, is transposed to the realm of profane history. No more is man's true destiny to be attained through grace in the Church on the individual level and collectively at the end of time with the general resurrection; political Gnosticism seeks to establish a paradisal realm on earth through human knowledge and power. As Gnostic suppositions gradually took root in Western Christendom during the second millennium, Gnostic elites grew sufficiently powerful to orchestrate political movements of sometimes tremendous, if short-lived, power.

> Gnostic speculation overcame the uncertainty of faith by receding from transcendence and endowing man and his intermundane range of action with the meaning of eschatological fulfillment.... The spiritual strength of the soul which in Christianity was devoted to the sanctification of life could now be diverted into the more appealing, more tangible, and, above all, so much easier creation of the terrestrial paradise.[50]

---

50   Voegelin, *The New Science of Politics*, 129.

Voegelin may not have been a practicing Christian,[51] but as a competent scientist he was able to appreciate the Orthodox Christian experience and therefore explicate its historical implications. The Gnostic "creation of the terrestrial paradise," while impossible in historical reality, nonetheless was psychologically "so much easier" because it unburdened the Gnostic of the "fear and trembling,"[52] of the life of "suffering and patience,"[53] of the necessity for faith as "the substance of things hoped for,

---

51   Author's conversation with Paul Caringella, Voegelin's former assistant. While perhaps strictly peripheral to our task, it seems appropriate to quote here Dr. Caringella's "*Manner of the Death of Eric Voegelin*," which stands as a poignant qualification to Voegelin's apparent nonacceptance of Christianity during his professional life.

The funeral plans were made by Eric himself in the presence of his wife Lissy and the Dean of Stanford Memorial Church, Robert Hamerton-Kelly, in Eric's room at the Stanford Hospital in early December of 1984. I was also present. Eric said that he wanted the Lutheran order to be followed for his funeral. The readings he requested were verses 15–17 of chapter 2 of the First Letter of John:

Do not love the world or the things in the world. If any one loves the world, love for the Father is not in him. For all that is in the world, the lust of the flesh and the lust of the eyes and pride of life, is not of the Father but is of the world. And the world passes away, and the lust of it; but he who does the will of God abides forever.

I remember Lissy asking Eric why those verses (after Robert had read them aloud to us) and Eric answering simply, "for repentance."

The gospel reading Eric wanted was even shorter, two verses, 24 and 25, in the 12th chapter of the Gospel of John:

Truly, Truly, I say to you, unless a grain of wheat falls into the earth and dies, it remains alone; but if it dies, it bears much fruit. He who loves his life loses it, and he who hates his life in this world will keep it for eternal life.

The short funeral service with no more than a dozen people present took place in the chapel of a funeral home in Palo Alto a few days after Eric's death on January 19th (of 1985) at his home on the Stanford campus.

http://watershade.net/ev/ev-remembered.html#manner_of_death. Accessed September 13, 2019.

52   Phil. 2:12.

53   James 5:10.

the evidence of things not seen"[54] of the genuine Christian life. Gnostics throughout history "achieved a certainty about the meaning of history, and about their own place in it"—albeit a gravely mistaken one—"which otherwise they would not have had."[55] Such Gnostic attitudes can be found throughout the myriad religious/political movements of the modern era and even among many self-professed Christians. In contrast, in the Orthodox Christian experience,

> The life of the soul in openness toward God, the wai-ting, the periods of aridity and dullness, of guilt and de-spondency, contrition and repentance, forsakenness and hope against hope, the silent stirrings of love and grace, trembling on the verge of a certainty which if gained is loss—the very lightness of this fabric may prove too heavy a burden for men who lust for massively possessive experience.[56]

Well did St. Paul instruct, "For you have need of endurance, so that after you have done the will of God, you may receive the promise."[57] Gnostics lack the faith to "endure hardship as a good soldier of Jesus Christ"[58] and require the consolation of world-immanent activity in place of faith in God's Providence and the interior struggle for salvation.

At the height of Orthodox civilization, the life of the Church absorbed great numbers of the best and brightest and directed them to labor not for this world but for the next. In Orthodoxy, the soul is directed on a primarily internal effort to cultivate the virtues of patience, humility, and love and to subdue the

---

54   Heb. 11:1.
55   Voegelin, *The New Science of Politics*, 122.
56   Ibid., 122.
57   Heb. 10:36.
58   2 Tim. 2:3.

passions of pride, lust, and avarice. As Western Civilization progressively abandoned its Orthodox orientation, huge energies were released for worldly activity. Even while the increasingly heterodox West retained an outwardly Christian form, its attentions were more and more focused on this world rather than the next. In particular, those souls thirsting for salvation, those most sensitive to the fallen nature of this world, instead of populating the monasteries and parishes of Orthodox society, were now directed to find their salvation, not through an inward transformation of the soul into the image of Christ, but through an outward transformation of this world into paradise. They had begun to forget that "the kingdom of God is within you."[59]

One of the recurrent Gnostic symbols Voegelin identifies is that of the "Third realm," a supposed future period of history in which mankind will enjoy the equivalent of Christian salvation on earth. Gnostic interpretations invariably divide history into three phases: the first, which is past, in which man lived in ignorance; the second, the present time, in which the Gnostic has discovered the knowledge that will provide for a transformation of the self and of the world; and the third, a future phase, when the transformative *gnosis* will have found fulfillment in a super-historical end-state. It then follows that it is the task of all good Gnostics to see that the *gnosis* finds fulfillment in history, an imperative that functionally replaces the Christian life of the spirit with historical action. "Civilizational action became a *divertissement*, in the sense of Pascal, but a *divertissement* which demonically absorbed into itself the eternal destiny of man and substituted for the life of the spirit."[60] Instead of working out one's salvation in the Church, one now was to "divert" oneself with various forms of historical action depending on the

---

59   Luke 17:21.
60   Voegelin, *The New Science of Politics*, 129.

particular Gnostic creed. But, as Voegelin points out, the "diversions" were far from innocuous; rather they came to replace the interior struggle for salvation with the idea—at first vague but over time with mounting force—of "ending" history and building an eternal civilization on earth. Gnostics began to distort the Christian symbols of salvation and paradise into inner-worldly objects within the power of human manipulation. By the time of the great totalitarian ideologies of the twentieth century, of "modernity without restraint,"[61] the Gnostic ambition for constructing the paradisal realm in one form or another had so overwhelmed the West's remaining genuine Christian tendencies that the civilization was pushed to the brink of existential collapse. Political action, and indeed revolution and world war, became the means of "diverting" oneself from the horror of having lost one's faith and of finding another path back to paradise.

> Nietzsche most tersely expressed the nature of this demonic diversion when he raised the question why anyone should live in the embarrassing condition of being in need of the love and grace of God. "Love yourself through grace—was his solution—you are no longer in need of your God, and you can act the whole drama of Fall and Redemption to its end in yourself." And how can this miracle be achieved, this miracle of self-salvation, and how this redemption by extending grace to yourself? The great historical answer was given by the successive types of Gnostic action that have made modern civilization what it is.[62]

---

61   See *The Collected Works of Eric Voegelin*, v. 5. (Columbia, University of Missouri Press, 1999).
62   Voegelin, *The New Science of Politics*, 129-30.

As the second millennium wore on, the civilizational centers of the West came up with their own responses to the questions that the Orthodox Church asks and answers but in sharply different ways. Having jettisoned Orthodoxy, such systems were forced to devise their own ideas of how meaning and salvation could be articulated in history. Early on, these systems of thought remained self-consciously Christian; as the centuries wore on, they grew ever more self-consciously antichristian. Generation after generation, the centers of Western thought moved further and further from an Orthodox orientation. By the modern age, the vanguard of Western thought was increasingly focused on how man might save himself and redeem the fallen world than on anything that could be recognized as the Orthodox struggle for redemption.

> The miracle [of self-salvation] was worked successively through the literary and artistic achievement which secured the immortality of fame for the humanistic intellectual [during the "Renaissance" of the fifteenth and sixteenth centuries], through the discipline and economic success which certified salvation to the Puritan saint [in the seventeenth], through the civilizational contributions of the liberals and progressives [in the eighteenth and nineteenth], and, finally, through the revolutionary action that will establish the Communist or some other Gnostic millennium [in the twentieth]. *Gnosticism, thus, most effectively released human forces for the building of a civilization because on their fervent application to intramundane activity was put the premium of salvation.* The historical result was stupendous. The resources that came to light under such pressure were in themselves a revelation, and their application to civilizational work produced the truly magnificent spectacle of Western progressive society. However fatuous the surface arguments may be, the widespread belief that modern civilization is Civilization in a pre-eminent sense is

experientially justified; *the endowment with the meaning of salvation has made the rise of the West, indeed, an apocalypse of civilization.*[63]

In the preceding paragraph we have, perhaps, the most perceptive observation on the rise of modern Western Civilization ever offered. "Apocalyptic" Western Civilization is, indeed, an astonishing historical revelation. What Voegelin has discovered is that the second millennium "Rise of the West" was made possible by the distortion of the meaning of Orthodox Christian salvation, which occurs in the Church in the realm of eternity, into the Gnostic heresy that salvation may be gained in this life through historical action. It is a process of "re-divinizing" terrestrial politics, which the first millennium Church had successfully "de-divinized" through becoming the representation of eternal order on earth. While it may be a tough fact to bear for Westerners proud of their heritage, the West is a fundamentally Gnostic, heterodox undertaking, and therein lies the secret of its great success. The acceptance of Gnostic ideologies in the West— at first under the guise of Christianity but eventually under various antichristian banners—unleashed previously unimagined power that in an Orthodox context was channeled into the Church and the struggle for salvation with only a tangential civilizational effect. The origin of this power is the soteriological truth of Christianity, the universal human thirst for God and for salvation, which the variations of Western Gnosticism diverted into the construction of an apocalyptic civilization, of imitation heavens-on-earth. The variations on this theme in our own time are too many to enumerate: from the massively destructive ideologies of Communism and National Socialism to the adulation of "democracy" that borders on religious faith; from the hubris of modern technical science to the growing

---

63   Ibid., 130. Emphasis added.

fascination with the occult in a civilization that prides itself on its rationalism—Gnosticism imbues virtually every aspect of the modern West. Unlike the Kingdom of God, the kingdom of the West *does* come with observation; the evidence is all around us.

But, as the Lord tells us, "You cannot serve God and mammon."[64] "On this apocalyptic spectacle, however, falls a shadow; for the brilliant expansion is accompanied by a danger that grows apace with progress."[65] The danger is that the building of an ever-progressing, ever-expanding civilization means trading God for mammon, of sacrificing salvation in the next world for power, glory, and comfort in this one. The "truly magnificent spectacle of Western progressive society" in our time is the result of more and more of its inhabitants committing themselves to the undertaking of self-salvation in this life, whether personally or politically, whatever the name that their particular creed happens to travel under, even so much modern "Christianity." It is as true now as when the Lord spoke it and St. Augustine and the Church clarified it: ultimately one can labor for the Kingdom of God or the kingdom of man, but not both. With the rise of each new Gnostic ideology, each new grand civilizational undertaking, the West has made its choice—even while looking upon the Orthodox East as "backward" because it has not set the same premium on historical progress. The consequence of that choice, made again and again through the centuries in myriad ways, is a growing spiritual disorder that manifests itself as societal breakdown even amidst the grand spectacle of technical-material advance.

The death of the spirit is the price of progress. Nietzsche revealed this mystery of the Western apocalypse when he announced that God was dead and that He had been

---

64   Matt. 6:24.
65   Voegelin, *The New Science of Politics*, 130.

murdered. This Gnostic murder is constantly committed by men who sacrifice God to civilization.[66] The more fervently all human energies are thrown into the great enterprise of salvation through world-immanent action, the farther the human beings who engage in this enterprise move away from the life of the spirit. And since the life of the spirit is the source of order in man and society, the very success of a Gnostic civilization is the cause of its decline. [67]

Gnostic Western Civilization is indeed an astounding spectacle, a miracle of history. It has advanced in ways unimagined by the brightest minds of the pre-modern world, yet it has simultaneously declined. The tremendous advances in the hard sciences, technology, and the provision of goods of the past several centuries have been paralleled by equally tremendous political disasters with no real precedent in history. While the twentieth century saw the development of modern medicine, electronic communication, air and space travel, and an enormous improvement in the standard of living in the Western world, it also saw the rise of ideologically driven tyrannies of unprecedented brutality, wars of unprecedented destructiveness, and entire industries apparently dedicated to the destruction of Christian society. Voegelin has shown us that the spectacle of the modern West in both its advancing and declining aspects is the result of its trading of God for mammon, of the widespread growth of world-immanent Gnosticism as its animating spirit, of inner worldly antichristianity displacing otherworldly Christianity. Voegelin's analysis provides us with a very different picture of the rise of modern Western Civilization than is usually offered.

---

66   Recall that Cain, the first murderer, was also the first city-builder, the founder of civilization. See Gen. 4:1-17.

67   Voegelin, *The New Science of Politics*, 131.

Conventionally, Western history is divided into periods with a formal incision around 1500, the later period being the modern phase of Western society. If, however, modernity is defined as the growth of Gnosticism, beginning perhaps as early as the ninth century, it becomes a process within Western society extending deeply into its medieval period. Hence, the conception of a succession of phases would have to be replaced by that of a continuous evolution in which modern Gnosticism rises victoriously to predominance over a civilizational tradition deriving from the Mediterranean discoveries of anthropological [philosophical] and soteriological [Christian] truth.[68]

Instead of the conventional picture of Western Civilization "progressing" or "evolving" toward a higher, nobler conception of man and society, we discern a progressive unraveling of the first-millennium Orthodox synthesis punctuated by episodes of violent disintegration.[69] In those latter cases, some ascendant power organization—the Crusading Latin church, the expansionary Protestant nations, revolutionary France, Soviet Communism, etc.—in a manner suggesting the self-understanding of the pre-Christian pagan empires, believed that it represented a cosmic truth in history that obliged it, in a nutshell, to conquer the world.

Not only does cosmological representation survive in the imperial symbols of the Western Middle Ages... its principle is also recognizable where the truth to be represented is symbolized in an entirely different manner. In Marxian dialectics, for instance, the truth of cosmic order is replaced by the truth of a historically immanent order. Neverthe-

---

68   Ibid., 133.
69   See ch. 5.

less, the Communist movement is a representative of this differently symbolized truth in the same sense... and the consciousness of this representation leads to the same political and legal constructions as in the other instances of imperial representation of truth.[70]

In short, Gnostic societies regard themselves as God's Church on earth, as unique representatives of truth in history, even if they employ very different language and may even eschew everything outwardly religious. Far from "separating" politics and religion, the decline of the Orthodox worldview in the West has allowed earthly polities to arrogate to themselves attributes of the Church. But whereas the faithful of Christ's Church are commanded to "love their enemies, to turn the other cheek," and that "all who take the sword will perish by the sword,"[71] the "faithful" of modern Gnostic movements have shown no such scruples. The bloodshed that so mars the history of the modern West testifies to this. We are thus brought to a difficult realization:

> A civilization can, indeed, advance and decline at the same time—but not forever. There is a limit toward which this ambiguous process moves; the limit is reached when an activist sect which represents the Gnostic truth organizes the civilization into an empire under its rule. Totalitarianism, defined as the existential rule of Gnostic activists, is the end form of progressive civilization.[72]

Toward what end is modern Western Civilization simultaneously "advancing" and "declining"? Answer: totalitarianism, and in our age of globalization, the logical end of a progressive

---

70   Voegelin, *The New Science of Politics*, 59.
71   Matt. 26:52.
72   Voegelin, *The New Science of Politics*, 132.

global civilization is global totalitarianism. The logic of the Gnostic activism of the Open Conspiracy will stop short of nothing less than a single economic, political, and religious order that, like totalitarian systems before, will brook no opposition. At the head of this global order will one day emerge the final "revelation" of "apocalyptic" Western Civilization, its own "savior" and incarnate "god." While Voegelin describes the historical process of the construction of a Gnostic, Western-dominated, global order, Orthodoxy illuminates its ultimate significance in the figure of the coming Antichrist. The age of Antichrist promises to fulfill, in outward form, the ancient Gnostic quest for the "Third realm," a time of great material wealth and unprecedented spiritual poverty; a golden age of "peace and safety" followed by "sudden destruction"[73] with the return of the True King at the Second Coming. It is not possible to know what form Antichrist's totalitarian regime will take; it may well prove less one of guns and gulags than of enticements and sophisticated psychological pressure, a "soft" totalitarianism, a despotism of souls, that may prove all the more damning for those who will succumb to it. But whatever form it takes, a global, totalitarian order is identifiably the end form of modern progressive Western society.

In order to understand the rise of the modern West as a global antichristian empire, we must turn to a more focused account of the thousand-year process by which Gnostic antichristianity progressively displaced genuine Christian consciousness in the West.

---

73   1 Thess. 5:3.

CHAPTER 5

A Brief History of Antichristianity

> Why do the nations rage so furiously together, and why do the people imagine a vain thing? The kings of the earth rise up, and the rulers take counsel together, against the LORD, and against His Christ, saying, "Let us break their bands asunder, and cast away their cords from us."
>
> Psalm 2:1-3

The incarnation of the transcendent God in the person of Jesus Christ was the seminal historical event that will continue to shape the meaning of history for as long as this world lasts. The centuries following the advent of Jesus Christ were marked by the ascent of the Church in history and the general expansion and consolidation of Orthodoxy throughout the Mediterranean world and beyond. During the first millennium, the Church evangelized the Middle East, Europe, Africa, and Asia; she clarified her doctrines and rites in the great Councils; and she won over the Roman Empire—the leading civilization on earth and formerly her greatest persecutor—and transformed it into her guardian on earth. A revolution the likes of which the world has never seen.

As the first millennium wore on, the Church's ascendancy was challenged from a variety of quarters. Persian, Assyrian, and

Coptic Christians rejected later Church Councils and entered into schism; barbarian invasions in Western and Northern Europe threatened Christian populations; and the rise of Islam cut off Christian societies in much of the Middle East and North Africa from imperial protection.

But it would be in the first century of the second millennium that the greatest disaster would occur: the rending of Christendom by the Great Schism. It was then that a leading patriarchal see, Rome, in contravention of the Church's historic collegium, insisted on imposing ecclesial and doctrinal innovations beyond her traditional jurisdiction and broke with Orthodoxy. Rome's defection set in motion additional innovations and heresies, which began the long process of unraveling Western Christendom and displacing it first by heterodox, and eventually by explicitly antichristian, belief systems. Following the Roman Schism, the Orthodox world spent the next thousand years struggling to resist the inroads of Western-inspired heresies, revolution, subversion, and invasion. That struggle continues to this day.

The ascendant phase of the Church's historical articulation corresponds to what Eric Voegelin has described as "de-divinization," the process by which terrestrial power structures such as the pagan Roman Empire lost their claim to represent transcendent order on earth. They were supplanted by the Church, which, by the era of the great Councils of the mid-first millennium, had arisen to become the sole representative of divine truth throughout Christendom. The descendant phase of the Church's historical articulation, which corresponds roughly with the second millennium, Voegelin terms "re-divinization," the process by which the Church progressively lost her status as the representative of eternal order, with terrestrial politics displacing her as the means by which man was to fulfill his ultimate destiny. While both phases comprise roughly one thousand years, there is no telling how far into the future the descendant phase will continue, even if it is possible to discern its ultimate outcome in the reign of Antichrist.

Efforts at "re-divinizing" earthly politics endeavor in effect to rebuild the old cosmological systems of the ancient pagan world but in a Christian/antichristian context. In Orthodox lands, the state power organization had come to be understood as a temporal aspect of existence that will pass away at the end of time. In the Church it is the individual human soul that is "divinized" through divine grace and spiritual struggle rather than by way of the fallen world of terrestrial political forms. But, as the West progressively departed from its Orthodox orientation, various ideologies arose that sought to replace the Church as the representative of truth, many of which gave rise to new political forms and ultimately to revolution. This process of "re-divinizing" terrestrial politics has continued to gain steam through the course of the second millennium into our own time of globalization. We saw clearly the "re-divinizing" of earthly politics in chapter two in the ideas of Wells, who regards the great enterprise of globalization as fundamentally a religious undertaking. The logical end of the historical process of "re-divinization" is the worship of the political leader as an ersatz Christ, an incarnate god, something intimated by the messianic posers of twentieth-century totalitarianism such as Lenin, Hitler, and Mao, and which aptly defines the future reign of Antichrist.

Earlier, we identified the historical movements that have shaped the modern West as essentially Gnostic in character. It is important to note that the

> conception of a modern age succeeding the Middle Ages is itself one of the symbols created by the Gnostic movement. It belongs in the class of the Third realm symbols.... By the immanent logic of its own theological symbolism, each of the Gnostic waves has as good a claim to consider

itself the great wave of the future as any other. There is no reason why a modern period should begin with humanism rather than with the Reformation, or with the Enlightenment rather than with Marxism.[1]

It is testimony to the success of Gnostic propaganda that the revolutions of the modern era—from the English interregnum to the French Revolution to Bolshevism—are widely seen as justifiable revolts against monarchical oppression. In fact, they were diabolical plots to destroy the bulwarks of Christian civilization—throne and altar—which failed in all of their stated popular goals, and which unleashed unprecedented suffering, war, and death in their time. Monarchies such as Bourbon France and Romanov Russia proved far more open, lenient, just, and effective in providing for the basic needs of their populations than the revolutionary regimes that overthrew and replaced them. Louis XVI's France and Nicholas II's Russia were vulnerable to revolution not because they were especially unjust and brutal but rather because they were the opposite. True despots never had any trouble with revolution; Louis and Nicholas did because they were unwilling to employ the severe repression of their revolutionary adversaries.

But a detailed examination of the history of revolutionary movements is beyond the scope of this study. We are here interested in the general historical process of "re-divinization," of the rise of Gnostic antichristianity and its displacement of Orthodox consciousness, and will thus confine ourselves to a brief historical survey with emphasis on specific episodes of Gnostic advancement and how they have helped to set the stage for modern globalization and ultimately the appearance of Antichrist.

---

1   Voegelin, *The New Science of Politics*, 133-4.

ISLAM

Islam was the first major antichristian attempt at globalization. Islam developed in the fecund religious atmosphere of late sixth-century Arabia, at the confluence of various Judaic, Christian, and pagan influences. According to St. John of Damascus (+749), an arabophone Christian who served at the court of the Muslim caliph, Islam, which accepts Christ as a prophet while denying His divinity, amounted to an outgrowth of the heresy of Arianism.

> There is also the superstition of the Ishmaelites [i.e., Arab Muslims, who claim descent from Ishmael[2]] which to this day prevails and keeps people in error, being a forerunner of the Antichrist.... From that time [the early seventh century] to the present a false prophet named Mohammed has appeared in their midst. This man, after having chanced upon the Old and New Testaments and likewise, it seems, having conversed with an Arian monk, devised his own heresy. Then, having insinuated himself into the good graces of the people by a show of seeming piety, he gave out that a certain book had been sent down to him from heaven. He had set down some ridiculous compositions in this book of his and he gave it to them as an object of veneration.[3]

Thirteen centuries later, St. John's adumbration of Islam still holds up. On the one hand, the god of Islam, Allah, can be neither known nor beheld by man but remains inaccessibly transcendent in sharp contrast to the Christian Incarnation.

---

2   See Gen. 16.
3   St. John of Damascus, *Critique of Islam*. http://orthodoxinfo.com/general/stjohn_islam.aspx. Accessed September 13, 2019.

On the other hand, Allah's dominion is properly of *this* world as much as of the next; hence is it the religious duty of the Islamic faithful to bring the law of Allah, the *Sharia* (Arabic شريعة), derived from the injunctions of the Koran and the precedents set by Muhammad in the *hadiths* (Arabic حديث), to the entire earth. A society not based on Sharia is ipso facto illegitimate; it exists in a state of rebellion with Allah, which the faithful are directed to bring into submission through force if persuasion fails.[4]

What brought such tremendous and relentless energy to Islam's conquests in the first millennium of its existence was the exceptionally powerful idea that one's salvation could be gained through military exploit. This was *jihad* (Arabic جهاد, "holy war") which transformed a hitherto unaccomplished people, the Arabs, into one of the greatest conquering races in history. Following a century of whirlwind victories that gained the Holy Land, North Africa, and southwestern Europe for *dar al Islam* [Arabic دار الإسلام, "the house of Islam"], the armies of Christendom finally stemmed the bloody Islamic tide, first in France at the battle of Tours in 732 and later in Anatolia (now Turkey).

Constantinople, the jewel of the Orthodox East, having resisted numerous Muslim sieges, finally fell to the Turkish Sultan Muhammed II in 1453 during the second great wave of Islamic conquest of Christian lands. Until the Balkan Wars of Liberation in the nineteenth and twentieth centuries, Islam enslaved, butchered, and persecuted Orthodox Christians of Asia Minor and the Balkans for nearly half a millennium and, to this day, oppresses millions of Christians throughout the Middle East, Africa, and Asia.[5]

---

4   For a summary treatment of Islam's main tenets see *House of War: Islam's Jihad Against the World, Facing Islam,* and the documentary *Islam: What the West Needs to Know.* For more in-depth analysis, see H. Lammens' *Islam: Beliefs and Institutions,* Srdja Trifkovic's *Sword of the Prophet,* and Ibn Warraq's *Why I am Not a Muslim.*

5   See Bat Ye'or's *Decline of Eastern Christianity under Islam.* It is also important to bear in mind that some of Islam's bloodiest acts occurred on its eastern boundary

Even while no Islamic power has successfully modernized to the extent that it could directly threaten the Western world as in times past, in recent years, the American-led West has shown a peculiar tendency to support various jihadist movements against relatively secular governments—in Afghanistan, Bosnia, Kosovo, Chechnya, Iraq, Egypt, Libya, Syria, etc.—even while claiming to prosecute a global "war on terror." This apparent contradiction is explained by the fact that jihad in the modern, terrorist form well suits the needs of Western-led globalization: modern jihad assists in the general program of undermining independent nation-states in order to bring them into global subservience. The rising Islamic tide—in Africa, Asia, and Europe—is acting as a powerful solvent for the traditional societies there. While many jihadists believe that they are furthering their salvation in fighting Western hegemony, their principal achievement is to weaken the few remaining holdouts of the Western-dominated New World Order. A weakened nation-state having to defend itself against recurring Islamic terrorism and subversion must naturally grow more dependent on the good will of the "international community," which will insist on its integration into that New World Order. Western Europe today is a good example of this. Hamstrung by political correctness of an increasingly Orwellian order, it has been reduced to fighting a rear-guard action against Islamic terrorism on its own soil. Adamantly refusing to identify Islam as the fundamental source of terrorist violence, and therefore unable to address the pool of potential

---

in Asia. "According to Prof. K. S. Lal, the author of the *Growth of Muslim population in India*, the Hindu population decreased by 80 million between 1,000 AD, the year Mahmud Ghazni [971-1030] invaded India and 1525 AD, a year before the battle of Panipat. One can safely add another 20 million Hindus to this list to account for the number that were killed during the Mughal rule or the rule of the Muslim rulers in the Deccan plateau. By all known accounts of world history, as pointed out by Koenard Elst in his book the *Negationism in India*, the destruction of about 100 million Hindus is perhaps the biggest holocaust in whole world history." [sic] http://www.hinduwebsite.com/history/holocaust.asp. Accessed September 13, 2019.

terrorists in its midst growing by the day through immigration, a higher birth rate, and, increasingly, conversion, the nation-states of Europe can only bring ever more indiscriminate totalitarian measures to bear. Islam in Europe (and elsewhere) is proving the perfect foil for police-state tactics, the destruction of traditional ordering institutions such as local government, and the consolidation of power at ever-higher levels beyond any kind of effective accountability. As Western Europe slides toward its likely denouement—civil war in the vein of Lebanon and Yugoslavia—it will find itself ever more at the mercy of the Open Conspiracy, who may even be willing to side with a possible right-wing reaction as long as it means continuing the erosion of Europe's traditional ordering institutions, which alone are capable of guaranteeing genuine self-government.

THE PAPAL REVOLUTION

While Islam showed itself to be a major force to be reckoned with on the Eurasian continent for many centuries, it has been utterly outclassed by the rise of the West in the modern era. The birth of what is now spoken of as Western Civilization may be traced to the rise of the see of Rome as an ecclesial and political monarchy that sees itself as the supreme representative of the divine order on earth. It was the rise of the Papacy that set the West on a very different trajectory from the rest of Christendom. The widespread idea that Western Civilization may be distinguished by its Greco-Roman heritage neglects the historical reality that the Byzantine and Orthodox East retained much greater continuity with Greek and Roman cultural and political forms. Indeed, the Byzantine Empire *was* the Roman Empire geographically transposed; the term "Byzantine" did not come into usage until after the fall of Constantinople. During the second half of the first millennium, the western provinces of the Empire, effectively beyond imperial protection from Constantinople, became the prey of Vikings, Goths, and other barbarian invaders that reduced life substantially to a struggle for physical survival—the Dark Ages.[6] As the first millennium wore on, the Christian West increasingly had to fend for itself, and Western ecclesial and political development increasingly diverged from the Greco-Roman Orthodox East.

It was in the eleventh century that the see of Rome, hitherto at the mercy of the powerful families that dominated the internecine politics of the Eternal City, forcefully addressed the problems of Western disorder. In a remarkably short space of time, Rome was able to consolidate the hitherto anarchic sees of Western Christendom under its leadership. Pope Leo IX (1049–1054) began the process of disentangling the Western Church from the imbroglio of feudal obligations that had reduced much of the clergy to vassals of the landed classes. But the process of reform did not stop there: it continued through the tenure of the powerful Gregory VII (1073-85), which transformed the see of Rome, the first among equals, into what is recognizable as the modern papacy: a supreme monarchy and the self-conscious arbiter of all matters spiritual and temporal. "In addition to the demand for *libertas* and spiritual renewal . . . a determined effort had been made by the papacy to see that its claims to a universal jurisdiction throughout Christendom were everywhere acknowledged."[7] To refer to the Gregorian "reforms" is "a serious understatement, reflecting in part the desire of the papal party itself—and of later Roman Catholic historians—to play down the magnitude of the discontinuity between what had gone before and what came later."[8] "Ecclesiologically, at any

---

6   See Aristeides Papadakis, *The Christian East and the Rise of the Papacy* (Crestwood, St. Vladimir's Seminary, 1994), 6.

7   Papadakis, *The Christian East and the Rise of the Papacy*, 46.

8   Berman, *Law and Revolution: The Foundation of the Western Legal Tradition* as quoted in Papadakis, *The Christian East and the Rise of the Papacy*, 55.

rate, the rapid transformation of the Western Church in the eleventh century was a revolutionary development."[9]

While disagreement on a variety of theological points arose between Rome and the Orthodox East, such as the former's formal inclusion of the *filioque* (Latin: "and the Son") into the Nicene-Constanipolitan Creed in 1014, the primary issue was and remains jurisdictional, i.e., Rome's claim to a universal authority over all other sees in contravention to the Church's historic collegium. In the wake of the papal revolution, "Obedience to Rome, in the last analysis, was the ultimate test of [Latin] orthodoxy."[10] It is this point that has proved over the centuries intolerable to Orthodox Christendom. The claim of Papal supremacy has time and again scuttled serious attempts to address the substantive theological differences between East and West. By insisting on supremacy, Rome in effect claims that substantive doctrinal differences are moot because it alone can ultimately decide such matters; as spelled out in Pope Gregory VII's *Dictatus papae*, "In obvious contrast to all other sees and patriarchates... [Rome] is actually incapable of error and infallible."[11]

The pretense to infallibility—while not codified until the First Vatican Council of 1869-70—turned the Orthodox understanding of the Church on its head. One of the most necessary virtues in Orthodox clerical circles is obedience—and this applies even to the most senior clergymen. In Orthodoxy, no man, even the highest-ranking member of the clergy, possesses the right to adjudicate the Church's received wisdom; only a council, whose decisions must also be accepted by the Church at large, possesses such authority.[12] It is only the Church as a whole, of

---

9   Ibid., 55.

10   Papadakis, *The Christian East and the Rise of the Papacy*, 56.

11   Ibid., 49.

12   See Acts 15 for the first Church council, held in Jerusalem. Though present, St. Peter, later the first Roman Pope, did not dictate his opinions but acted in accordance

which Christ is the Head, that may be considered "infallible."
All that any man or body of men can do is to endeavor to apply
the received wisdom of the Church to their own lives and, if
called to do so, serve in the clergy as its interpreter to others.
The only genuinely independent power that any man possesses
is the personal freedom to reject aspects of Church Tradition
or to add to them, in which case all that he achieves is to cut
himself off from the Body of Christ. "If anyone adds to these
things, God will add to him the plagues that are written in this
book; and if anyone takes away from the words of the book of
this prophecy, God shall take away his part from the Book of
Life…"[13]

By the turn of the second millennium, the West was enjoying a
time of relative quiet and prosperity while eastern Christendom
was increasingly in a life-or-death struggle with *dar al Islam*. The
deteriorating strategic situation put the Eastern Empire, on both
the political and ecclesial levels, at a decided disadvantage. The
West was increasingly able to press its claims on the Empire and
the Eastern Church, which, in their distress, repeatedly sought
to come to a workable understanding that would enable strategic cooperation against the Islamic threat battering at their
door. Islamic depredations in the Holy Land, and especially
attacks on Western pilgrims, set the stage for a Western military
response, which would be led by one of the great conquering
races of history, the Normans. It had been first German and
then Norman power that had helped support the "papal revolution" that had successfully vaulted the Roman see to the top
of both the Western ecclesial and political pyramids. With a
papal blessing, the Normans had conquered Byzantine territory
in Italy and installed Latin bishops over Orthodox populations.

---

with others present. A conciliar epistle was issued not in his name but in the name
of all of those present, "the apostles, the elders, and the brethren." (Acts 15:23)
13   Rev. 22:18-19.

With their final victory over Byzantine forces in Italy in 1071, the Normans set their sights on Imperial holdings in the Balkans. "That these Norman ventures both resemble and anticipate the first crusade is obvious."[14]

It would be the Crusades that would render the Schism of 1054, in the first centuries of the second millennium still inchoate, into vivid historical reality. In 1095, Pope Urban II called for the Western faithful to defend Christian interests in the East in response to a request for aid against the Turks by the Byzantine Emperor Alexios I Komnenos. It would be the form that military assistance took that would prove both unprecedented in the Christian world and, ultimately, disastrous. Rather than simple military assistance provided by Western powers with the blessing of the Pope, Urban called for an "armed pilgrimage" that would unite religious and strategic objectives. Urban's "own novel contribution or his suggestion that ideological warfare and religious pilgrimage together join forces, was, in the final analysis, both unprecedented and crucial to the crusading idea."[15] His "armed pilgrimage," however, soon turned into a full-blown holy war bent on capturing the Holy Land for the Roman church: "feudal Europe in point of fact was to make the conquest of Jerusalem and the liberation of the Holy Sepulchre instead [of protecting pilgrims] its primary target. Popular pressure regarding the matter was apparently so persuasive that the pope himself was forced to abandon his own objective."[16]

The Byzantines were uneasy from the start about an armed rabble meandering across imperial territory with hazy objectives— "for the empire the concept of holy war—ideologically and psychologically—was unknown;"[17] it sounded all too reminiscent of *jihad*, but they were in no position to determine the

---

14   Papadakis, *The Christian East and the Rise of the Papacy*, 72.
15   Ibid., 82.
16   Ibid., 84.
17   Ibid., 88.

form that Western support against the Turks should take. In time, the Byzantines' worst fears were realized. While ostensibly directed against the Turks, the Crusades' "ultimate victim was the Byzantine state and not Islam."[18] As in the earlier case of the Norman conquests of Byzantine Italy, rather than restoring Orthodox authority in sees liberated from Islam, the Crusader armies set up Latin bishoprics and refused to recognize the legitimacy of the indigenous Orthodox hierarchy.

But the true nadir of the Crusades would occur in 1204 and result in one of the greatest crimes ever committed by people claiming to be acting as Christians against their brethren. It was then that the Venetian armies of the Fourth Crusade, fed up with what they saw as a lack of cooperation on the part of the Byzantine emperor, laid siege to Constantinople under the pretext of placing Alexios Angelos, son of the deposed Isaac II Angelos, on the imperial throne. After indecisive fighting and the restoration of Emperor Isaac II, the Crusaders broke into the city and subjected the jewel of the Christian East to a three-day orgy of massacre, pillage, rape, and sacrilege. Countless treasures including icons, relics, and gold and silver adornments of the city's numerous churches were destroyed or plundered and hauled back to the West, where many remain to this day. An eyewitness to the carnage, the scholar and statesman Nicetas Choniates, observed bitterly, "Even the Saracens [Muslims] are merciful and kind in comparison to these creatures who bear the cross of Christ upon their shoulders. They come from the West to fight the infidel Turk, but diverted to plunder the greatest of Christian Cities." Pope Innocent III (1198–1216), who had set the Fourth Crusade in motion, learning of the crime, reprimanded his legate, Cardinal Peter, who had seen fit to absolve the Crusaders of their vows not to harm fellow Christians and thus allow the assault on the city to go forward:

---

18   Ibid., 86.

As for those who were supposed to be seeking the ends of Jesus Christ, not their own ends, whose swords, which they were supposed to use against the pagans, are now dripping with Christian blood they have spared neither age nor sex. They have committed incest, adultery, and fornication before the eyes of men. They have exposed both matrons and virgins, even those dedicated to God, to the sordid lusts of boys.... They have even ripped silver plates from the altars and have hacked them to pieces among themselves. They violated the holy places and have carried off crosses and relics.[19]

While Pope Innocent may have condemned the act, he accepted the result, namely, the establishment of a (short-lived) Eastern Latin empire and patriarchate with its seat in Constantinople. The Fourth Crusade remains the signal example of Rome's policy to effect union with the Orthodox East through "reduction." Whatever the original vision for the Crusades, the fact is they turned into an anti-Orthodox rampage that, in the end, proved little more than a nuisance to *dar al Islam*, but which significantly hastened the downfall of Constantinople.

The Crusades were an attempt to remedy an ecclesial problem—disunity within Christendom—through decidedly worldly means. In the spirit of the papal revolution, the Latin see, confusing its temporal extension with the transcendent life of the spirit, believed it could further the Christian mission by expanding its worldly authority through conquest. But, as the Lord admonished, "all who take the sword will perish by the sword,"[20] and it would not be long before other Western centers of power

---

19   Pope Innocent III, Ep 136, Patrologia Latina 215, 669–702, translated by James Brundage, *The Crusades: A Documentary History* (Milwaukee, Marquette University, 1962), 208-09.
20   Matt. 26:52.

would arise to challenge Papal supremacy. Following the Great Schism, the struggle to maintain Latin hegemony in the West soon turned into a running political and military struggle that would lead directly to the rending of Europe by the Protestant Reformation in the sixteenth century and the ensuing Wars of Religion that would kill millions.

THE GROWTH OF GNOSTICISM IN THE WEST

The Papacy's departure from Orthodoxy and the rapid development of heterodox ideas such as Christian holy war and Papal infallibility were both symptoms of the rise of Gnostic speculation in the West as well as contributing factors in its further development. With the Orthodox East taking the brunt of the *jihad*, the West, free of the need to conform to the received wisdom of Orthodoxy, began to indulge in novel, if still nominally Christian, forms of speculation. The forms Gnosticism would take during the course of the second millennium would regularly manifest themselves as variations on infallibility: from the Roman Popes in the eleventh century possessed of a special charism that permitted them to pontificate without error to "The Party" of Communist regimes in the twentieth that could do no wrong because they were in the vanguard of history—the sure knowledge afforded by the various Gnostic systems would brook no rebuttal. Indeed, from the torture chambers of the Latin Inquisition to the torture chambers of the Bolshevik gulags, the results of such Gnostic "certainty" have been predictably, and disastrously, the same.

As in the history of all ideological movements, Gnosticism had been incubating beneath the surface of Western Christendom for some generations before it gained real efficacy.

> A suitable date for its formal beginning would be the
> activation of ancient Gnosticism through Scotus Eriugena
> [+877] in the ninth century, because his works, as well as
> those of [Pseudo] Dionysius Areopagita which he trans-
> lated, were a continuous influence in the underground
> Gnostic sects before they came to the surface in the
> twelfth and thirteenth centuries.[21]

While it is not fair to lay the full blame for the revival of
Gnosticism in the West at the feet of Eriugena (an Irish scholar
who spent most of his productive life in France and in whose
writings there is both good and bad), it is worth remember-
ing that he was condemned in his time by Church councils at
Valence (855) and Langres (859) and later by some of the more
conservative post-schism popes. During Eriugena's time, the
West was still a part of the Orthodox fold, and his ideas failed
to gain much traction. The Gnostic seed, however, had been
planted—by him and others; it would bear fruit in the Latin
scholastic movement of the first half of the second millennium.
Scholasticism sought to reconcile Church tradition and dogma
with Aristotelian (and even neoplatonic) philosophy by way of
human reason. The highest authority was no longer the received
wisdom of the Church but a supposed "synthesis" of tradition,
revelation, philosophy, and reason achieved through dialectics.
"Theology" became no longer the interior knowledge of God in
the *nous*, or heart, which it remains to this day in Orthodoxy, but
the reduction of knowledge of God to a "system" comprehended
by the mind. The "schoolmen," who mastered the scholastic
methods, became the new Gnostic elite in the Latin church.

A key figure in scholasticism, and the first Gnostic political
thinker to garner papal support, was Joachim of Fiore (1135–
1202). Born less than a century after Rome's formal break with

---

21   Voegelin, *The New Science of Politics*, 128.

Orthodoxy, his Gnostic speculation significantly took a historical bent: he advanced a "trinitarian" theory of history in which the latter could be divided into three sequential ages, each reflecting the Persons of the Holy Trinity. The first age, from the creation of the world to the advent of Christ, was that of the Father; the second age, from the advent of Christ to Joachim's own time in the twelfth century, was that of the Son; the third age, of the Holy Spirit, was yet to come. A critical aspect of Joachim's speculation was that "The three ages were characterized as intelligible increases in spiritual fulfillment,"[22] which meant that it was now possible to discern an ultimate meaning to the course of profane history, which the Orthodox formulation had reserved for the Church and for eternity.

Joachim, a priest-monk whose works received the support of Pope Lucius III (1181-85) and who is venerated in Roman Catholicism as a "beatus," a lesser saint, had produced a major theoretical deviation from the Orthodox conception of history. Instead of mankind finding ultimate fulfillment in the Church and eternity, Joachim saw the coming "age of the Holy Spirit" as a future paradise-on-earth that would supersede any form of institutionalized Christianity. He believed that the institutional Church would—foreshadowing Marxist language regarding the state—"wither away," marriage would cease, and Christians would live an angelic life on earth. Joachim's idea of a coming "new age" of history that would provide universal material and spiritual fulfillment mirrors the chiliastic heresies of the early Church that St. Augustine had refuted and the Church had suppressed. With Rome's defection from Orthodoxy, the chiliastic fantasy was allowed to climb back out of its box.

In his work on Joachim, Eric Voegelin isolates four key elements, or symbols, of Joachim's "trinitarian eschatology" that would reappear in political thought over the course of the

---

22   Ibid., 111.

succeeding centuries.[23] The first of these symbols, as we have seen, is that of the "Third" or "final realm" of history, a permanent end-state or "golden age" to be reached through an evolutionary or revolutionary process beyond which there would be no further change. The second symbol is that of the "leader," who ushers in the "end" of history, the "Joshua" who leads his people into the promised land of the Third realm. The leader is presaged by the "prophet," the third symbol, who paves the way for the leader and the Third realm by expressing theoretically the principles of history that the latter will fulfill. It is through the Gnostic vision of the prophet—the discovery of the hitherto hidden knowledge that will transform history—that is key to the entire process. Finally, there is the fourth symbol, what Voegelin calls the "brotherhood of autonomous persons," who make up the inhabitants of the Third realm. The brotherhood live in harmony in the Third realm thanks to their transformation by the process of history (as expressed by the prophet and implemented by the leader) into effectively angelic or superhuman beings able to live without the need for conventional ordering institutions. In his own time, Joachim apparently regarded himself as the prophet and Francis of Assisi (c. 1181–1226) as the leader of the coming "age of the Holy Spirit," which he foresaw as beginning in the year 1260.

Joachim's thought is significant not so much for its particular claims (like countless predictions about the end of history, 1260 came and went with little fanfare) but for the symbols that Voegelin identifies that would recur with increasing intensity through the history of the West. While Joachim developed his theory in a medieval Latin context, in succeeding centuries, it permeated Western political culture and eventually found its most spectacular historical expression in the antichristian revolutions of the twentieth century. Communism and National

---

23   See Ibid., 111-13.

Socialism both had their prophets (Marx and Engels; Hegel and Nietzsche), their leaders (Lenin and Stalin; Hitler), and their conceptions of a utopian Third realm (the Communist "withering away of the state"; the National Socialist "Thousand Year Reich") inhabited by a new brotherhood of the "chosen people" (the revolutionary proletariat; the Aryan *Volk*). But Joachitic elements can be found throughout the political thought of the modern West. In fact, the fantastic power manifested by modern Western Civilization in its technical advancement and cultural and material hegemony is a direct result of its abandonment of the Orthodox understanding of the two realms of history, the sacred and the profane, and its "re-divinizing" of intramundane reality with an eschatological telos in the vein of Joachim. "In his trinitarian eschatology, Joachim created the aggregate of symbols which govern the self-interpretation of modern political society to this day."[24] Eight centuries ago, the basic parameters of modern politics were laid out by a Roman Catholic monk.

Joachim's speculation, while Gnostic, is still identifiably Christian in that it posits a new irruption into history by the Spirit of God that will usher in the Third realm; it is, however, also antichristian in that it implicitly denies the Church as the manifestation of eternity, as the extant "final realm," already present, and proposes a future realm of historical existence without her. As the years and centuries went by, the West drifted ever further from its pre-schism, Orthodox orientation, and Western speculation on the meaning of history incrementally shed its Christian attributes. Simple chiliasm—the anticipation of an earthly reign of Christ—slowly gave way to Gnostic activism in which man himself was to build the "final realm" through his own intelligence and power. Both chiliasm and Gnosticism commit the same theoretical error of trying to "immanentize the eschaton," i.e., make concrete in history what properly

---

24   Ibid., 111.

belongs only to eternity. In Orthodox Christianity, the end of history comes with the Second Coming of Christ, of which "no man knows the day nor hour."[25] Chiliasm and Gnosticism, in contrast, insist on forcing eternity into history and reject the necessary patient waiting in the Church for the return of the Lord. In the Joachitic symbols of leader, prophet, Third realm, and brotherhood of autonomous persons we can clearly descry the outlines of Antichrist, the False Prophet, and Antichrist's regime promising a golden age and a universal brotherhood of mankind. The antichristian historical process, so evident in our time of globalization, was set in motion a long time ago.

> Gnostic experiences determine a structure of political reality that is *sui generis*. A line of gradual transformation connects medieval with contemporary Gnosticism. And the transformation is so gradual, indeed, that it would be difficult to decide whether contemporary phenomena should be classified as Christian because they are intelligibly an outgrowth of Christian heresies of the Middle Ages or whether medieval phenomena should be classified as anti-Christian because they are intelligibly the origin of modern anti-Christianism. The best course will be to drop such questions and to recognize the essence of modernity as the growth of Gnosticism.[26]

Voegelin here makes an observation key to our study of the antichristian historical process underway in our own time: in the post-schism West, it is very difficult to tell where Christianity ends and antichristianity begins; the two intermingle and overlap; the latter bears characteristics of the former. While Voegelin identifies modernity as essentially Gnostic, Gnosticism is evident

25   Matt. 24:26; Mark 1:32 pm.
26   Voegelin, *The New Science of Politics*, 125-6.

as far back as Rome's break from Orthodoxy in the eleventh century and the heresies that erupted in the Schism's aftermath. In general, the deviations from Orthodoxy have grown more marked with time: the later in history that a particular movement has arisen, the less Christian and more explicitly antichristian it has shown itself. The running debate among some Western scholars over whether the West is more Christian or Greco-Roman in its culture and institutions may be effectively put to bed by realizing that the West is primarily Gnostic. The West is a civilization devoted to the ill-fated pursuit of paradise through worldly knowledge and power. The successive Western heresies, from Roman Catholicism to Catharism to Lutheranism to Calvinism to Anabaptism, etc., retain, with decreasing force, Christian attributes, and evince, with increasing force, Gnostic, antichristian ones. Even Communism, which came late in the process, while violently antichristian, promises a golden age of the brotherhood of men, the end of want, and the "withering away" of state power, i.e., a fake Christian paradise. The blending of Christianity into antichristianity speaks directly to the difficulty that the world will have in recognizing Antichrist and his regime for what they will be.

THE FRAGMENTATION OF THE LATIN WEST

The thirteenth century saw the theory of the universal monarchy of the Pope—that all the land in the world belongs to the Pope as Christ's representative on earth, and he gives it to landholders. The climax of this point of view occurred at the jubilee of 1300 in Rome, when Pope Boniface VIII seated himself on the throne of Constantine, arrayed himself in a sword, crown and scepter, and shouted aloud: "I am Caesar—I am Emperor." This was not just an act but an indication of something extremely deep in the whole of modern thought: the search for a universal monarch, which will be Antichrist.[27]

The fruit of Rome's defection from Orthodoxy soon became apparent in the unraveling of Western Christendom. Once the Papacy arrogated to itself the characteristics of a temporal monarchy, political rebellion against Papal authority became possible. Now, ecclesial and theological disputes inevitably acquired political dimensions and vice versa. Disagreements in the West over doctrine and religious practice quickly became political and military struggles in a zero-sum contest. It was only a question of time before men outside the Papacy arrogated to themselves the right to (re) define the Church as the Roman popes had done. Fighting heresy soon became a full-time problem for Rome, which was now in the position of trying to reign in the revolutionary logic that it had set in motion when it left Orthodoxy. Rome wanted the exclusive right to define what the Church was; the problem was, now everybody else did, too.

> The eleventh, twelfth and thirteenth centuries were marked by resurgence in Europe of spiritual movements of clearly Gnostic character. During the late eleventh century, a Gnostic religion that had survived orthodox persecution for many centuries in the Byzantine Empire and on the Balkan Peninsula—the Bogomil religion—found its way to the Languedoc region of southern France and to areas of northern Italy. There it took root and flourished over the next three centuries as the Cathar religion—the tradition of the Good and True Christians, the *Bons Hommes*.[28]

---

27   Damascene, *Father Seraphim Rose*, 623.
28   "Cathar Texts and Rituals." http://www.gnosis.org/library/cathtx.htm. Accessed September 13, 2019.

The rise of the Cathars and the related Albigensians and Waldensians in France in the twelfth century was the first instance of Western anti-Papal movements to achieve sustained efficacy. Echoing Joachim's conjectures about a coming "new age" in which Christian virtue and salvation could be achieved personally apart from the institutional Church, the Cathars (from Greek καθαρός, *katharos*, "pure") rejected established episcopal authority as well as traditional Christian sacraments and endeavored to live as "free spirits" in a way suggested by the idea of the brotherhood of autonomous persons.

The Papacy, having demonstrated its willingness to wage a foreign war in the service of supposedly religious ends, now undertook what was effectively a civil war against heretics at home. It was the same Pope Innocent III who had sanctioned the Fourth Crusade who launched the Albigensian Crusade against the Cathars in southern France in 1209. On one memorable, and infamous, occasion, after an attempted sortie by Catharite forces from the town of Beziers, the Crusaders pursued the Cathars into the town where they took refuge in the church of St. Mary Magdalene. It was then that the Papal legate, the Abbot of Citeaux, Arnaud-Amaury, when asked how to tell Catholics from Cathars, issued his notorious order, "Kill them all, the Lord will recognise His own." Catholic forces massacred the inhabitants, slaughtering, torturing, and dismembering thousands.

The successful prosecution of the Albigensian Crusade by 1229 was followed by the establishment of the Papal Inquisition as a standing body to root out heresy. As Papal consciousness grew more worldly, Pope Innocent IV in 1252 issued a bull permitting the use of torture to obtain confessions. Crusade and Inquisition largely succeeded in suppressing further heresies until the Hussite explosion of the early fifteenth century. The Latin priest, John Huss (1369–1415), rector of the University of Prague, had become enamored of the writings of the English priest, John Wycliffe (1320-84), posthumously condemned for heresy in 1415. Both men were writing at a time when the worldly excesses of the Latin church were attracting widespread antipathy. Wycliffe and Huss deplored the transformation of the Latin church into an increasingly secular institution: bishops, for example, had become landed magnates with huge incomes, very often absent from their sees. While the Latin church had confused the spiritual and temporal spheres in practice, Wycliffe and Huss proceeded to develop an ecclesiology of their own that would do so in principle. Their key innovation was the idea that the secular realm, the "regnum," apart from the church, itself comprised "a salvationary community."[29] Theirs represented a truly revolutionary spirit that sought to turn European civilization upside down.

> The political ecclesiology of Wycliffe had defined the body politic of the realm as an ecclesia, an autonomous section of the Church Militant and had seen the secular powers of the realm as also the rulers of the church.... Wycliffe does not distinguish between Church and State. He uses "Regnum," "ecclesia" [church] and "respublica" interchangeably.[30]

Whereas the Popes and bishops of the Latin church had set themselves up as princes, so it now seemed princes would set themselves up as popes—and, if princes were unwilling to lead the laity in holy rebellion against Rome, then it fell to charismatics like John Huss who believed themselves possessed of special knowledge of God's plan for mankind.

> Huss and his followers ... described the Czechs as a "holy nation." Unlike the "New Israel," warned by Jesus that

---

29   E. Michael Jones, *The Jewish Revolutionary Spirit and Its Impact on World History* (South Bend, Fidelity, 2008), 150.
30   Kaminsky, *A History of the Hussite Revolution* as quoted in Jones, *The Jewish Revolutionary Spirit,* 150.

those who lived by the sword would die by it, the Bohemian zealots who conflated *"regnum"* and *"ecclesia"* could spread the gospel with the sword because Bohemia was their *"ecclesia,"* and their religion, derived from the messianic politics which revolutionaries from the time of Simon bar Kokhba[31] had gleaned from the Old Testament. Since there was only one "holy nation," Bohemians became the "New Israel" by default.[32]

While some secular authorities supported Huss' sermons against clerical empire-building, they would come to regret giving public space to his revolutionary logic. Following Huss' exile from Prague, Jerome of Prague kept the movement going and made even more explicit what the newly emboldened laity were supposed to do: "All should kill so that we can make our hands holy in the blood of the accursed ones, as Moses shows us in his books; for what is written there is an example to us."[33] Soon the movement splintered and infighting began among self-proclaimed Taborites, Adamites, etc., all of whom had their charismatic leaders and glosses on how holy war against the Roman church should be waged. Prefiguring the twentieth century Communists, who believed that paradisal socialism could only be brought about through revolutionary violence, sword-wielding priests exhorted their flocks to "religious, orgiastic, ritualistic"[34] bloodshed that would, supposedly, usher in an earthly paradise free from all necessity and constraint.

---

31   Simon bar Kokhba led the Third Jewish-Roman War of AD 132-5 and was proclaimed messiah by Rabbi Akiva (referred to in the Talmud as "Rosh la-Chachamim," Head of all the Sages). Both bar Kokhba and Akiva were executed by the Romans following the failure of the rebellion. See ch. 9.

32   Jones, *The Jewish Revolutionary Spirit*, 153.

33   Kaminsky, 88 as quoted in Jones, *The Jewish Revolutionary Spirit*, 158.

34   Ibid., 177.

> The Elect ... will be brought back to the state of innocence
> of Adam in Paradise, like Enoch and Elijah they would
> be without any hunger or thirst, or any other spiritual or
> physical pain.... In this renovated kingdom there will be
> no sin, no scandal, no abomination, no falsehood, but all
> will be the chosen sons of God, and all the suffering of
> Christ and of His lambs will cease. . . Women will give
> birth to children without pain and without original sin
> ... and children born in the kingdom, if they are of the
> kingdom, will never die, because death will no longer be.[35]

The "Adamite" sect, led by a self-proclaimed "Moses-Adam,"
believed that they now lived in a pre-fallen, sinless state; they
shunned clothes and engaged in fornication whenever it suited
them—a lifestyle that hardly proved innocuous. "As if to prove
that the concupiscible and irascible passions were closely connected, the Adamites 'went out at night, surprising the villages
in the neighborhood, taking food and pitilessly killed all inhabitants, men, women, children, even the babies in their cradles.' "[36]
Pre-figuring Napoleon Bonaparte, a military genius who would
spread revolution through Europe four hundred years later, the
warrior-priest Prokop the Bald led Hussite armies to numerous victories in central Europe and disseminated revolutionary
propaganda throughout Western Christendom. The Hussites
and their related sects were finally defeated in 1437 by the Holy
Roman Emperor, Sigismund. Order had been restored thanks
to vigorous repression and widespread horror at the crimes
of the rebels, but it would not last long. Control of Western
Christendom was slipping from Rome's grasp. The Reformation
was just around the corner.

---

35   Ibid.
36   Ibid., 188.

THE REFORMATION

> While none of the [religious-political] movements [of the
> Late Middle Ages] deserves preference by the content of
> its truth, a clear epoch in Western history is marked by
> the Reformation, understood as the successful invasion of
> Western institutions by Gnostic movements. The move-
> ments which hitherto existed in a socially marginal posi-
> tion—tolerated, suppressed, or underground—erupted
> in the Reformation with unexpected strength on a
> broad front, with the result of splitting the universal
> [Latin] church and embarking on their gradual conquest
> of the political institutions in the national states.[37]

There was nothing terribly novel about Luther's famous nine-
ty-five theses, which he nailed to the Castle church in Wittenberg
in 1517. Before him, various reformers had protested against
the worldliness of the Roman church, clerical elitism, Papal
aggrandizement, and the sale of indulgences. Circumstances
had changed, however, from the time of Wycliffe and Huss.
Luther's attack on the landed monasteries found critical support
among the German princes, who were keen on finding means
of countering what they saw as interference in civil affairs by the
enormously rich and powerful Roman church. A key aspect of
the Reformation's success would be the confiscation of church
lands by secular authorities, who instantly had a powerful economic incentive to support the Reformers and to resist Papal
countermeasures.

Like all revolutionary movements, the Reformers soon
splintered into moderates and radicals. Very soon, the issue was
not "reform" at all but revolution, not rectifying the errors of the

---

37   Voegelin, *The New Science of Politics*, 134.

Latin church but the turning over of society. Luther desired to hold the Reformation at the point of casting off Papal supremacy and appropriating church lands by established secular authorities, whereas men like Thomas Müntzer sought wholesale revolution and the eradication of all formal hierarchy, ecclesial and social. Luther held to *sola scriptura*, the notion that Scripture alone was the final authority; Müntzer used personal visions to substantiate his positions.[38] As the Papacy had cast off the historic Orthodox collegium in the eleventh century in preference for "infallibility," now Luther cast off the "infallible" Pope, and Müntzer cast off *sola scriptura*. In all three cases, as in revolutions everywhere, the Gnostic certainty claimed by each party had to be imposed through force. Luther may have condemned Müntzer's radical Peasants' Revolt of 1524, but Latin observers

> held Luther responsible for the Peasant's Revolt, even though Luther urged the princes to crush it, because Luther prepared the way by eliminating the Church as the guarantor of Scripture and the legitimate basis for social order. Luther, "the seducer of the people," was horrified by Müntzer's actions because in them he saw his own principles carried to their logical conclusion.[39]

Within a year, Müntzer and 100,000 peasants lay dead thanks to the violence of the revolutionary logic that Luther had set in motion and, subsequently, the zeal with which he exhorted his princely supporters to eradicate it.

> Luther would ultimately solve the problem of competing interpretation and competing authority in the same way [the Hussite] Jan Zizka did earlier in Bohemia and Oli-

---

38   Jones, *The Jewish Revolutionary Spirit*, 278.
39   Ibid., 265-6.

ver Cromwell and Stalin did later, which is to say, by *force majeure*. Like Zizka, Luther used military might to end the debate over doctrine. Two and a half centuries later, Friedrich Nietzsche, the son of a Lutheran pastor, would distill the lessons of Protestantism and Revolution into one distinct phrase: will to power.[40]

As the Reformation gathered momentum, it fractured into rival factions and central Europe became locked in a deadly struggle of competing Gnostic sects: Rome's "infallible" Pope, Luther's "infallible" Scripture, Müntzer's "infallible" visions, etc. The only arbiter would be the battlefield as the seemingly endless religious wars of the sixteenth and seventeenth centuries would testify. The Reformation would continue to take ever more bizarre and bloody turns.

> On February 8 [1534] Bokelzoon [a preacher from Leyden] received a vision from the Lord announcing that Münster had become the New Jerusalem. He ran naked through the streets of Münster announcing that vision to the town's inhabitants, calling them to repentance. Soon the town's population, swollen with renegade monks and nuns who had put off their habits and taken on the new baptism, began to imitate Bokelzoon. The liberated nuns had visions of the coming apocalypse so intense that they would tear off their clothes and roll around in mud and dung, frothing at the mouth, screaming the end times had finally arrived.[41]

Once the "godless" were expelled [from Münster], the Elect celebrated in an orgy of drunkenness and destruction.

---

40   Ibid., 266.
41   Ibid., 301.

Bursting into the Cathedral, the mob of the Elect destroyed ancient manuscripts, including the Bible, and smeared paintings of the Blessed Virgin with excrement.[42]

"Luther and [his collaborator] Melanchthon were horrified by what they saw in Münster because events there showed the inadequacy of the idea that the Bible could interpret itself."[43] Certainly, the "Reformers" demonstrated, at best, "zeal not according to knowledge,"[44] and, in supposing themselves capable of interpreting Scripture on their own, neglected the admonition of St. Peter that in Scripture "are some things hard to understand, which untaught and unstable people twist to their own destruction, as they do also the rest of the Scriptures."[45]

As the Reformation drifted from the original idea of reforming the Roman church, it grew more worldly and political in nature. Its supporters, still trying to justify their increasingly repressive and bloody actions by way of Holy Scripture, were naturally drawn to the Old Testament for support. Torn from the centuries-long interpretative Tradition of the Church, which understands the Old Testament through the lens of the New, the Reformers were able to cherry-pick from the Pentateuch to justify their most worldly and sanguinary undertakings. Soon they cast themselves as modern day Moses and Joshuas, chosen by God to lead the chosen people into the promised land—and to eradicate the heathen in the process. As God had commanded Moses to "utterly destroy" the nations of Canaan lest "they turn your sons away from following Me," so many Reformers arrogated to themselves the status of "a holy people, a special treasure above all peoples on the face of the earth,"[46] possessed of the right and

---

42   Ibid., 303.
43   Ibid., 299.
44   Rom. 10:2.
45   2 Pet. 3:16.
46   Deut. 7:2.

duty to take up the sword in the name of God. The "rediscovery" of Scripture by the Reformers, especially those of the Old Testament, proved not an advance in the understanding of the Law of God but a signal disaster that shattered the provisional peace achieved by Rome through Inquisition and Crusade and which permanently rent Western Christendom asunder.

For the purposes of this study, there is no need to go deeper into the particulars of the Reformation and its attendant conflicts and infighting; it is enough to come to a summary assessment:

> Truth and salvation are bestowed upon love, i.e., the Church—such is [Orthodox] Church consciousness. Latinism, having fallen away from the Church, changed this consciousness and proclaimed: truth is given to the separate person of the Pope, and the Pope manages the salvation of all. Protestantism only objected: Why is truth given to the Pope alone?—and added: truth and salvation are open to each separate individual, independently of the Church. Every individual was thus promoted to the rank of infallible Pope.[47]

The Wars of Religion sparked by the Reformation did not wind down until the mid-seventeenth century, when Protestant and Roman Catholic Europe, wearied from more than a century of bloodletting, agreed to disagree about what form Western Christianity ought to take. European conflicts following the Treaty of Westphalia of 1648, which concluded the gigantically destructive Thirty Years' War, were generally limited affairs for limited ends. No more were the contestants fighting to establish God's order on earth, an enterprise by nature unlimited in scope and unamenable to compromise. Not until the French Revolutionary Wars of the 1790s would Western Europe again

---

47   St. Ilarion Troitsky, *Christianity or the Church?* 26.

be consumed by unlimited ideological warfare and an attempt to impose a revolutionary doctrine across the continent. Following the twenty-five-year effort to subdue Revolutionary France and Napoleon, monarchical Europe managed to contain the revolutionary virus for another hundred years until the catastrophe of 1917, when Revolutionary Communism seized control of the last Orthodox Christian Empire, Russia.

THE PURITANS AND AMERICA

A key step in the development of Gnostic Antichristianity in the West was the establishment of Puritan colonies in North America. The Puritans, who sought a "pure" form of Christianity reminiscent of the Cathars half a millennium earlier, agitated widely in Continental Europe and Britain against royal and episcopal prerogatives and were largely driven out of Europe after the restoration of the English monarchy in 1660. Like Huss, Müntzer, and revolutionaries before and after, they sought to build ideal societies on earth. Rejecting the Church but remaining self-consciously Christian, Puritans often referred to themselves in ways evoking Israel of the Old Testament, the "chosen people" possessed of a divine commission to found a godly society that would not be subject to the forces of historical decline.

Drawing on the Puritans' greatest contemporary critic, Church of England priest Richard Hooker (1554–1600), Eric Voegelin convincingly portrays the Puritans and other Gnostic activists as afflicted with a sort of madness, which, while not a mental illness, effectively walled them off from reality and all arguments and evidence that would induce a reasonable man to reconsider his position. The Puritans remain a classic case of what would be described today as "fundamentalists," men

suffering from "a peculiar pneumopathological state,"[48] a disease
of the spirit. In the Puritan case, this led to the belief that "the
faithful" have a political and even military mission to hasten the
coming of the Kingdom of God on earth, a foreshadowing of
the "revolutionary violence" required to usher in the Communist
millennium. The Puritan sect of the "Fifth Monarchy Men"—so
named for their belief that the four monarchical regimes named
in the Book of Daniel had come and gone and Christ would
soon reign with His (Puritan) saints on earth—attempted armed
insurrections in England in order to prepare the world for the
reign of Christ. "In chapter 20 of Revelation an angel comes
down from heaven and throws Satan into the bottomless pit
for a thousand years; in the Puritan Revolution, the Gnostics
arrogate this angelic function to themselves."[49]

A major figure in the developing Puritan consciousness in
America was the governor of the Massachusetts Bay Colony,
John Winthrop (1588–1649). A wealthy English lawyer who
emigrated to New England in 1630, Winthrop helped define the
Puritan cause in the New World. The Puritan millennialist streak
is especially evident in Winthrop's famous shipboard sermon in
which he describes the foundation of Puritan colonies in New
England as an undertaking sanctioned by God that will bring
either happiness and salvation or ruin and perdition. Winthrop
copiously employs Old Testament language evocative of God's
call to ancient Israel:

> The Lord will be our God, and delight to dwell among
> us, as his own people, and will command a blessing upon
> us in all our ways. So that we shall see much more of his
> wisdom, power, goodness, and truth, than formerly we
> have been acquainted with. We shall find that the God of

---

48   Voegelin, *The New Science of Politics*, 139.
49   Ibid., 145.

Israel is among us, when ten of us shall be able to resist a thousand of our enemies; when he shall make us a praise and glory that men shall say of succeeding plantations, "the Lord make it like that of New England." For we must consider that we shall be as a city upon a hill. The eyes of all people are upon us. So that if we shall deal falsely with our God in this work we have undertaken, and so cause him to withdraw his present help from us, we shall be made a story and a by-word through the world.[50]

Since the European discovery of America at the end of the fifteenth century, European intellectuals such as Sir Thomas More (1478–1535) had speculated on the possibility of an ideal society in the New World. More's *Utopia* described a hypothetical New World island nation marked by religious tolerance and the absence of private property. The idea of America as a land of plenty, particularly blessed by God, proved powerful during the Enlightenment and perdures to this day in the self-conscious "exceptionalism" of the United States. The American spirit, in which no problem is too great or complex to yield to human resourcefulness, has become one of the leading Gnostic attitudes of our time. While Winthrop's Christian rhetoric has largely gone, the idea of America as "the last best hope of earth"[51] continues to show staying power as does the unfortunate consequence of tending to frame practical political problems in all-or-nothing terms.

---

50   John Winthrop, *A Modell of Christian Charity*. 1630. *Collections of the Massachusetts Historical Society*. (Boston, 1838, 3rd series), 7:31-48. http://history.hanover.edu/texts/winthmod.html. Accessed September 13, 2019. See 2 Chr. 7:20.

51   President Abraham Lincoln. "Annual Message to Congress," December 1, 1862. https://www.presidency.ucsb.edu/documents/second-annual-message-9. Accessed September 13, 2019.

> [T]he leaders of the United States of both parties still subscribe to the notion of America's exceptionalism and to the propositional creed rooted in Puritan millenarianism.
>
> In world affairs this neurosis translates into self-appointed missions of "spreading democracy" and "humanitarian interventionism." There is precious little to choose between the neoliberal interventionists . . . and their neoconservative counterparts.... They are but two sides of the same coin.[52]

America's hugely impressive material achievements of the twentieth and early twenty-first centuries have tended to reinforce the idea of a nation specially destined to subdue the earth with her principles and culture. It is her continued self-consciousness as a chosen nation with a destiny to remake the world in her image—to bring the blessings of American-style capitalism and democracy to the world, even to those nations and peoples that may not want them, that singles her out as the leading globalizing force in the world today. But with numerous overseas strategic commitments that risk bringing her into conflict with regional powers, welfare and defense programs whose costs threaten to spiral out of control, as well as the ongoing erosion of her

---

52   Trifkovic, Srdja. "Beyond the Strategic Partnership," *Chronicles Magazine.* September 15, 2011. https://www.chroniclesmagazine.org/beyond-the-strategic-partnership/. Accessed September 13, 2019. Just one example of America's tendency to see herself as specially appointed to adjudicate the affairs of the world was offered by then Secretary of State Madeline Albright, who famously justified American military involvement in Iraq in 1998 by asserting that "... if we have to use force, it is because we are America; we are the indispensable nation. We stand tall and we see further than other countries into the future, and we see the danger here to all of us." (Interview on NBC-TV, Transcript, February 19, 1998, USIS Washington File, https://quotes.yourdictionary.com/author/madeleine-albright/. Accessed April 23, 2020.) From an outsider's point of view, it is not hard to see why other nations, less blessed with material resources, geographic isolation, or sheer military might, might regard America as less truly exceptional and more prosaically arrogant.

Christian culture, how long she will remain effective as a nation state—weakened and dependent, if not even disintegrated—only time will tell. However exceptional the United States may be, she is a human construction that, like all things of this world, must one day pass away.[53]

THE RISE OF RUSSIA

Following the breakdown of imperial order in the West during the Dark Ages, attempts were made to reorganize the fragmented West into a new Christian empire that would rival the Roman East as the imperial protector of Christian truth. The establishment of the Holy Roman Empire in Central Europe in the year 800 constituted an attempt to "resurrect" the Roman Empire even while a Roman emperor still sat on the throne in Constantinople. While the Holy Roman Empire enjoyed some success, its efficacy was fatally compromised by the contemporaneous development of the Papacy as a self-conscious universal monarchy and the European religious wars that broke out in the wake of the Great Schism and Reformation.

> Precisely at the time when the Western imperial articulation ultimately disintegrated, when Western society re-articulated itself into the nations and the plurality of churches, Russia entered on her career as the heir of Rome. From her very beginnings Russia was not a nation in the Western sense but a civilizational area, dominated ethnically by the Great Russians and formed into a political society by the symbolism of Roman continuation.[54]

---

53 We will have more to say about American democracy in ch. 7.
54 Voegelin, *The New Science of Politics*, 115.

As Voegelin observes, during the first half of the second millennium, the Holy Roman Empire, while it would endure, at
least in name, until 1806, was breaking down into what would
become the modern European nation-states, distinguished by
centuries of religious, ethnic, and national conflict. At the same
time, after seven centuries of trying, Islam finally managed to
overwhelm the Eastern Roman Empire in 1453 with the capture of Constantinople. With the fall of Constantinople and the
earlier loss of Rome and the West to schism, Orthodoxy was
deprived of its historical center and imperial protector. The
question then was: now that the Second Rome had fallen, would
there be a Third? Who would succeed Constantinople as the
champion of Orthodoxy? It was then that Moscow picked up
the baton and became the "Third Rome," the imperial guardian
of the Church on earth. "That Russian society was in a class by
itself was gradually recognized by the West."[55]

> Transcendentally Russia was distinguished from all
> Western nations as the imperial representative of Christian
> truth; and through her social re-articulation, from which
> the tsar emerged as the existential representative, she was
> radically cut off from the development of representative
> institutions in the sense of the Western national states.
> Napoleon, finally, recognized the Russian problem when,
> in 1802, he said that there were only two nations in the
> world: Russia and the Occident.[56]

Russia proved a problem for the West because she stood out
as the symbolic successor to the Christian Roman Empire, a
mantle that various power centers in the West would like to have
arrogated exclusively to themselves, but which their infighting

---

55   Ibid., 115
56   Ibid., 116.

and Russian ascendancy effectively prevented. Ten years after issuing his complaint, Napoleon endeavored to "solve" the Russian problem by force. Napoleon remains one of the great antichrists of history: a young man who rose to astonishing heights with meteoric speed, the incarnation of the antichristian ideology of his time ("the world-spirit on horseback" according to Hegel), who set out to destroy the world's foremost Orthodox civilization. The Napoleonic invasion of Russia of 1812 was a genuine "clash of civilizations" in which nominally Christian nations of Western Europe, assembled into a gigantic multinational army under the Gnostic banner of *Liberté, Egalité, Fraternité*, attempted to snuff out Orthodox imperial representation once and for all. As in the case of all Gnostic fantasies, reality eventually intervened and sent Napoleon's *Grand Armée* reeling westward with losses of eighty percent.[57]

Moscow's assumption of the title of the Third Rome may seem little more than a public relations exercise, but the symbolism of Roman continuity was by no means trivial.

> Rome was built into the idea of a Christian society by referring to the Danielic prophecy of the Fourth Monarchy to the *imperium sine fine* as the last realm before the end of the world. The church as the historically concrete representation of spiritual destiny was paralleled by the Roman Empire as the historically concrete representation of human temporality. Hence, the understanding of the medieval empire as the continuation of Rome was

---

57 Arnold Toynbee's "Russia's Byzantine Heritage" remains probably the best outline of the centuries-long struggle between Russia and the West in English. Composed in 1947, it rings as true as ever (though Toynbee, like many Western scholars, oversimplifies Byzantium). Of some relevance to our own time, Toynbee observes, "In the annals of the centuries-long warfare between the two Christendoms, it would seem to be the fact that the Russians have been the victims of aggression, and the Westerners the aggressors, more often than not." http://www.unz.com/print/Horizon-1947aug-00082/. Accessed September 13, 2019.

more than a vague historical hangover; it was part of the conception of history in which the end of Rome meant the end of the world in the eschatological sense.[58]

In other words, the prevalent Orthodox conviction has been that, if the Church were to lose her temporal protector—an Orthodox Empire in the vein of Rome—then the end of the world, entailing the reign of Antichrist and the Second Coming, would be at hand. With the fall of the Russian Empire to militant atheism in 1917, it seemed to many that the age of Antichrist had come.

THE ENLIGHTENMENT AND WORLD REVOLUTION

By the seventeenth century, a new wave of Western intellectuals was seeking to expand human knowledge without having to take sides on religious matters. It was during this time that modern science came into its own. "Enlightened" men were those smart enough not to waste time in the sort of theological and ecclesiological disputes that had, evidently, been the source of the bloodshed of preceding centuries. While many remained nominally Christian, these new "men of science" eschewed the wisdom of tradition and sought knowledge and power over nature beyond the boundaries of traditional Christianity. No longer content with assimilating the Truth of Revelation, they sought undiscovered truths in nature. Intellectuals such as Voltaire ridiculed traditional Christian faith, while a scientist and alchemist such as Newton sought to reduce creation to a "clockwork" model and to wrest occult gnosis from Scripture along "scientific" lines.

---

58   Voegelin, *The New Science of Politics*, 110.

With the progressive Western abandonment of the Orthodox worldview following the Great Schism, a broad current of innerworldly opinion and action began to develop amidst an outward shell of Christianity. "By the mid sixteenth century, it was possible to talk about a revolution, an international political movement bent on overthrowing the medieval view of the world and replacing it with something new."[59] The Enlightenment was a key step in the development of what we can identify as the Modern Revolution, the multi-generational turning over of traditional Christian society by movements that rejected the Church as the repository of truth and sought to build political societies on earth that would promise a return to paradise. While the Modern Revolution took clear shape in the Enlightenment, over time it morphed into myriad variants, eventually shedding Christian consciousness in the deism of the French Revolution of the late eighteenth century, which itself proved but a forerunner to the militant atheism of Communism in the twentieth. While "something new" would vary according to historical circumstances, in fact, the successive political explosions of the second millennium were all manifestations of the same revolutionary spirit.

> The Gnostic revolution has for its purpose a change in the nature of man and the establishment of a transfigured society. Since this program cannot be carried out in historical reality, Gnostic revolutionaries must inevitably institutionalize their partial or total success in the existential struggle by a compromise with reality; and whatever emerges from this compromise, it will not be the transfigured world envisaged by Gnostic symbolism. If, therefore, the theorist would study the Gnostic revolution at the level

---

59   Barbara Tuchman, *Bible and Sword*, 54 as quoted in Jones, *The Jewish Revolutionary Spirit*, 330.

of its temporary stabilization, of its political tactics, or of the moderate programs which already envisage the compromise, the nature of Gnosticism, the driving force of the Western revolution, could never come into view. The compromise would be taken for the essence, and the essential unity of the variegated Gnostic phenomena would disappear.[60]

What possibly connects the Papal revolution of the eleventh century with the Bolshevik Revolution of the twentieth? The Hussite rebellion of the fifteenth century with the National Socialist half a millennium later? The comparatively benign American Revolution with the sanguinary French one, championed by many of the same men? They were all manifestations of the spirit of Gnosticism that rejected the Lord's message of salvation, "Take up the cross and follow me,"[61] and sought in various ways a manmade shortcut back to paradise. The common aim of building a utopia through a given formula— Papal infallibility, *sola scriptura*, "visions," pseudo-scientific laws of history in the thought of Hegel and Marx, etc.—is the overarching theme even while, to the casual observer, the successive phases of the Revolution each seem to produce something genuinely novel.

A clear understanding of these experiences as the active core of immanentist eschatology is necessary, because otherwise the inner logic of Western political development from medieval immanentism through humanism, enlightenment, progressivism, liberalism, positivism, into Marxism [and beyond] will be obscured. The intellectual symbols developed by the various types of immanentists

---

60   Voegelin, *The New Science of Politics*, 152.
61   Mark 10:21.

will frequently be in conflict with one another, and the various types of Gnostics will oppose one another.[62]

In other words, while various political movements would rise and fall through the course of the second-millennium West, many of which would explicitly oppose one another—such as Communism and National Socialism—they nevertheless evince the same basic symbols and trajectory. Possessed of a total certainty of the rightness of their cause and of the wickedness of their enemies, Gnostic revolutionaries effectively declared war on reality. The only way of defeating such movements, as with National Socialism, has been through the application of greater force, or, as in the case of Communism, of having to wait for the internal disintegration of the Gnostic fantasy even while it lays waste to the civilization around it.

The World Revolution in our time of globalization, however, is no longer "revolutionary" in the sense of seeking the "turning over" of society because, in much the way that H. G. Wells described, it has become the establishment: it has successfully colonized the world's centers of power such that it now intends not the overturning of an old, Christian order, but the consolidation of a new, antichristian one.

> The Revolution, perhaps, begins to move out of its malevolent phase and into a more "benevolent" one— not because it has changed its will or direction, but because it is nearing the attainment of the ultimate goal which it has never ceased to pursue; fat with its success, it can prepare to relax in the enjoyment of its goal.[63]

---

62   Voegelin, *The New Science of Politics*, 125.
63   Damascene, *Father Seraphim Rose*, 153.

In our time, the World Revolution has successfully overturned the old Christian-monarchical order in favor of pseudo-democracies, which themselves are dominated by a supranational oligarchy and the ideologues of the Open Conspiracy.[64] A genuine revolution in our time would not involve the continued pursuit of a unified world order but a return to national or regional independence and the rejection of the Gnostic ideologies that permeate contemporary culture.

COMMUNISM

From the days of Spartacus, Weishaupt,[65] Karl Marx, Trotsky, Bela Kun, Rosa Luxemburg and Emma Goldman, this world conspiracy has been steadily growing. This conspiracy played a definite recognizable role in the French Revolution. It has been the mainspring of every subversive movement during the 19th century. And now at last, this band of extraordinary personalities from the under-world of the great cities of Europe and America have gripped the Russian people by the hair of their head

---

64   See chs. 6 and 7.

65   "Brother Spartacus" was the pseudonym of Johann Adam Weishaupt, founder of the "Order of Illuminati," a subversive secret society discovered and proscribed by the Bavarian government in 1784. Weishaupt drew unreservedly on both his Jesuitical education and his extensive knowledge of the occult and the Kabala to develop a Gnostic system based on the perfection of human nature, which he endeavored to infiltrate into Freemasonry, into which he had been initiated in 1777 in Munich. Following exile from Bavaria, he continued working in Gotha, where he died in 1830, though the course of his later life, as well as his continuing influence on Illuminism and Freemasonry, are disputed. For definitive works on the Illuminati and their role in the World Revolution, see Nesta Webster's *Secret Societies and Subversive Movements, World Revolution: The Plot Against Civilization*, and *The French Revolution: A Study in Democracy*.

and have become the undisputed masters of that enormous empire.[66]

The foregoing might be dismissed as the ravings of a "conspiracy theorist" if not for the fact that it was written by one of the twentieth century's leading statesmen. Winston Churchill was describing the Communist takeover of Russia and the systematic brutality it unleashed upon the people of the Russian Empire. While a series of Gnostic disasters rent the West from the Great Schism to the rise of German National Socialism nine hundred years later, the greatest disaster occurred in Russia in 1917, when a small, disciplined band of Communist revolutionaries, the Bolsheviks, heavily supported by Western centers of influence, seized power during the crisis of the First World War. With the transformation of the world's leading Christian power, Orthodox Russia, into the leading antichristian power, the Communist Soviet Union, an earthquake in history occurred equivalent to the fall of Rome in 476 and Constantinople in 1453. The era of Imperial Christianity, in which state power recognized the Church and the law of God as greater than itself, was over. It had begun with the legalization of the Church by Emperor St. Constantine I in the early fourth century; it ended with the murder of the last Orthodox Christian Emperor, St. Nicholas II Romanov, sixteen centuries later. Priest-Confessor Gleb Yakunin, in a letter to the Russian Orthodox diaspora, interpreted the significance of the murder of the Tsar and his family:

> The meaning for world history of the martyr's death of the Imperial Family, something that likens it to the most significant Biblical events, consists of the fact that here

---

66   Winston Churchill, "Zionism versus Bolshevism." *The Sunday Herald*. February 8, 1920. http://www.fpp.co.uk/bookchapters/WSC/WSCwrote1920.html. Accessed September 13. 2019.

the Constantinopolitan period of the existence of the Church of Christ comes to an end, and a new, martyric, apocalyptic age opens up. It is begun with the voluntary sacrifice of the last anointed Orthodox Emperor and his family. The tragedy of the Royal Family has lain like a curse on the Russian land, having become the symbolic prologue of Russia's long path of the Cross—the death of tens of millions of her sons and daughters.[67]

Indeed, Communism proved the most violently destructive manifestation of the Modern Revolution. Courtois, et al., estimate the number of victims who died worldwide as the direct result of Communist policies conservatively at one hundred million, the equivalent of a September 11-scale attack every day for one hundred years.[68] Tens of millions of Orthodox Christians

67   Taken from a lecture given at the Youth Conference of the Russian Orthodox Church Outside of Russia, San Francisco, August 3, 1981 by Blessed Hieromonk Seraphim Rose. http://www.orthodoxphotos.com/readings/seraphim/russia/. Accessed September 16, 2019.
68   See Stéphane Courtois, et al., *The Black Book of Communism: Crimes, Terror, Repression* (Cambridge, Harvard University, 1999). Even greater than the staggering death toll directly inflicted by Communism through systematic incarceration, brutality, and murder, were the implications of Communist policies on the most helpless members of society, namely, the unborn. In 1920, the Communist Soviet Union became the first country to legalize abortion, a policy that would remain in place until the fall of Communism in 1991, save for a hiatus during the period of 1936-55 when abortion was made illegal again, largely over concerns about weak population growth. In the 1950s and 1960s, the Soviet Union had some of the highest abortion rates in the world, amounting to perhaps six to seven million abortions per year, far eclipsing the number of live births, and amounting to perhaps an almost incredible 200 million total abortions. ("Historical Abortion Statistics, Russia." http://www.johnstonsarchive.net/policy/abortion/ab-russia.html; "Abortion in Russia." https://en.wikipedia.org/wiki/Abortion_in_Russia#1920-1936; "What is the Abortion Situation in Europe?" https://www.hli.org/resources/abortion-situation-europe/ Accessed October 1, 2019.) Westerners should not feel too complacent, however, as democratic capitalism has managed to produce some fifty million abortions in the United States alone since 1973. ("FACT CHECK: 50 Million Abortions Claim Checks Out." https://www.desmoinesregister.com/story/news/politics/reality-check/2015/03/06/million-abortions-claim-checks/24530159/ Accessed October 1, 2019.) For

went to their deaths in the gulags of the overwhelmingly Orthodox Soviet Union, Romania, Bulgaria, and Yugoslavia, suffered starvation through state-inflicted famine, or were murdered outright on suspicion of "counterrevolutionary activities." Ancient monasteries, once bastions of Orthodox piety, were turned into prisons and factories, icons and holy objects were desecrated, destroyed, or sold abroad, churches were closed, and great cathedrals were dynamited. Agents of the Communist state infiltrated the Orthodox hierarchy and clergy, sowing treachery, discord, and distrust among the faithful, the scars of which are visible to this day.

Ironically, it was the unprecedented calamity of atheistic Communism that scattered much of the Orthodox Church to the winds and planted the seeds of an Orthodox revival in the West nine hundred years after the schism of Rome.

> In chastising, the Lord at the same time also shows the Russian people the way to salvation by making it a preacher of Orthodoxy in the whole world. The Russian Diaspora has made all the ends of the world familiar with Orthodoxy; the mass of Russian exiles, for the most part, is unconsciously a preacher of Orthodoxy.... To the Russians abroad, it has been granted to shine in the whole world with the light of Orthodoxy, so that other peoples, seeing their good deeds, might glorify our Father Who is in heaven, and thus obtain salvation for themselves.... The Diaspora will have to be converted to the path of repentance and, having acquired forgiveness for itself through prayer to God and through being reborn

---

all their outward differences, one thing modern forms of government tend to share is an enormous body count.

spiritually (will) become capable also of giving rebirth to our suffering homeland.[69]

The ongoing disintegration of Western Christianity, which grows ever more difficult to ignore for any serious person, is driving many Westerners to the True Church, the fulness of the Faith, Holy Orthodoxy. Truly, the Lord works in mysterious ways.

THE AGE OF SCIENCE

During the long, dark night of Communism, the most virulently antichristian thought-system in history, it was easy to imagine that nihilistic atheism would prove the final victor at the end of history in a global Communist tyranny; but the official atheist state proved temporary. With the collapse of Eastern European Communism in the late twentieth century, Orthodox lands re-oriented themselves westward in the hope of partaking of the fruits of "democracy." Materialistic Communism gave way to materialistic capitalism. Now, in the post-Communist world, an Orthodox revival is attempting to gain steam even while a tidal wave of Western materialism and heterodoxy threatens to swamp it. "If in our times there are signs that the era of violence and negation is passing, this is by no means because Nihilism is being 'overcome' or 'outgrown,' but because its work is all but completed and its usefulness is at an end."[70] With the fall of Communism and the triumph of the West, there apparently remains only to bring the "delights of modernity" to the few dark corners left in the world. Slowly but surely is the West wearing down the cultural resistance of the Islamic,

---

69   Archbishop St. John Maximovich, in a report to the All-Diaspora Sobor of 1938, as quoted in Rose, *The Future of Russia.* http://www.orthodoxphotos.com/readings/seraphim/russia/. Accessed September 13, 2019.
70   Damascene, *Father Seraphim Rose*, 153.

Asian, and Orthodox worlds even while it undergoes the internal disintegration characteristic of an ascendant Gnostic civilization. While the West's Gnostic tendencies have often been hidden beneath Christian language or other ideological facades, in our age of globalization, "knowledge" itself is increasingly paraded as the key to, in effect, human salvation.

> Modern science was born [in the Renaissance] out of the experiments of the Platonic alchemists, the astrologers, and magicians. The underlying spirit of the new scientific worldview was the spirit of Faustianism, the spirit of magic, which is retained as a definite undertone of contemporary science.... Descartes, who formulated the mechanistic scientific worldview, said that man was to become "the master and possessor of nature." It should be noted that this is a religious faith, which takes the place of Christian faith.[71]

A widespread notion, which has continued to gain momentum since the Enlightenment, is that technical science possesses unlimited potential to improve the human condition. Everywhere science and technology are proposed as the answers to the world's ills: from bad health, physical and mental, to poverty, political strife, social decay, even mortality itself[72]—whatever problem that plagues the human condition, there exists now a "science" that holds out the promise of "solving" it.

---

71   Ibid., 625.

72   "The conference [Global Future 2045 International Congress] took a surreal turn when Martine Rothblatt – a lawyer, author and entrepreneur, and CEO of biotech company United Therapeutics Corp. – took the stage. Even the title of Rothblatt's talk was provocative: 'The Purpose of Biotechnology is the End of Death.'" While the title of Mr. Rothblatt's talk may well have provoked his audience, it is merely candid. http://www.livescience.com/37499-immortality-by-2045-conference. html. Accessed September 13, 2019.

> Scientism has remained to this day one of the strongest Gnostic movements in Western society; and the immanentist pride in science is so strong that even the special sciences have each left a distinguishable sediment in the variants of salvation through physics, economics, sociology, biology, and psychology.[73]

Outwardly, the present world is being rapidly reduced to a technocracy in which, supposedly, the only "real" problems are technical problems that in principle admit of a solution. Other matters such as religion, truth, and meaning itself are regarded as irrational and irrelevant—everything that the pre-modern world once regarded as paramount. Like Voegelin, we might term this prevailing belief or ideology (perhaps "faith"), which seems to permeate every corner of contemporary life, "scientism," but really it is just an especially powerful wave on the antichristian Gnostic tide that surges through the modern world. Indeed, ours is an age of explicit, self-conscious Gnosticism. The contemporary cult of education and fascination with technical knowledge belies the abandonment of revealed, transcendent truth, which by nature cannot be reduced to a technical system. That which remains of revealed truth in the Western consciousness, such as the Bible, is itself subjected to "scientific" analysis that seeks to explain transcendent phenomena in naturalistic terms or to "decode" Scripture to divulge some new, occult meaning. However,

> ...if there is no Revealed Truth, there is no truth at all; the search for truth outside of Revelation has come to a dead end.... The multitude demonstrates this by looking to the scientist, not for truth, but for the technical applications of a knowledge which has no more than a practical value,

---

73   Voegelin, *The New Science of Politics*, 127.

and by looking to other, irrational sources for the ultimate values men once expected to find in truth. The despotism of science over practical life is contemporaneous with the advent of a whole series of pseudo-religious "revelations"; the two are correlative symptoms of the same malady: the abandonment of truth.[74]

Few appreciate the irony of such a "scientific" and "advanced" civilization as ours devouring all sorts of pseudo-scientific rubbish in an attempt to satisfy its spiritual hunger. Ghost-hunting, neo-paganism, witchcraft, UFOs, and an endless stream of ever-weirder science-fiction fantasy constitute modern man's misguided efforts to summon a mystical reality that now eludes him. When he does manage to connect with something genuinely "spiritual," it is not the Spirit of Truth, but a manifestation of the demonic, which in his blindness he is unable to recognize.

The idea that science will somehow, someday, surpass its reductionist boundaries and emerge into a realm of transcendent meaning is a common theme in much science fiction and increasingly an article of popular faith. In such fantasies, technical advance eventually permits man to transcend the limits of science itself and become, or make contact with, god-like beings, thus providing a connection with what is, in effect, a mystical realm of existence.

> The future world and humanity are seen by science fiction ostensibly in terms of "projections" from present-day scientific discoveries; in actuality, however, these "projections" correspond quite remarkably to the everyday reality of occult and overtly demonic experience throughout the ages.... Science fiction in general is usually

---

74   Damascene, *Father Seraphim Rose*, 141.

not very scientific at all, and not really very "futuristic" either; if anything, it is a retreat to the "mystical" origins of modern science—the science before the age of the 17th- and 18th-century Enlightenment, which was much closer to occultism.[75]

Both [modern technical science and magic] are preoccupied with phenomena and their manipulation, with wonders, with results. Both are an attempt at wish fulfillment, an attempt to bend reality to one's own will. The difference is simply this: science (modern science) is *systematic* magic; science has found a method, where magic works in fits and starts.... [D]o not the results of science today resemble a magical landscape?[76]

It is not hard to imagine that an Orthodox Christian of the first millennium—or even most anyone from only a few centuries ago—transported to our time of air and space travel, electronic communication, atomic energy, virtual reality, X-ray and MRI machines, etc. would imagine himself on an altogether different planet, one dominated by occult and magical forces that have utterly hypnotized its inhabitants. While modern technological advances may be used for good or for evil, that we today take for granted the technical marvels of our time to such an extent that we have trouble living without them testifies to the power they hold over us. Gnostic assumptions are today so widespread, so woven into the fabric of modern life, that it is likely impossible for us to appreciate how profoundly they shape our lives and how distorted from the true Orthodox Christian worldview ours has become.

---

75   Rose, *Orthodoxy and the Religion of the Future*, 75-6.
76   Damascene, *Father Seraphim Rose*, 139.

In this chapter, we have only been able to touch on some of the key phases in the displacement of Orthodox Christian consciousness in the West and its progressive eclipse by various forms of Gnostic antichristianity. An authoritative lesson from even our very brief survey is that the greatest disasters in world history have proven to be not acts of God but acts of men. The glorious promise of the Gnostic Revolution has consistently resulted in violence, war, death, and social and spiritual desolation. The chasing after false ideals and the concomitant fallacious construction of political society can prove far deadlier than any earthquake, typhoon, or pestilence. It is the gravest of errors to surmise that political forms are mere projections of the human will, that man possesses an unlimited capacity to shape the world he inhabits. The Greek philosophers and the Fathers of the Church possessed a much sounder understanding of the limits of human power than their modern successors. History attests that there is nothing more disastrous than politics done badly.

In sum, we see what is typically defined as historical "progress" to be generally the opposite: not an ascent to greater wisdom and understanding but a progressive—and highly destructive—falling away from the light of Orthodoxy to inner-worldly delusions that seek salvation without the Cross. We must be clear, however, that we are not issuing a blanket condemnation of Western Civilization. Much in the West is objectively good, including what remains of the Greco-Roman tradition and genuine Christian consciousness. The West's astonishing technical advances, like most things, may be used for good or ill: to facilitate the easing of suffering through love; to take life or to preserve it; to instill gratitude to God for medicines and comforts; or to become ends in themselves and idols to man's own greatness. Many of the great lights of the Orthodox Church in modern times have emphasized the importance of seeking out the nobler elements that remain in contemporary culture as crucial supports of Christian life. "Finally, brethren, whatever things are true, whatever things are noble, whatever things are just, whatever things are pure, whatever things are lovely, whatever things are of good report, if there is any virtue and if there is anything praiseworthy—meditate on these things."[77] St. Paul's exhortation is as relevant today as it was in his own time—even while the world's slide into global antichristianity renders it increasingly difficult to carry out.

Having surveyed the millennium-long growth of antichristianity in the West that has set the stage for modern globalization, we will now turn to a more detailed examination of globalization in our time at the economic, political, and religious levels.

---

77 Phil. 4:8.

PART III

THE AGE OF CONFUSION

CHAPTER 6

THE GLOBALIZATION
OF ECONOMICS

[T]he powers of financial capitalism had [a] far-reaching aim, nothing less than to create a world system of financial control in private hands able to dominate the political system of each country and the economy of the world as a whole. This system was to be controlled in a feudalist fashion by the central banks of the world acting in concert, by secret agreements arrived at in frequent private meetings and conferences. The apex of the system was to be the Bank for International Settlements in Basle, Switzerland, a private bank owned and controlled by the world's central banks which were themselves private corporations.

Professor Caroll Quigley (1910-77)
Tragedy and Hope, p. 324[1]

The globalization of economics is today most evident in the removal of traditional restrictions between economic zones, particularly between nation-states. The idea of distinct national economies is increasingly antiquated. Economic cycles of expansion and contraction, of boom and bust, are ever more global

---

1 Caroll Quigley, *Tragedy and Hope: A History of the World in Our Time* (New York, MacMillan, 1966).

in nature. Workers in one part of the globe must now compete with others thousands of miles away, making the same product or providing the same service. The dislocations wrought on individuals, accustomed to living in a certain, familiar area, whose personal concerns transcend the mere economic, can be enormous. The old allegiances to family, country, and local culture continue to give way before the juggernaut of global capitalism's "bottom line."

The intricacies of the modern global economic system are far too great to receive a thorough treatment in this work; here we will only be able to touch on some of its major aspects and its relevance to our central thesis. We know that the world economic system will be of special significance under the regime of Antichrist thanks to the Apocalypse of St. John, which tells us that, during Antichrist's reign, "he causes all, both small and great, rich and poor, free and slave, to receive a mark on their right hand or on their foreheads, and that no one may buy or sell except one who has the mark or the name of the beast, or the number of his name.[2]" During this time, official exchange will require allegiance to the regime of Antichrist, and it is particularly worth noting that this will entail a *number.* Already in our time it is hardly possible to "buy or sell" without an identifying number of some kind such as a social security, bank account, or credit card number. The world's currencies themselves all bear unique serial numbers. Antichrist's regime will take the numericization of exchange to its final conclusion.

Antichrist's control of global commerce implies control of the medium of exchange in the world's markets, which is to say control of a global currency regime. To come to understand how such extraordinary power could be exercised on a global basis, we will examine the underpinnings of the increasingly centralized international banking system.

---

2   Rev. 13:16-17.

THE MONEY REVOLUTION

Some of the greatest innovations of the modern world have been in the area of finance, and in particular of money itself. Money may be broadly defined as any medium of exchange. Historically, gold and silver, by virtue of their scarcity, durability, and portability served as universally accepted money. Gold and silver coins, usually bearing a government emblem, were the most common forms of money. Banking originated with goldsmiths and bullion depositories, who, for reasons of convenience, began to issue notes of redemption against their physical stores of precious metals so that they need not be transported. These redeemable notes began to be traded and over time evolved into paper currency. Governments and later central banks began to issue their own notes against their bullion supplies. Modern currencies such as the dollar and the pound sterling derive their names from designated measures of weight even while they no longer retain any connection to precious metals.

The great prophet of globalization, H. G. Wells (see ch. 2), writing at a time when most currencies in the world were still based on a metallic standard, foresaw that a new global order would require the development of a new kind of money. The "new world money" that he described sounds very similar to the unbacked currencies of today:

> it becomes plain that a collectivist world order ... will have to carry on its main, its primary operations at least with a new world money, a specially contrived money, differing in its nature from any sort of money conventions that have hitherto served human needs. It will be issued against the

total purchasable output of the community in return for the workers' services to the community.[3]

In *The Shape of Things to Come*, an imaginary retrospective from the year 2106, Wells outlines this "new world money" and its deliberate disconnection from traditional forms.

[Modern paper currency] had indeed grown out of a barterable commodity, a thing in itself, silver or gold or the like, but it had ceased to be this, and it was the difficulties in the transition of money from the former to the latter status that had released those diseases of the economic system which had in succession first destroyed the Roman imperialism and then the European sovereign states. A completely abstract money, a money as abstract and free from association with any material substance as weight or measure, had to be contrived for mankind. Human society could not be saved from chaos without it. It had to be of worldwide validity. . .[4]

The key difference between the old metallic standards of money of the past and the new paper/electronic currencies of today is that there is no inherent limit on the latter. Gold and silver are by nature limited in quantity; not so with today's currencies, which are commonly referred to as *fiat* — "let it be done"—which is to say that they may be created in indefinite quantities by their issuers. On the old metallic standards, the only way to expand the money supply was through the issuance of new metallic coin or through alloying extant coin with baser metals. This latter tactic allowed governments to pay their bills through

3   Wells, *The New World Order*, ch. 12. https://www.voltairenet.org/IMG/pdf/Wells_New_World_Order.pdf. Accessed September 13, 2019.
4   Wells, *The Shape of Things to Come*, bk. III, ch. 1. http://gutenberg.net.au/ebooks03/0301391h.html. Accessed September 13, 2019.

sleight-of-hand. Debased coinage invariably led to devaluation of the coinage and price inflation. At some point, prices would skyrocket uncontrollably and coin debasement could effectively go no further; then the responsible government would be forced to recall its coin, melt it down, and issue new coins of genuine quality—or face collapse. Rather than coin, issuing redeemable notes against bullion supplies was a means of expanding the money supply more efficiently but still with fundamental limits. Today, by abandoning redeemability and moving to fiat currencies, no physical limit remains on the creation of currency.

> Like gold, U.S. dollars have value only to the extent that they are strictly limited in supply. But the U.S. government [in conjunction with the Federal Reserve, the U.S. central bank—more anon] has a technology, called a printing press (or, today, its electronic equivalent), that allows it to produce as many U.S. dollars as it wishes at essentially no cost. By increasing the number of U.S. dollars in circulation, or even by credibly threatening to do so, the U.S. government can also reduce the value of a dollar in terms of goods and services, which is equivalent to raising the prices in dollars of those goods and services.[5]

We will examine in a moment how governments and their central banks issue currency, but the everyday issuance of ordinary bank loans is the most common method of increasing the money supply. Whereas borrowing $1,000 from a non-bank party merely entails the transfer of $1,000 from one place to another, borrowing from a bank is quite different. Obtaining a bank loan of $1,000 seems to imply that there is $1,000 worth

---

5   Benjamin S. Bernanke, "Remarks Before the National Economists Club, Washington, D.C., November 21, 2002." http://www.federalreserve.gov/boarddocs/speeches/2002/20021121. Accessed September 13, 2019.

of deposits somewhere inside the bank that is being loaned out, but that would be misleading. The relationship between a bank's deposits and the amount it lends out is actually quite indirect and can vary substantially. When a party obtains a $1,000 loan from a bank, the $1,000 becomes an entry in a physical or electronic ledger that comes literally from nowhere. Before the loan is made, the $1,000 simply does not exist; it comes from nothing. The aggregate money supply is enlarged each time a loan is made and contracts as the loan is paid back. As the debtor repays the bank (with interest, which the bank profits), the entry in the ledger shrinks until it finally vanishes back into the nothingness from which it sprang. A modern bank thus has a unique legal existence that amounts to a special charter to create money through what is known as "double-entry book-keeping"—a privilege not extended to the rest of us.

However, there exists an even greater power in the financial system today, that of the central banks. Central banks set a basic interest rate that governs lending among commercial banks through the purchase and sale of government securities (and increasingly other forms of securities as well, such as corporate bonds and exchange traded funds). Central banks are virtually unlimited in their power to increase or decrease the aggregate money supply. Among other things, they serve as a "lender of last resort" for commercial banks, which correspondingly have great incentive to lend recklessly in the hope of profit because, should their loans turn bad, the central bank can always bail them out. While governments have often established central banks with the idea of providing a safety net for their financial systems, in fact, central banks act first and foremost for the benefit of the commercial banking system they are supposed to regulate.

Contrary to widespread belief, central banks are in fact private corporations—legally protected monopolies—granted a special charter by their respective governments to control the money supply. The central bank monopolies are in reality cartels of the major private banks. Whereas governments have often acted to break up cartels, trusts, and monopolies, they have gone out of their way to establish and enshrine in law the central bank cabals. Like all private corporations, the central banks act in the interests of their owners, namely, the major private banks and the governments that oversee them. One ostensible hope of establishing such "independent" central banks was to deprive governments of the power of simply printing money to pay their bills. The fact is, however, that in the era of central banking, governments have been far more willing and able to spend beyond their means. Instead of paying their bills with their own newly created money, governments now must borrow by way of selling bonds that are purchased largely by the creation of new money from the central banks. The process is effectively the same—governments paying their debts with newly created money—with the difference that governments now become debtors to the major banks.

The tremendous power afforded by the legal right to create money by issuing debt was ably summed up by one of the twentieth century's leading bankers, Sir Josiah Stamp, a director of the Bank of England, in 1927, in what is for a banker an atypically candid admission:

> The modern banking system manufactures money out of nothing. The process is perhaps the most astounding piece of sleight of hand that was ever invented. Banking was conceived in iniquity and born in sin... Bankers own the earth. Take it away from them but leave them the power to create money, and, with a flick of a pen, they will create enough money to buy it back again...[6]

---

6   Quoted in Silas Walter Adams, *The Legalized Crime of Banking and a Constitutional Remedy*, ch. 1. https://archive.org/details/ LegalizedCrimeOfBankikngAndItsConstitutionalRemedy/page/n5. Accessed September 13, 2019.

The ongoing increase in the money supply permitted by fiat currency and central banking greatly increases banks' profitability by allowing them to lend far more than if they were confined to a simple metallic standard. The ongoing expansion of the money supply leads to price inflation and the progressive devaluation of the currency, which in turn encourages further borrowing and debt and harms responsible savers who see the real value of their savings decline. The financial independence traditionally afforded by saving can be readily wiped out through a bout of central bank-induced inflation. The modern fiat currency system renders entire populations dependent on the good will of the central banks whose interests are in many ways opposed to the economically productive members of society. A remarkably able diagnosis of the dangers posed by fiat currencies was, surprisingly, given by Alan Greenspan, one of our time's leading central bankers.

> In the absence of the gold standard, there is no way to protect savings from confiscation through inflation. There is no safe store of value. If there were, the government would have to make its holding illegal, as was done in the case of gold [in 1933; rescinded in 1974].... The financial policy of the welfare state requires that there be no way for the owners of wealth to protect themselves.
> ... Deficit spending is simply a scheme for the confiscation of wealth. Gold stands in the way of this insidious process. It stands as a protector of property rights. If one grasps this, one has no difficulty in understanding the statists' antagonism toward the gold standard.[7]

---

7   Alan Greenspan. *Gold and Economic Freedom*. 1966. https://www.constitution.org/mon/greenspan_gold.htm. Accessed September 13, 2019.

And that the ramifications of the inflation-oriented fiat system spill over into all aspects of society was pointed out by one of the twentieth century's most influential economists, John Maynard Keynes (1883–1946).

> Lenin is said to have declared that the best way to destroy the capitalist system was to debauch the currency. By a continuing process of inflation, governments can confiscate, secretly and unobserved, an important part of the wealth of their citizens. By this method they not only confiscate, but they confiscate arbitrarily; and, while the process impoverishes many, it actually enriches some. The sight of this arbitrary rearrangement of riches strikes not only at security but at confidence in the equity of the existing distribution of wealth.
>
> … Lenin was certainly right. There is no subtler, no surer means of overturning the existing basis of society than to debauch the currency. The process engages all the hidden forces of economic law on the side of destruction, and does it in a manner which not one man in a million is able to diagnose.[8]

The ascendancy of modern global finance and the de facto rule by banks has proven not merely destructive in the social dimension but violates injunctions set down by God Himself. Usury, the practice of lending at interest, now universal through-out the contemporary banking industry, was something that the Lord explicitly condemned.

---

8   John Maynard Keynes, *The Economic Consequences of the Peace*, 235. https:// oll.libertyfund.org/titles/keynes-the-economic-consequences-of-the-peace. Accessed September 13, 2019.

> If one of your brethren becomes poor, and falls
> into poverty among you, then you shall help him, like a
> stranger or a sojourner, that he may live with you. Take
> no usury or interest from him; but fear your God, that
> your brother may live with you. You shall not lend him
> your money for usury, nor lend him your food at a profit.
> I am the LORD your God, who brought you out of the
> land of Egypt, to give you the land of Canaan and to be
> your God.[9]

The temptation to treat others as objects of gain through
usury has been a perennial problem, which has broken out into
hitherto unimagined dimensions in our time. Despite the Lord's
proscription, the problem recurred throughout the history of
ancient Israel, which various prophets were compelled to address.
"After serious thought, I [Nehemiah] rebuked the nobles and
rulers, and said to them, 'Each of you is exacting usury from his
brother.' So I called a great assembly against them…. 'Please,
let us stop this usury!' "[10] The problem became so grave that
God included lending on usury along with idolatry and robbery
with violence as offenses worthy of death.

> If he has oppressed the poor and needy, robbed by violen-
> ce, not restored the pledge, lifted his eyes to the idols, or
> committed abomination; if he has exacted usury or taken
> increase—shall he then live? He shall not live! If he has
> done any of these abominations, he shall surely die; his
> blood shall be upon him.[11]

---

9   Lev. 25:35-8.
10   Neh. 5:7, 10.
11   Ezek. 18:12-13.

When one reflects that usury, once forbidden by divine command on pain of death, has become the foundation stone of the modern global economy, one begins to appreciate the true significance of the "money revolution." The Lord Himself expelled from His temple "the money changers doing business,"[12] and the Church for centuries greatly limited usury throughout Christendom.[13] It seems safe to say that the global banking system constitutes a gigantic affront to the will of God and His command to treat fellow humans as brothers rather than as objects of gain.

While there have been many revolutions through the ages that have transformed the historical landscape, none has been so tremendous yet so unremarked as the revolution in finance effected by modern banking. Money was once an asset, gold or silver, but is now a form of debt created by banks. This financial revolution stands the traditional understanding of money on its head. The existence of money in one place implies the existence of debt bondage in another. The ever-increasing money supply resulting from fiat currencies represents an ever-expanding web of debt that enslaves the economically productive members of society to the issuers of this debt-money, the banks and those who administer them. The old gold standard amounted to a highly democratic monetary system: gold and silver were always good regardless of who possessed them; no power could systematically control their supply. Now, the global monetary system revolves around the interests of the highly centralized financial sector and the decrees of the central bankers.

---

12   John 2:14.
13   See Michael Hoffman, *Usury in Christendom: The Mortal Sin that Was and Now is Not* (Coeur d'Alene, Independent History and Research, 2012).

THE NEW ECONOMIC WORLD ORDER

Today's fiat currencies are exactly the sort of specially contrived, new world money foreseen by Wells that are key to the new world order. In many ways, the modern banking system and its heads, the central banks of the world, are institutions more powerful than any government. On the one hand, they enjoy the attributes of sovereignty in possessing the sole right to issue currency that all members of society are legally bound to accept; however, as independent, non-governmental entities, they are bound by none of government's mechanisms of accountability such as popular elections and separation of powers.

While independent, private corporations, the world's central banks are often considered as extensions of their respective governments, and in some way this is true: governments and central banks routinely coordinate fiscal and monetary policy; but it is probably more apt to think of the situation in reverse, that the world's governments are extensions of their central banks. A bank makes money lending at interest; it is therefore desirable by the banks that governments borrow as much as possible in order to maximize interest payments to them. Wars and non-productive social programs are special favorites from the banks' point of view because they are very costly and create no new, independent wealth that would escape the banks' orbit. From the banker's perspective, a good government is one that spends and spends—what it chooses to spend on is less important. Governments of the right or the left are indistinguishable as long as they are profligate. An agreeable right-wing government might spend huge sums on national defense, an agreeable left-wing one might spend huge sums on domestic social programs, and an agreeable centrist one on both. As the arch-financier Amschel Mayer Rothschild observed in 1838, "Permit me to issue and control the money of a nation, and I care not who makes its laws." The colossal debt generated by government spending is guaranteed by the governments' compulsory taxing power, which drastically reduces the risk of default to the banks. The banks' incentive, then, is to foment an ever-expanding cycle of government spending and taxing. The process only ends with either the destruction of the currency through uncontrolled inflation and/or political collapse. With massive deficits now a commonplace, the world's governments are clearly playing the bankers' game at the expense of the economically productive taxpayers who must ultimately foot the bill.

The implications of the tremendous concentration of power in the hands of the central banks and their constituents, the major private banks, are profound for an age in which power is supposedly exercised by, for, and of the people.

> The central banking system has, from its inception, acted in ways which monopolize industry (thus negating Adam Smith's concept of a free market and competition); militarize nations (financing wars and conquest, imperialism); merging the interests of both the economic and political realms into a holistic ruling class (modeled upon the dual nature of a central bank itself—holding the authority and power of a government body, but representing the interests and submitting to the ownership of private individuals)...
>
> The central bank of a nation finances monopoly industry and imperial states, both of which are created out of debt bondage to the central bank. Both the commercial/industrial elites and political elites merge their interests... This makes up the ruling class of a nation, the capitalists, or owners of the means of production, merging with the political rulers of the nation. One does not represent or

overpower the other, but rather, both serve the interests, and are owned through interest, by a tiny international elite.[14]

While the foregoing summary has an almost Marxian ring, it captures well the state of the political economy today among the world's great nations. Significantly, one of the ten planks of Karl Marx's (1818-83) Communist Manifesto (along with a progressive income tax and public schooling) was the establishment of a central bank, something that all capitalist nations eventually adopted.

Even military power, which in theory would be able to resist financial power, in practice is bought and sold by the latter. The greatest military leader in modern history, Napoleon Bonaparte, who would succumb to the financial strength of a far inferior military adversary, Great Britain, observed, "When a government is dependent upon bankers for money, they and not the leaders of the government control the situation, since the hand that gives is above the hand that takes. . . Money has no motherland; financiers are without patriotism and without decency; their sole object is gain."[15] In a world in which real power is exercised by a small, unaccountable, supranational oligarchy, democracy as such is reduced to little more than an elaborate Punch and Judy show (see also ch. 7). "Democratic" statesmen become front men for the stateless ruling cabal; their job description is to sell in plausible terms to their constituents the massive government spending programs and concomitant deficits that are the banks' bread and butter. The French political theorist

---

14   Andrew Gavin Marshall, *Global Power and Global Government: Evolution and Revolution of the Central Banking System, Part 1*. http://www.globalresearch.ca/index.php?context=va&aid=14464. Accessed September 13, 2019.

15   *Goodreads*. https://www.goodreads.com/quotes/296162-when-a-government-is-dependent-upon-bankers-for-money-they. Accessed April 22, 2020.

Montesquieu (1689–1755), who perhaps more than any thinker inspired the framers of the US Constitution, observed that a key component of popular freedom is the ability of the people's representatives to withhold funds from the executive branch of government: the famous "power of the purse." Increasingly, however, governments depend for their financial existence more on the stateless banking industry that purchases their debt than on the goodwill of the people's representatives. A profound, if quiet, revolution, or indeed coup d'etat.

Under a monetary regime in which prices remain generally stable, profitable speculation is difficult; one must resort to generating real wealth in order to turn a profit. It is only through the cycles of boom and bust and the ensuing huge swings in asset prices that great fortunes can be made. The huge oscillations of the "business cycle" have the tendency to turn ordinary people into speculators, who, of course, then become the prey of the insiders. The owners of the central banks—the major private banks, who directly influence the cycles of boom and bust—profit immensely from their inside positions, which allow them to anticipate the mysterious cycle. And, if something does go wrong, it is always possible to create new money by fiat and bail themselves out.

The world's economies, governments, and peoples are increasingly enslaved to the highly centralized supranational banking system, which lies at the heart of globalization. The process of enslavement has by no means occurred overnight. Numerous statesmen of the past centuries have sought to warn their countrymen of the perils of allowing financial institutions to dominate the legal channels of government. American statesmen alone afford many such examples. In a letter written shortly before he became the first president of the United States, General Washington (1732-99) commented on the use of paper money in the state of Rhode Island: "Paper money has had the effect in your state that it will ever have, to ruin commerce, oppress the honest, and open the door to every species of fraud and injustice."[16] Then there is President Thomas Jefferson (1743–1826):

> And I sincerely believe with you that banking establishments are more dangerous than standing armies; and that the principle of spending money to be paid by posterity, under the name of funding, is but swindling futurity on a large scale.[17]

President Abraham Lincoln (1809-65):

> The money powers prey upon the nation in times of peace, and conspire against it in times of adversity. It is more despotic than monarchy, more insolent than autocracy, more selfish than bureaucracy.... Corporations have been enthroned, an era of corruption will follow and the money power of the country will endeavor and prolong its reign by working upon the prejudices of the people, until the wealth is aggregated into a few hands and the republic is destroyed.[18]

And President Andrew Jackson (1767–1845), who perhaps did more than any American statesman to resist the encroachments of the money power on responsible government:

---

16   *Goodreads.* https://www.goodreads.com/quotes/161884-paper-money-has-had-the-effect-in-your-state-that. Accessed April 22, 2020.

17   "Thomas Jefferson to John Taylor, May 28, 1816." https://founders.archives.gov/documents/Jefferson/03-10-02-0053. Accessed September 13, 2019.

18   *OpEd News.* https://www.opednews.com/Quotations/The-money-powers-prey-upon-the-by-Lincoln-Abraham-111016-448.html. Accessed September 13, 2019.

It is one of the serious evils of our present system of banking that it enables one class of society—and that by no means a numerous one—by its control over the currency, to act injuriously upon the interests of all the others and to exercise more than its just proportion of influence in political affairs.... The mischief springs from the power which the moneyed interest derives from a paper currency which they are able to control, from the multitude of corporations with exclusive privileges which they have succeeded in obtaining in the different States, and which are employed altogether for their benefit; and unless you become more watchful in your States and check this spirit of monopoly and thirst for exclusive privileges you will in the end find that the most important powers of Government have been given or bartered away, and the control over your dearest interests has passed into the hands of these corporations.[19]

The myriad warnings issued through history to free peoples to beware the ascendancy of financial power have in our time gone unheeded. Antichrist, while promising freedom, will complete the enslavement of mankind that is well underway with the aid of Wells' specially contrived, new world money that grows more comprehensive day by day.[20]

---

19   Andrew Jackson, *Farewell Address*. http://www.presidency.ucsb.edu/ws/index.php?pid=67087. Accessed September 13, 2019.

20   Significantly, a digital "Synthetic Hegemonic Currency" was recently proposed by the outgoing Governor of the Bank of England, Mark Carney, to replace the US dollar as the world reserve currency – yet another step toward a comprehensive global currency regime along the lines of Wells. https://www.bankofengland.co.uk/-/media/boe/files/speech/2019/the-growing-challenges-for-monetary-policy-speech-by-mark-carney.pdf?la=en&hash=01A18270247C456901D4043F59D4B79F09B6BFBC. Accessed September 13, 2019.

The Sorcery of Finance

For reasonable, well-intentioned people whose aspirations extend to providing for their families and enjoying the fruits of honest labor, it is difficult to grasp the fantastic revolution that has occurred through the creation of the modern banking system. It is a product of an almost otherworldly dimension of ambition and greed. In a "democratic" age, such a concentration of unaccountable power, beyond the reach of any law or government, with effectively unlimited resources to influence, bribe, and subvert legitimate centers of power and opinion, is almost unimaginable.

> The study of money, above all other fields in economics, is one in which complexity is used to disguise truth or to evade truth, not to reveal it. The process by which banks create money is so simple the mind is repelled. With something so important, a deeper mystery seems only decent.[21]

While "enlightened" modernity is accustomed to look back with horror at the arbitrary power wielded by the pharaohs, emperors, shahs, and tsars, the fact is that we have permitted a far greater and more arbitrary power to be built up in our midst, which now bestrides the globe. The private, independent central bank cartels, able to avail themselves of the sovereign power to create money with none of government's encumbering accountability, constitute what is arguably the greatest power ever seen on earth.

---

21   John Kenneth Galbraith, *Money: Whence It Came, Where It Went* (Princeton, Princeton University, 1975). https://monneta.org/en/money-whence-it-came-where-it-went/. Accessed September 13, 2019.

The modern banking system is best described as "supra-national" rather than "international" because it exists effectively above and beyond the reach of nations. Its full power is difficult to grasp because it does not conform to "enlightened" ideas about how the world works. There is no modern concept that adequately describes its strange hold on the nations of the world. The "mystery of banking"[22] is only adequately captured by pre-modern concepts, in particular the medieval concept of alchemy, a branch of sorcery in which it was believed that base metals could be transmuted into gold, the monetary standard of the day. The medieval alchemists failed for a time, but in the modern banking system their elusive dream has become a reality: it is now possible to create money from nothing. Modern banking is alchemical and its creation of money *ex nihilo* a modern form of sorcery. The bankers' ability to summon money from thin air is a fantastic, magical power that the kings and pharaohs, high priests and wizards of the pre-modern world could only dream of. The most powerful men on earth are now the wizards—literally sorcerers—of high finance. Like wizards and sorcerers of the past, they possess occult gnosis that gives them special power over men without the latter's knowing it. Today's bankers are the magicians who control the world by way of their financial black arts.

The global financial octopus that dominates the nations of the earth in our time seems to be described in the Apocalypse of St. John "as a great harlot who sits on many waters, with whom the kings of the earth committed fornication, and the inhabitants of the earth were made drunk with the wine of her fornication."[23] Furthermore, this harlot sits "on a scarlet beast which was full of names of blasphemy, having seven heads and

---

22   See Murray Rothbard, *The Mystery of Banking* (Ludwig von Mises Institute, 2008).
23   Rev. 17:1-2.

ten horns,"[24] the same number as "the beast rising up out of the sea, having seven heads and ten horns,"[25] Antichrist.

> The woman was arrayed in purple and scarlet, and adorned with gold and precious stones and pearls, having in her hand a golden cup full of abominations and the filthiness of her fornication. And on her forehead a name was written: MYSTERY, BABYLON THE GREAT, THE MOTHER OF HARLOTS AND OF THE ABOMINATIONS OF THE EARTH. I saw the woman, drunk with the blood of the saints and with the blood of the martyrs of Jesus. And when I saw her, I marveled with great amazement… And the woman … is that great city which reigns over the kings of the earth… And the waters which I saw, where the harlot sits, are peoples, multitudes, nations, and tongues.[26]

While the world's political leaders engaged in illicit intercourse with her, "the merchants of the earth have become rich through the abundance of her luxury,"[27] trading in all forms of goods and delicacies and "even the bodies and souls of men."[28] Like the proud and self-satisfied men of our time whose financial power renders them effectively above any temporal law or justice, this whore of Babylon "glorified herself and lived luxuriously," and said "in her heart, 'I sit a queen, and am no widow, and will not see sorrow.' " However, "her plagues will come in one day—death and mourning and famine. And she will be utterly burned with fire, for strong is the Lord God who judges her."[29] The modern world's delights and entertainments—its material

---

24   Rev. 17:3.
25   Rev. 13:1.
26   Rev. 17:4-6, 15, 18.
27   Rev. 18:2-3.
28   Rev. 18:13.
29   Rev. 18:7-8.

riches and the adoration they elicit; the power and glory of its "great men" who move proudly through the medium of global finance—all sustained by modern financial sorcery, will all end in destruction at the Last Judgment.

> Then a mighty angel took up a stone like a great millstone and threw it into the sea, saying, "Thus with violence the great city Babylon shall be thrown down, and shall not be found anymore... For your merchants were the great men of the earth, for by your sorcery all the nations were deceived. And in her was found the blood of prophets and saints, and of all who were slain on the earth."[30]

"Banking was conceived in iniquity and born in sin," and the sorcerous quality of the modern banking system indicates its basic antagonism with the Church, which regards all forms of magic—black or white—as demonic in provenance. By the "sorcery" of the global financial system in our time have "all the nations [been] deceived." Antichrist, the great sorcerer, will avail himself of the alchemical power of global finance to consolidate his world empire and, save for a miracle of God, entrap the majority of mankind into accepting his specially contrived, new world money, his mark, at the cost of their souls.

---

30   Rev. 18:21, 23-4.

CHAPTER 7

THE GLOBALIZATION OF POLITICS

> Democracy… while it lasts is more bloody than either aristocracy or monarchy. Remember, democracy never lasts long. It soon wastes, exhausts, and murders itself. There is never a democracy that did not commit suicide.
>
> US President John Adams (1735–1836)[1]

Democracy has become the shibboleth of political legitimacy in our time. No government can be considered legitimate if it does not cater to the idea of democracy in some way. Even hereditary dictatorships adorn themselves in the trappings of democracy, e.g., holding regular "elections." "Democracy" itself implies the rule of the people (Greek: δῆμος *demos*, "people;" κράτος, *kratos*, "rule"), a particular form of government in which the ruled select their rulers as opposed to other forms such as monarchy or aristocracy in which political office is usually hereditary. Democracy implies the popular basis of governmental authority, that power flows upward from the people to their governors.

But, as we have discussed in the previous chapter, the supranational money power that dominates the nations of the world makes a fiction of their pretense to self-government. The great nations of the world today have been co-opted by a supranational

---

1   "Letter to John Taylor, December 17, 1814." https://founders.archives.gov/documents/Adams/99-02-02-6371. Accessed September 18, 2019.

oligarchy fueled by unprecedented concentrations of wealth. Power in the democratic nations of today, rather than flowing upward as is commonly thought, flows ever more effectively downward, from the rulers and opinion-makers to the masses. This downward flow of power is all the more effective because of the widespread perception of the opposite. The more that people are persuaded that political legitimacy originates with them, the more empowered they feel, the more effectively power may be exercised upon them and the more cooperative they are in their own subjugation. Systems of government such as monarchy or aristocracy, in which power is openly wielded by one or a few, must by nature be more sensitive to the actual needs and desires of their people precisely because such regimes' power base is narrow and because their policies are not made in the name of "the people." From the English Republic to Revolutionary France to Bolshevik Russia, we see that the most tyrannical regimes invariably claim to represent the people as a matter of course even while they wield the most arbitrary and oppressive power.

For most of history, the masses were effectively excluded from participation in governance. They still are, but in modern democracy they are induced to believe otherwise. While a handful of people wield power—as always—the masses have come to believe that, through voting, public opinion polls, and the prevalence of democratic rhetoric, they participate in the process of governance. Even while they are excluded from power, yet they feel themselves participants in it. This is an astonishing revolution but not as customarily understood. It is, one might say, a psychological or even spiritual revolution, in that now huge numbers in the world's great nations—their nominal electorate—believe that they meaningfully participate in the governance of their societies even while they are cajoled and compelled into ever more profound servitude. As German writer Johann

Wolfgang von Goethe said, "None are more hopelessly enslaved than those who falsely believe they are free."

The "democratic" revolutions of the modern era—especially those of 1789 and later—aimed at concentrating power in a single center based on an exclusive claim to represent the people. As crimes were sometimes committed in the name of God by Christian monarchs, so far greater crimes came to be committed in the name of the people by the revolutionary regimes that overthrew them. In the modern age, as long as a regime can effectively present its actions as done in the name of the people (or, couched slightly differently, the workers in the case of Communist regimes or the *Volk* in the case of German National Socialism), it can get away with anything.

Modern democracy is a means of giving the ruling power direct access to the masses without interfering intermediary institutions. Authority in pre-modern societies was distributed among the central government as well as numerous associations and institutions—the Church, clubs, guilds, local councils, communes, etc.—that served to disseminate and temper the exercise of central power. Increasingly, modern democracy has denuded society of these mediating institutions and left the individual exposed to the unbridled glare of modern central state power. Those independent institutions that remain—large corporations and banks, for example—can so effectively manipulate "democratic" institutions that they act virtually above the law. Modern democracy's ostensible characteristics, with its professed goals of building coalitions, incorporating varied opinions, and of not permitting any one representative institution or figure too much power, make it necessarily vulnerable to non-democratic sources of power—large businesses, wealthy individuals, media interests of broad reach, secret societies—that act out of self-interest and possess none of democracy's scruples. Such a government naturally becomes the tool of powerful special interests whose power is all the more magnified because they can shelter behind the democratic façade. Increasingly, the individual has nowhere to turn, no institution in which he may find shelter against the prehensile power of the "deep state," the integrated network of effectively unaccountable financial, corporate, and bureaucratic interests whose power grows apace.

DEMOCRACY AND THE CHURCH

The Western perception of Christ has evolved with the development of democratic sensibilities. From the Supreme Monarch Who will judge the nations and Who reigns in His Church and in the hearts of His faithful now and forever, the democratic age has reduced Christ to a feel-good Messiah distributing worldly delights to the "saved" and Who will not reign until the "thousand years" begins on earth sometime hence. The dethronement and "democratization" of Christ made way for the regicides who deposed and murdered the Christian royal houses in the revolutions of the modern age. The age of democracy has rendered kingship, as a meaningful or operative idea, kaput in both a political and a spiritual sense.

The fact that the world may have rejected Christ as King, however, does not mean that the throne remains empty. The revolutions of the modern era testify to the fact that kingly authority is the only true authority: no matter how "democratic" the aspirations of modern revolutionaries, a king figure has always arisen to bring order to the chaos that revolution inevitably brings. Having deposed a rightful king, sooner or later a pretender will take up the mantle: the murder of Charles I gave way to the tyranny of Cromwell; the murder of Louis XVI to the tyrannies of Robespierre and Napoleon; the murder of Tsar Nicholas II to Lenin and Stalin; the deposition of the Karadjordevic dynasty in Yugoslavia to Tito; the expulsion of the Turkish Sultan by the Young Turks to the dictatorship of Atatürk and the Armenian Genocide; the end of the Hohenzollern dynasty in Germany to the invidious Weimar Republic and to Hitler; the deposition of the Iranian Shah to the Ayatollah Khomeini; etc. In time, Antichrist will arise to bring order to a confused world that, like the wayward Israelites of the Prophet Samuel's day and revolutionaries throughout the ages, will have rejected the Lord and will be desperate for "a king to judge us."[2]

In the contemporary, democratic world, technology provides a special connection between ruler and ruled. In ancient times, few saw the actual faces of their rulers with any frequency. Thanks to electronic communication, it is now possible for most anyone to see on a daily or hourly basis the faces of his ostensible governors. Modern media permit a sort of intimate participation with power—albeit a highly superficial and misleading one—on a mass level that is without precedent. Even the empires of the ancient world, in which the autocrat was considered divine, never enjoyed the sort of direct influence over their subjects that modern technology affords. When the time comes, Antichrist's face will appear on every computer, on every television screen, on every personal electronic device (or whatever then prevails) and will afford a direct and instantaneous connection with his world subjects.[3]

The figure of the coming Antichrist illumines the larger purpose that modern democracy serves. Democracy is a logical concomitant of globalization because, by nature, it seeks to include all people in political life rather than merely a designated minority. Globalization amounts to a horizontal form of political integration, whereas democracy is vertical. Democracy provides a direct connection between the masses and the rulers—again, not to enable ordinary people to participate in governance but to permit ever more unimpeded and comprehensive control

---

2 1 Sam. 8:5.
3 See Rev. 13:15.

by central power over its subjects. Yet Antichrist's kingdom, as total a tyranny as will have ever existed, may retain all the trappings of democracy, which will be a key to the completeness of his mastery. The people of the world will truly identify with their master and will give him their hearts and minds to an extent that the tyrants of the ancient world would envy. Democracy permits a peculiar connection between rulers and ruled; while trumpeting the separation of the religious and the temporal, it confuses them to an unprecedented degree. The mass rallies of the Protestant megachurches, the colossal papal masses, the prayer services of the megamosques, and the huge political rallies and conventions—all possessed of the same massive aesthetic that overwhelms individual reason—are increasingly indistinguishable.

Living in a self-styled enlightened and democratic age, it may be difficult to believe that the world will someday accept an individual as its king and savior. Indeed, the reign of Antichrist would not be possible in a world of sane, rational people with their reason unbefogged. But because ours is an age of confusion in which evil masquerades as good, the ugly as the beautiful, the false as the true, in which nothing is stable and everything is jumbled together, so Antichrist will be able to pull off his great deception by appearing as the one true, good, and able man left.

PROPAGANDA

Key to the formation of beliefs and the stimulus to action in the democratic age is propaganda, an instrument employed to tremendous effect in the modern globalizing world. A simple definition of propaganda is "ideas, facts, or allegations spread deliberately to further one's cause or to damage an opposing cause" as well as "a public action having such an effect."[4] Jacques Ellul, however, cogently demonstrates that what distinguishes propaganda from mere "ideas, facts, or allegations" is its very deliberate intention to induce an action. Propaganda is not about getting people to think differently; in fact, *thinking* is the last thing the propagandist wants to stimulate in his target audience. Propaganda is intended to produce a reflex of certain actions or the acceptance of certain propositions *without* rational consideration. As soon as the target starts *thinking* in anything other than a reflexive or conditioned way the propagandist has failed for the simple reason that propositions accepted through rational thought may just as readily be discarded in the same manner. The field of rational thought, of reasoned argument and the deliberate weighing of evidence, is far too uncertain a playing field in the results-oriented, high-stakes game of social control. Propaganda is about bringing about a desired result notwithstanding what people think. Propaganda, as opposed to reasoned argument, shapes beliefs through the discouragement, rather than encouragement, of thought. As often as not, beliefs follow from induced action rather than the other way around. Successful propaganda stimulates an action—a vote, say, or some other political act—which then demands rationalization. Propagandized belief systems are by nature the engineered result of induced action and rationalization rather than of reasoned consideration.[5]

Lest we imagine that propaganda is the instrument only of totalitarian governments and evil despots, Edward Bernays, the great mass psychologist and father of modern propaganda (and Sigmund Freud's nephew) assures us otherwise.

---

4   Merriam-Webster Dictionary. http://www.merriam-webster.com/dictionary/Propaganda. Accessed September 14, 2019. An adequate definition.
5   Jacques Ellul, *Propaganda: The Formation of Men's Attitudes* (New York, Alfred A. Knopf, 1973), 29.

The conscious and intelligent manipulation of the organized habits and opinions of the masses is an important element in democratic society. Those who manipulate this unseen mechanism of society constitute an invisible government which is the true ruling power of our country.

We are governed, our minds are molded, our tastes formed, our ideas suggested, largely by men we have never heard of. This is a logical result of the way in which our democratic society is organized. Vast numbers of human beings must cooperate in this manner if they are to live together as a smoothly functioning society.

… Whatever attitude one chooses toward this condition, it remains a fact that in almost every act of our daily lives, whether in the sphere of politics or business, in our social conduct or our ethical thinking, we are dominated by the relatively small number of persons . . . who understand the mental processes and social patterns of the masses. It is they who pull the wires which control the public mind.[6]

Propaganda by nature endeavors to be total; it employs all forms of media at its disposal in order to inundate the individual and the mass and thereby fosters a comprehensive, self-contained worldview that leaves no aspect of life untouched. A man is fed propaganda at breakfast by the newspaper he reads, at work by a computer, at home by the television, in the evening by the cinema, at bedtime by a novel—and now in between by all manner of advertising and electronic media. These apparently different sources of opinion, on the surface appearing to make unrelated or even contrary points, reinforce the fundamental

---

6   Edward Bernays, *Propaganda* (Brooklyn, Ig Publishing,1928, 2005), 37.

propaganda myth without the target audience becoming conscious of it.[7]

> Propaganda tries to surround man by all possible routes, in the realm of feelings as well as ideas, by playing on his will or on his needs, through his conscious and his unconscious, assailing him in both his private and his public life. It furnishes him with a complete system for explaining the world, and provides immediate incentives to action. We are here in the presence of an organized myth that tries to take hold of the entire person. Through the myth it creates, propaganda imposes a complete range of intuitive knowledge, susceptible of only one interpretation, unique and one-sided, and precluding any divergence. This myth becomes so powerful that it invades every area of consciousness, leaving no faculty or motivation intact. It stimulates in the individual a feeling of exclusiveness, and produces a biased attitude. The myth has such motive force that, once accepted, it controls the whole of the individual, who becomes immune to any other influence.[8]

To a great extent, propaganda has come to fulfill the traditional role of religion. It is comprehensive; it provides a point of reference for all incoming information; it colors the entire outlook of the individual with respect to all aspects of reality. The successfully propagandized audience is fully capable of thinking one thing and acting in a totally contrary manner without cognizance of any contradiction. Modern, "democratic man"—perpetually bombarded by propaganda to buy something, sell something, vote for somebody, support a cause, etc.—is reduced to a ganglion of irreconcilable contradictions

---

7   Ellul, *Propaganda*, 113.
8   Ibid., 11.

of which he is mostly unaware. To try to point out the contradictions, to encourage rational and independent reflection as
to why he acts the way he does and believes what he does, is to
risk provoking a hostile reaction.

By nature, propaganda cultivates in its target audience an
extravagant confidence, a false certainty with respect to the
propaganda myth—indeed, a Gnostic attitude—that is directly
opposite to the humility that is at the heart of all true wisdom
and understanding. Propaganda constantly flatters modern
man as the most sophisticated, intelligent, highly evolved representative of the species, far savvier than his credulous and
superstitious forbears, enslaved to priests and despots. To try to
encourage thoughtful reflection outside the propaganda myth
threatens to overturn modern man's worldview and expose
that he has actually been sold a bill of goods, that he is a dupe.
The instinctive reaction, a consequence of propaganda itself,
is to shoot the bearer of such unwelcome news. Propaganda
encourages the growth of "fundamentalists," "true believers"
whose personalities become so intertwined with a given propaganda myth that any criticism—even reasoned, well-meaning
questions—is met with hostility.[9] Any skeptic, or even anyone
merely unwilling to champion the accepted myth, becomes
not an interlocutor but an enemy.[10] The extent to which an
individual has been successfully propagandized is often revealed
by the degree of emotional aggression he shows to lines of
reasoning that cut against his worldview. A man whose beliefs
and actions are grounded in thoughtful reflection will be able
to engage contrary evidence and argument in a sober fashion;
a man whose actions and beliefs are shaped by propaganda will
instinctively wall himself off from reasoned discussion because
it is by nature the enemy of his propagandized worldview (even

---

9   Ibid., 166.
10   Ibid., 213.

if that worldview happens to contain some truthful elements). Propaganda effectively turns its target audience into neurotics who must "stop their ears"[11] when presented with ideas that conflict with their own or, indeed, to kill the messenger.

Modern democratic man, conditioned to believe that he is more perceptive than his ancestors, free from prejudice and fallacy, and both able and entitled to participate in the shaping of the world he inhabits, finds himself in the midst of irresoluble tension when his induced assumptions make contact with reality.[12]

> To the average man who tries to keep informed, a world emerges that is astonishingly incoherent, absurd, and irrational, which changes rapidly and constantly for reasons he cannot understand.... Man cannot stand this; he cannot live in an absurd and incoherent world . . . nor can he accept the idea that the problems, which sprout all around him, cannot be solved, or that he himself has no value as an individual and is subject to the turn of events.... And the more complicated the problems are, the more simple the explanations must be; the more fragmented the canvas, the simpler the pattern; the more difficult the question, the more all-embracing the solution; the more menacing the reduction of his own worth, the greater the need for boosting his ego. All this propaganda—and only propaganda—can give him.[13]

In our present age of confusion, propaganda amounts to a necessity for those "fearful" and of "little faith"[14], who thirst for someone to sort out modernity's complexities and contradictions for them. Propaganda, thus, is not just a question of evil

---

11   Acts 7:57.
12   Ellul, *Propaganda*, 92.
13   Ibid., 145-6.
14   Matt. 8:26.

manipulators leading the masses by their noses; propaganda fills a social need, a void left by the evacuation from society of authentic Christianity.

But a few of the major propaganda myths of our time include democracy, progress, evolution, and climate change.[15] Because they are products of propaganda, however, and may be fairly categorized as myths, they are not for that reason false. Ellul points out that, while propaganda is by nature manipulative, it is not synonymous with "lie" as is customarily supposed. Of course, propaganda often will be untrue, but it can just as easily be true even if it is by nature misleading. Merely because propaganda is used in support of an end does not therefore make that end false or wrong. Employing genuine, verifiable facts (when available) is indispensable to the propagandist because it lends to his larger purpose the veneer of truth and authority.

In a popular context, in which political action largely succeeds or fails on the reaction of the public, propaganda becomes the indispensable connection between institutional power and the masses. Even genuinely "true" or "right" causes must engage in propaganda if they are to be politically effective. No matter how right one's cause may be, to refuse to engage in propaganda is to relegate it to political irrelevance. The unhappy consequence is that, in the public square, what is true and what is false, what is virtuous and what is ignoble, are reduced to competing propagandas. The only way to make an independent judgment on real merits is to cut through the propaganda and engage in genuine, reasoned, independent thought. But the findings of such an endeavor, the product of non-propagandized reflection, will by nature be rendered politically irrelevant. Truth, then, in modern democratic circumstances, is either compromised and tainted through its incorporation into propaganda or it is forced to the

---

15   The Gnostic certainty surrounding "climate change" has a special role to play in the ongoing centralization of power in our time, about which more anon.

political sidelines. For Christianity to compete in the modern political arena requires it to abandon its otherworldliness and submit to a propagandistic framework, which is the essence of the various attempts by Western denominations to be "relevant" to the "problems of today," etc., and ultimately to make peace with the world. For otherworldly Orthodoxy to try to make itself relevant in such a sense is by nature self-defeating.

Democracy and the Passions

A key mechanism by which propaganda exerts its influence over the mass mind is through the manipulation of human passions. The passions may be thought of as the irrational quality of the human nature as opposed to the rational, noetic nature that man originally possessed unblemished in paradise. By appealing to the passions, the propagandist seeks to circumvent the rational side of man and minimize the risk of the target becoming cognizant of his being manipulated. By triggering a passion and thus short-circuiting rationality, the propagandist induces the target to imagine that he himself has decided on the desired action in an independent and rational manner; an impassioned mind readily manufactures its own excellent reasons for doing what its carnal self has already decided. The target whose passions have been adroitly enflamed in fact becomes the propagandist's most ardent cheerleader, conjuring all sorts of reasons why doing the propagandist's will is the clear, expedient, rational choice.

By stimulating a passion—pride, lust, greed, envy—and then proffering a means of satisfying it, the propagandist achieves a peculiar power over his target. The process is analogous to poisoning someone and then offering him the antidote. The most obvious examples of the widespread manipulation of public passions today may be seen in the realm of commerce. The supplier of some good or service seeks through advertising to incite a given passion in the target audience while simultaneously providing the means of sating it: buy a car, feel rich, look better than the next guy, get the girl, etc. The process is a simple one and is designed to short-circuit human rationality such that the target responds in a Pavlovian manner. Much commerce today is certainly not about supplying an existing public need or even an existing want; rather, it is about injecting the public with a toxic passion such that purchasing the intended product (or voting for the intended candidate) appears to be the only possible means of satisfying the particular passion.

That today the term "passion" enjoys positive connotations itself speaks volumes about the extent to which the public's passions are systematically manipulated. In the classical tradition, "passion" possessed decidedly negative connotations; in simple terms, it meant pain or suffering as in the "passion of Jesus Christ." More generally, a "passion" was a vice, a crippling weakness that enslaved the mind and body, which (as the classical tradition was well aware) did indeed cause suffering. But "passion" now is used in almost wholly positive ways: to be a "passionate person", for example, or to "follow your passion," is a very good thing: it connotes one wholly alive, energetic, and "ambitious" (another word turned upside-down). A salient example of how modern society has revolutionized—literally, revolved, turned upside down—the traditional understandings of vice and virtue, pride, once the cardinal sin, is now a capital virtue. Pride rather than humility has become in contemporary society the supreme mark of mental and spiritual health. That passion and pride are now understood as good rather than evil testifies to the broad success of generations of propagandists who have plied their trade to such effect that the public has come to accept the very weaknesses that the propagandists exploit as strengths.

The systematic cultivation of public passions in modern democracies bears directly on what is self-consciously the pre-eminent democratic virtue, "freedom."[16] "Freedom" in the modern sense implies the ability to do what one chooses: freedom of worship, of speech, of association, etc. But, contrary to modern sentiments, classical and Christian civilization understood freedom as primarily an internal, rather than an external, state in which man had overcome the vicissitudes of his carnal nature. Freedom was attained through the acquisition of the virtues, which liberated the soul from enslavement to fleeting worldly things and restored the *nous*—man's highest rational faculty reflecting the divine image—to its rightful pre-eminence. The man who had conquered his passions could think, speak, and act in accordance with his noetic reason irrespective of his outward circumstances. As St. Augustine put it sixteen centuries ago,

> the good man, although he is a slave, is free; but the bad man, even if he reigns, is a slave, and that not of one man, but, what is far more grievous, of as many masters as he has vices; of which vices when the divine Scripture treats, it says, "For of whom any man is overcome, to the same he is also the bond-slave."[17]

In a democracy, as the acknowledged source of political legitimacy, the people may be said to reign, yet, if they are ruled by their passions, do they remain slaves. Indeed, those who reign, in whatever circumstances, are vulnerable to pride, the most insidious of the passions. Acton's adage that power corrupts applies as much to democracies as other forms of government.

---

16   See, for example, Plato's *Republic*, bk. VIII, "Freedom, I replied; which, as they tell you in a democracy, is the glory of the State—and that therefore in a democracy alone will the freeman of nature deign to dwell." http://www.gutenberg.org/files/1497/1497-h/1497-h.htm#link2H_4_0011. Accessed September 14, 2019.
17   St. Augustine, *City of God*, bk. IV, ch. 3. http://www.newadvent.org/fathers/120104.htm. Accessed September 14, 2019. See also, 2 Pet. 2:19.

Because he sees himself as self-governing, with no man his natural superior, democratic man can in time come to resent all limitations on his freedom, no matter how necessary or reasonable, as unjust impingements on his sovereignty. One of Plato's greatest insights into democracy was its tendency to flatter its people and to engender a pride that in time can subvert the authority of democratic government itself.

> And above all … see how sensitive the citizens [of democracy] become; they chafe impatiently at the least touch of authority and at length, as you know, they cease to care even for the laws, written or unwritten; they will have no one over them.[18]

In a democracy, the prideful effect of power threatens to infect not just the one or the few but the populace at large. Whereas it is possible, in principle, to replace a bad king with a better one or to reconstitute an ineffectual aristocracy, there is little to be done with a corrupted public when it considers itself the fount of political legitimacy. A prideful public will not abide uncomfortable realities that reflect poorly on the character of the polity even if facing those realities is necessary to its survival. Policy then becomes a function of appealing to public passions, which in turn transfers real power from the people at large to those few who possess the resources to manipulate public passions on a grand scale. A democracy that cannot control its passions amounts in fact to an oligarchy ruled by the directors of public opinion—as Bernays described above.

When the public's passions grow to such an extent that they refuse all legitimate authority, no democratic government can be effective. Whereas in times of strength and self-confidence a

---

18   Plato, *The Republic*, bk. VIII. http://www.gutenberg.org/files/1497/1497-h/1497-h.htm#link2H_4_0011. Accessed September 14, 2019.

democracy exalts freedom above all, in cases when its logic has laid waste to constituted authority, it is willing to sacrifice every-thing for order. It is then that the tyrant emerges, a strongman who can restore order in the only way possible, through force. While promising freedom, most "democratic" revolutions of the modern era followed a common trajectory of increasing license leading to chaos and bloodshed culminating in despotism—the suicide mentioned by Adams above.

> The excess of liberty, whether in States or individuals, seems only to pass into excess of slavery.... And so tyranny naturally arises out of democracy, and the most aggra-vated form of tyranny and slavery out of the most extreme form of liberty.[19]

Thus Plato theorized that democracy, while exalting freedom, sows the seeds of its own eventual disintegration into tyranny. While the emergence of a tyrant is the logical conclusion of a democracy run amuck, the erosion of liberty itself is often a gradual process that parallels the growth of unchecked public passions. As individuals lose their willingness to restrain them-selves, they in turn must be restrained; when self-control departs from a society and passion gains the upper hand, compulsive power must correspondingly increase to provide the necessary ordering force. In a tyranny, the passions of the people are constrained by force; in a free society, they are held in check by public morals. Moral self-restraint is the true means by which a people realize self-government—it is the true basis of freedom.

> Men are qualified for civil liberty in exact proportion to their disposition to put moral chains upon their own appetites... Society cannot exist unless a controlling

---

19   Ibid., bk. VII.

power upon will and appetite be placed somewhere, and the less of it there is within, the more there must be without. It is ordained in the eternal constitution of things that men of intemperate minds cannot be free. Their passions forge their fetters.[20]

But "evil communications corrupt good manners"[21] and the moral chains that once bound human appetite have come unstuck in our time. The propagandists achieved a tremendous victory when they successfully persuaded modern man that moral behavior constituted an impediment to his freedom rather than its guarantor. The classical and Christian tradition knew that morality served not to impair individual freedom but to strengthen it. Moral behavior bridles the passions and liberates man's higher, God-given reason; on a social level, it inures a society from systematic manipulation by forestalling propaganda's chief operative mechanism, namely, the manipulation of the passions. The man in control of his mind, body, and soul, who can see clearly and does not succumb to passionate provocation, is a man truly free and the only type capable of governing himself.

However, a soul that has emerged victorious over the passions, whose *nous* is once again in control of its lesser faculties, is problematic for the interests who would prey upon the public for their private advantage. A self-controlled, self-governing public is poor soil for propaganda. To have its proper effect, propaganda requires a public square in which the passions have as free a play as possible. If allowed sufficient opportunity, private commercial and political interests will in time progressively eviscerate a society's moral principles, which are the primary

---

20   Edmund Burke, *Reflections on the Revolution in France*, ch. 4. https://www.goodreads.com/quotes/293641-men-are-qualified-for-civil-liberty-in-exact-proportion-to. Accessed September 14, 2019.
21   1 Cor. 15:33

obstacle to the successful manipulation of public sympathies. And that, indeed, brings us to today. While modern democratic man may appear outwardly free to choose, his capacity for rational choice lies prostrate before his enflamed passions and those who manipulate them.

> A vitiated state of morals, a corrupted public conscience, is incompatible with freedom. No free government, or the blessings of liberty, can be preserved to any people but by a firm adherence to justice, moderation, temperance, frugality, and virtue; and by a frequent recurrence to fundamental principles.[22]

Since freedom and liberty in the modern sense connote the unrestricted right to do whatever one pleases, they show themselves as fundamentally self-destructive because they breed precisely the opposite of the moderation and temperance necessary for their sustained continuation. The unrestricted right to satisfy one's passions is not a mark of liberty at all but a short stop on the way to tyranny. When liberty in the traditional sense—freedom from passion—morphs into liberty in the modern sense—freedom to indulge passion—an Orwellian point is reached where freedom becomes slavery.

> Once gratification of passion becomes the definition of liberty, then liberty becomes synonymous with bondage because he who controls the passion controls the man. Liberty, as defined by [the Marquis de] Sade, becomes a prelude to the most insidious form of control by man precisely because it is based on the stealthy manipulation of his passions. This was the genius of Enlightenment

---

22   Patrick Henry. http://quotes.liberty-tree.ca/quote_blog/Patrick.Henry. Quote.7125. Accessed September 14, 2019.

politics, which is in reality nothing more than a physics of vice: Incite the passion, control the man.[23]

The freedom to satisfy one's passions implies the freedom to enflame the passions of others, and those who can enflame the public's passions most effectively constitute the invisible government of which Bernays spoke, those "who pull the wires which control the public mind."

Plato, St. Augustine, Burke, Adams and other men of wisdom knew that the key to a free society was not arithmetic—whether the many or the few made the laws—but virtue. Men will control themselves or they will be controlled by others, a fact that those enamored of power intuitively grasp even if their modern subjects no longer do. The Christian societies of past taught their people to accept established authority as Providential and to free themselves from the illusion that true freedom could be achieved through any external agency. Modern democracy instead encourages a fictive political freedom while discouraging the cultivation of virtue and self-control, which alone fosters genuine liberty. The current fetish for democracy tickles the pride of modern man, who is reluctant to acknowledge any power greater than himself and who disdains past wisdom, which knew that no system of government is incorruptible or permanent. No matter how exquisitely an instrument of government may be designed, no matter how noble the intentions of its progenitors, it will in time succumb to human passions if not for the continuous insistence on the cultivation of virtue and self-control.

It is in vain to say that democracy is less vain, less proud, less selfish, less ambitious, or less avaricious than aristocracy or monarchy. It is not true, in fact, and nowhere appears

---

23   E. Michael Jones, *Libido Dominandi: Sexual Liberation and Political Control* (South Bend, Fidelity, 2000), 59.

in history. Those passions are the same in all men, under all forms of simple government, and when unchecked, produce the same effects of fraud, violence, and cruelty.[24]

The fate of modern democracy was cogently prophesied by one of our time's most trenchant observers, who foresaw both the oligarchical nature of political power as well as the repressive function of propaganda. Much as Alexis de Tocqueville wrote a century before in describing a soft form of totalitarianism and said that, in a modern democracy, "The will of man is not shattered, but softened, bent, and guided.... Such a power does not destroy, but it prevents existence; it does not tyrannize, but it compresses, enervates, extinguishes, and stupefies,"[25] so Aldous Huxley, in the conclusion to his 1958 work, *Brave New World Revisited*, forewarned:

> by means of ever more effective methods of mind-manipulation, the democracies will change their nature; the quaint old forms—elections, parliaments, Supreme Courts and all the rest—will remain. The underlying substance will be a new kind of non-violent totalitarianism. All the traditional names, all the hallowed slogans will remain exactly what they were in the good old days... Meanwhile the ruling oligarchy and its highly trained elite of soldiers, policemen, thought-manufacturers and mind-manipulators will quietly run the show as they see fit.[26]

---

24   John Adams. "Letter to John Taylor, December 17, 1814." https://founders. archives.gov/documents/Adams/99-02-02-6371. Accessed September 15, 2019.

25   See ch. 2.

26   Aldous Huxley, *Brave New World Revisited*, 1958. https://libertyblitzkrieg. com/2014/01/21/brave-new-world-revisited-key-excerpts-and-my-summary/. Accessed September 15, 2019.

It is hard to deny that a progressive "non-violent totalitarianism" fairly describes the political and social life of much of the developed world today.

THE ANTICHRISTIAN TENDENCY OF DEMOCRACY

Popular politics have always possessed a messianic, and therefore, antichristian quality, a tendency to produce antichrists who, explicitly or implicitly, promise to save their people from their existential plight. This is especially true in modern democracies, in which power is necessarily bound up with a direct appeal to the people. While public opinion (the "opinion of incompetents"[27]) rarely drives policy, it is nonetheless an imperative consideration to policy-makers. They must pay great heed to public opinion because to transgress it can prove fatal in a "democratic" age. Propaganda serves to shape and guide public opinion and make it amenable to policy[28] (to "manufacture consent" in the words of Walter Lippmann and Noam Chomsky). It is the shrewd propagandist who is able to determine how far he may push public opinion before it rebounds against him.

The successful democratic politician uses propaganda to attract a broader, more committed following than his competitors. The logic of democratic contests leads to the emergence of candidates who elicit feelings of total loyalty from the widest possible following. This is the natural aim of almost any modern political campaign. Demagogues (literally: "teachers of the people") such as Napoleon and Hitler are classic examples of this principle, but even indifferent figures such as contemporary American and European presidents and prime ministers also

---

27   Ellul, *Propaganda*, 125.
28   Ibid., 124-6.

fill this category. The almost irresistible tendency is to promise, even if only implicitly, more than one's competitors so as to attract the largest, most committed following. This logic will predictably lead, in time, to political figures who will promise more and more to win support until they are finally promising a virtual paradise on earth. Popular feeling toward a man whom one believes can deliver an earthly paradise will, by nature, be total, reverential, worshipful. Such a political figure then is by nature a messiah figure, an antichrist, promising salvation for his faithful who have handed over to him their votes along with their hearts and minds. As globalization progressively transforms the world into a single polity that functions as one, the opportunity grows for a popular leader to arise who will persuade the mass of the world to regard him as their savior, as God come to earth.

As a case in point, we will briefly examine the victorious 2008 presidential campaign of Barack Obama. Our point here is not to single out President Obama or to make a partisan point. As we have noted, all democratic politics are at least somewhat antichristian, and Mr. Obama perhaps only played the game better than his rivals, but he provided a striking example of democracy's antichristian tendencies. During his campaign for his party's nomination, then-Senator Obama said in a speech to a New Hampshire audience, "My job this morning is to be so persuasive . . . that a light will shine through that window, a beam of light will come down upon you, you will experience an epiphany, and you will suddenly realize that you must go to the polls and vote for Barack." Even if considered meta-phorically, the word "epiphany" and the unmistakably religious imagery coupled with the language of command ("you *must* go to the polls") bespeak a man who is playing a messianic role and, furthermore, is not shy about it. This latter point is especially significant. As we have said, almost any successful democratic politician today evinces antichristian characteristics, but it is something of a novelty for a candidate to integrate it consciously into his campaign strategy.

At a Catholic Charities dinner during his campaign, Senator Obama joked, "I was not born in a manger. I was actually born on Krypton and sent here by my father, Jor-el, to save the Planet Earth," in a reference to the story of the comic book hero Superman. It would presumably have been unacceptable to have said the opposite, that he was indeed born in a manger and is Jesus Christ, but the savior idea is clearly implied especially in conjunction with the Superman reference and saving the earth. While it may be said that this was only a joke, it is important to bear in mind that jokes serve as important political tools. Through them, it is possible to broach topics still inaccessible to non-facetious comment. If one causes offence through touching a taboo, one can always beat a retreat by saying that it was only a joke. Over time, insinuating an idea through humor paves the way for eventual, more explicit, acceptance. Jokes about Obama's messiahship further a process of intimating the idea that a political figure could someday actually be the messiah.

While Mr. Obama generally limited himself to implicit messianic references, many of his supporters were quite explicit. Various graphic artists portrayed Obama in unmistakably messianic ways. These images would often show beams of light emanating from the candidate or coronas surrounding his head. Even major mainstream news magazines ran covers with Obama surrounded by heavenly light; one leading US journal of opinion ran on its cover an explicitly iconographic portrait of Obama gesturing as Christ complete with halo.[29] A major German publication featured Obama on its cover during the 2008 campaign with the title, "The Messiah Factor: Barack Obama

---

29   *The New Republic*, January 30, 2008. https://enacademic.com/dic.nsf/enwiki/161544. Accessed September 15, 2019.

and the Yearning for a New America."[30] Additionally, Obama's campaign surrounded their candidate with simple, emphatic, religious-sounding language such as "Believe," "Yes We Can," "Change," "Hope," and finally a mystical "O" suggestive of the candidate's surname and the halo in which he was often seen. In an era in which public relations has reached the level of an advanced science with nothing left to chance, it is implausible to argue that these messianic comparisons were merely fortuitous.

During his campaign, Obama went out of his way to court overseas public opinion to an extraordinary degree. Uniting in himself a varied racial and religious background, he presented himself as not merely an American seeking his nation's highest office but as a man above all nations with whom all of the world's peoples could identify. His widespread overseas appeal and his protean ability to be all things to all people, to unite in himself people from across the globe, was remarkable. And certainly President Obama proved a great believer in globalization. As he pronounced in a speech in Berlin, Germany, while campaigning for the presidency:

> Partnership and cooperation among nations is not a choice; it is the one way, the only way, to protect our common security and advance our common humanity. That is why the greatest danger of all is to allow new walls to divide us from one another. The walls between old allies on either side of the Atlantic cannot stand. The walls between the countries with the most and those with the least cannot stand. The walls between races and tribes; natives and immigrants; Christian and Muslim and

---

30   *Der Spiegel*, July 2008. https://www.dialoginternational.com/dialog_international/2008/02/der-spiegel-cov.html. Accessed September 15, 2019.

Jew cannot stand. These now are the walls we must tear down.[31]

The messianic overtones to Obama's campaign were apparent enough to his competitor, the Republican Senator from Arizona, John McCain (1936-2018), whose campaign ran a television commercial mocking Obama's messianic insinuations. The calculation on the part of the McCain campaign was, presumably, that the American electorate was still sufficiently Christian or otherwise sensible enough to find offensive a presidential candidate comparing himself to Jesus Christ. Surely, many Americans did find Obama's messianic posturing and the quasi-worship of his followers offensive, but he nonetheless won decisively. Following his victory, some official White House photographs continued to follow a messianic theme, employing the presidential seal as a background halo.

Obama's youth, his meteoric rise to high office, his obscure background, and not least his peculiar magnetism are all traits that Antichrist will possess. While he has certainly advanced the antichristian program, President Obama and his advisors in some way merely discerned the spirit of the times better than their political peers and exploited it more nimbly. In light of Obama's impressive success, it seems likely that other political entrepreneurs will adopt his tactics in future.

A chief component of the age of confusion is unhealthy, impassioned conjecture as to who precisely Antichrist might be. During the 2008 campaign, speculation in some Protestant circles that Obama himself might actually be the Antichrist was sufficiently widespread to attract the attention of at least one major television news channel, which devoted a short piece to

---

31   Speech given in Berlin, Germany, July 24, 2008. https://www.nytimes.com/2008/07/24/us/politics/24text-obama.html. Accessed September 15, 2019.

the question.[32] While Barack Obama certainly partook of the antichristian spirit of the times, the idea that he could have been Antichrist himself hugely underestimates the power of the deception that Antichrist will embody when he finally appears.

President Obama certainly was not the first, nor will he be the last, statesman to cultivate a messianic aura (predictably, much of the messianic sheen wore off once candidate Obama made contact with the terrestrial realities of day-to-day governance). In examining President Obama, we are not trying to make a partisan point; he is merely a recent incarnation of the antichristian spirit that moves with mounting force through global democratic politics. America alone offers plenty of other examples: Presidents Franklin Roosevelt, Kennedy, and Reagan come to mind. That messianic figures appear from time to time on the American political stage should not be surprising in light of America's long-standing. self-conscious "exceptionalism" as a land specially favored by God.

That American messianic politics is truly bipartisan is attested to by Presidents Kennedy and Reagan, both fond of referring to the United States as the "shining city on a hill" destined to lead the world in truth, justice, and righteousness. While their conscious reference was to John Winthrop's sermon of 1630 written aboard the ship Arbella,[33] the original reference (if they knew it—certainly Winthrop did) was the words of the Lord to His disciples that they "are the light of the world. A city that is set on a hill cannot be hidden."[34] While Winthrop, Kennedy, and Reagan were thinking of Anglophone America as the "shining city," the Lord had in mind the Church: on the one hand, a terrestrial political organization built by men; on the other, the

---

32   *CNN*, August 15, 2008. https://www.newsbusters.org/blogs/nb/matthew-balan/2008/08/15/cnn-mccain-trying-make-voters-think-obama-biblical-antichrist. Accessed September 15, 2019.

33   See ch. 5.

34   Matt. 5:14.

eternal "Kingdom not of this world" founded by the blood of Jesus Christ. That leaders of a self-consciously "Christian" nation such as America could confuse the eternal, invincible Church of Christ with the temporal state they represent testifies to the extent to which true Christian principles of order have been supplanted in our time by antichristian ones. Shortly before assuming the highest office in the land, President-elect Kennedy had this to say:

> During the last sixty days, I have been at the task of constructing an administration.... I have been guided by the standard John Winthrop set before his shipmates on the flagship Arbella three hundred and thirty-one years ago, as they, too, faced the task of building a new government on a perilous frontier. "We must always consider," he said, "that we shall be as a city upon a hill—the eyes of all people are upon us." Today the eyes of all people are truly upon us—and our governments, in every branch, at every level, national, state and local, must be as a city upon a hill—constructed and inhabited by men aware of their great trust and their great responsibilities.[35]

There is less antichristian sentiment in President Kennedy's use of Christ's words than in Winthrop's. Recognizing that political office is indeed a "great trust" is a genuinely Christian sentiment. Still, Kennedy's words imply the clear tendency to confuse a temporal polity, the United States, for the Church. The antichristian sentiment in President Reagan's invocation twenty-eight years later of Winthrop is more apparent:

---

35   "Address of President-Elect John F. Kennedy Delivered to a Joint Convention of the General Court of the Commonwealth of Massachusetts." The State House, Boston, January 9, 1961. https://www.jfklibrary.org/archives/other-resources/john-f-kennedy-speeches/massachusetts-general-court-19610109. Accessed September 15, 2019.

I've spoken of the shining city all my political life, but I don't know if I ever quite communicated what I saw when I said it. But in my mind it was a tall proud city built on rocks stronger than oceans, wind-swept, God-blessed, and teeming with people of all kinds living in harmony and peace, a city with free ports that hummed with commerce and creativity, and if there had to be city walls, the walls had doors and the doors were open to anyone with the will and the heart to get here. That's how I saw it, and see it still.[36]

Though he was surely not aware of it, the "tall proud city" that President Reagan was describing amounts to an anti-christian paradisal vision. It contains the elements of a Christian view of paradise (with the addition of the distinctively American element of bustling commerce) transposed from the realm of eternity to that of profane history. While the political rhetoric of Winthrop, Kennedy, and Reagan compares favorably with the mounting illiteracy of twenty-first century politicians, the formers' concept of America nevertheless displaces Christ's Church as the proper object of Christian veneration.

---

36   "Farewell Address to the Nation," January 11, 1989. https://www. reaganfoundation.org/media/128652/farewell.pdf. Accessed September 15, 2019.

A Word on "Climate Change"

It is appropriate here to touch on a topic of great relevance to globalization in our time, that of "climate change." Climate change has developed into a truly global concern that is uniting peoples from across the globe into a worldwide crusade to save the planet from deleterious human activity. But before enquiring into the truth or validity of "climate change," i.e., whether it meaningfully represents real climatic conditions, it is both possible and necessary to analyze the theory itself for scientific and logical rigor. It is here that climate change falls short. However politically fashionable it may be, as a substantive scientific claim, the theory of climate change lacks merit because it fails to make specific predictions that may be empirically tested. Because the climate is always changing—from day to day, season to season, year to year—any meteorological observation may be said to agree with it: if it is extraordinarily warm somewhere, this may be attributed to climate change; extraordinarily frigid, likewise. Climate change is thus "unfalsifiable", which is to say that there exists no even hypothetical evidence that could be said to refute it, which renders it meaningless as a scientific theory.

> One of the tenets behind the scientific method is that any scientific hypothesis and resultant experimental design must be inherently falsifiable…. Most scientists accept and work with this tenet, but it has its roots in philosophy and the deeper questions of truth and our access to it.

> Falsifiability is the assertion that for any hypothesis to have credence, it must be inherently disprovable before it can become accepted as a scientific hypothesis or theory… Importantly, falsifiability doesn't mean that there are currently arguments against a theory, only that it is possible

to imagine some kind of argument which would invalidate it.... It is only the minimum trait required of a claim that allows it to be engaged with in a scientific manner— a dividing line between what is considered science and what isn't.[37]

Because there is no even hypothetical observation that might be said to refute climate change, it is unfalsifiable and amounts to a form of pseudo-science that may be made to agree with any observable evidence. Any meteorological phenomenon— hot, cold, wet, dry, calm, stormy, etc.—may be advanced as confirmation that the climate is somehow changing, while no phenomenon may be said to run contrary to it. Climate change thus cannot be empirically tested, it lacks theoretical merit, and it consequently fails to rise to the level of a scientific hypothesis.

The related notion of "global warming" possesses some- what more scientific rigor. Because global warming implies a measurable trajectory to global temperatures, it can at least in principle be tested and implicitly falsified; it thus qualifies as a scientific hypothesis. Practically, however, measuring tempera- tures worldwide on an ongoing basis with accuracy presents enormous difficulties, which have tended to overestimate observed warming.[38] Furthermore, even a cursory examination of temperature records shows that the earth's climate fluctu- ated substantially in the ages before human industrialization, and that modern day warming lies within pre-industrial his- toric patterns.[39] Thus, changes to the climate now, in and of

37   *Explorable.com.* "Falsifiability." https://explorable.com/falsifiability. Accessed December 29, 2019.

38   *Cfact.com.* "Measuring Global Temperatures: Satellites or Thermometers?" https://www.cfact.org/2016/01/26/measuring-global-temperatures- satellites-or-thermometers/. Accessed January 13, 2020.

39   *Long Range Weather, Harris-Mann Climatology.* "Long Range Temperature Trends from 2500 BC to 2040 AD." http://www.longrangeweather.com/global_ temperatures.htm. Accessed September 18, 2019. "Holocene Temperature

themselves, do not substantiate the "anthropogenic" theory of global warming, even according to the US government's own figures.[40] The scientific weaknesses of climate change and global warming are routinely evinced by the tendency of climate change "believers" to persecute and shout down "deniers" when the latter object to the prevailing dogma.[41] As in the case of globalization itself, some have been so heavily propagandized that climate change has become effectively a religion. " 'Climate is not a separate issue,' said Senator Cory Booker. 'It is the issue, the lens, through which we must see everything that we do.' "[42] One former UN under-secretary general went so far as to pen a hypothetical retrospective from the year 2031 with bold antichristian attributes describing a decade (the 2020s) of catastrophic climatic events that ultimately gives rise to a global mystic, Tadi, who unites all of the world's religions into one in order to save mankind.[43] Furthermore, however dramatic the predictions about climate change and global warming, it is important to bear in mind that the recent historical record

---

Variations," *Wikipedia.* https://en.wikipedia.org/wiki/Global_temperature_record#/media/File:Holocene_Temperature_Variations.png. Accessed September 18, 2019.

40   *NOAA.* "Temperature Change and Carbon Dioxide Change." https://www.ncdc.noaa.gov/global-warming/temperature-change. Accessed January 13, 2020.

41   "Chief of World Meteorological Organization Castigates Climate Alarmists," *The Epoch Times.* https://www.theepochtimes.com/chief-of-world-meteorological-organization-castigates-climate-alarmists_3073666.html. Accessed September 18, 2019.

42   "The Left Has Reframed Democrats' Climate Debate," *The Atlantic.* https://www.theatlantic.com/science/archive/2019/09/why-2020-climate-primary-like-2008/597694/. Accessed September 13, 2019.

43   "Climate 'Religion' Is Fueling Australia's Wildfires," *The Hill.* https://thehill.com/opinion/energy-environment/478769-climate-religion-is-fueling-australias-wildfires. Accessed January 20, 2020. Maurice Strong, *Where on Earth Are We Going?* (Texere, 2001). See ch. 8 for discussion of "ecumenism" and the ongoing amalgamation of the world's religions into one.

is full of apocalyptic claims about the environment that never came to pass.[44]

But if climate change and global warming lack scientific merit, what then is the basis of their continued sway over the public mind? The answers to that question are varied, but one important element appears to lie with the Open Conspiracy identified by Wells and its program of building a global political structure able to overpower local centers of governance—as well as a satanic hatred for the crown of God's creation, man.

> In searching for a common enemy against whom we can unite, we came up with the idea that pollution, the threat of global warming, water shortages, famine and the like, would fit the bill. In their totality and their interactions, these phenomena do constitute a common threat which must be confronted by everyone together. But in designating these dangers as the enemy, we fall into the trap, which we have already warned readers about, namely mistaking symptoms for causes. All these dangers are caused by *human* intervention in natural processes, and it is only through changed attitudes and behaviour that they can be overcome. The real enemy then is humanity itself.[45]

The foregoing words, proffered by the Club of Rome, one of our time's leading arms of the Open Conspiracy, sum up neatly the utility of climate change and global warming to the general program of globalization. By inculcating the idea that human toxification of the global environment is the overriding

---

44   "Doomsdays That Didn't Happen," *Fox News*. https://www.foxnews.com/politics/failed-climate-change-predictions. Accessed September 18, 2019.

45   Alexander King and Bertrand Schneider, *The First Global Revolution: A Report by the Club of Rome* (Orient Longman, 1991), 75. https://ia600202.us.archive.org/33/items/TheFirstGlobalRevolution/TheFirstGlobalRevolution.pdf. Accessed December 28, 2019.

Antichrist: the Fulfillment of Globalization

danger of our time—and by extension humanity itself—the Open Conspiracy is laying the groundwork for global control of every aspect of human life, because every aspect of human life may be said to have global environmental implications.

In short, whatever their scientific merits, climate change and global warming, in the political and economic spheres, amount to a huge power grab by national governments and supranational bodies that intend to regulate everything that affects the environment from automobiles to air travel to diet. On the pretense of saving the planet, virtually every human activity can be scrutinized, controlled, or even outlawed.[46] But, however shaky its scientific legs, we need not dispense with the idea of climate change entirely. An Orthodox perspective would affirm that, through sin of all kinds, man is forever disturbing God's beneficent ordering of creation on both the spiritual and physical planes. Just as the primordial sin led to man having to live by the sweat of his brow and broke the perfect communion between him and nature,[47] so have successive sins through history caused further deterioration in both spiritual and physical existence. Increasingly disruptive climatic conditions could well reflect mankind's increasing sinfulness and lack of repentance rather than man's direct physical interaction with the environment. Climate change could thus well have human origins but not in the sense that the secular world believes, and the solution would lie less on the environmental plane than on the spiritual one. Global repentance and a return by the peoples of the world to God's True Church, more than restrictions on CO_2 emissions, would be the answer.

In discerning antichristian tendencies in contemporary politics, we must not lose our cool. Much heterodox "end times"

46   See "The Green New Deal." https://ocasio-cortez.house.gov/gnd. Accessed September 18, 2019.
47   See Gen. 3:17-19.

speculation, far from fulfilling St. Peter's command to be "sober, and watch unto prayer for the end of all things is at hand,"[48] only fosters greater confusion and disorientation, which renders people more susceptible to deception of all kinds. While the anti-christian tendencies of modernity grow increasingly prevalent, and the world abounds in false messiahs of myriad stripes, we must "not be deceived"[49]: we must succumb neither to fantasies about saving the world nor to unbalanced speculation as to the who/when/where of Antichrist. While the secular world sleeps in obliviousness, much of the "Christian" world is overcome with febrile speculation about how the end of the world is supposed to play itself out. It is hard to know which is the greater error. A danger is that, when Antichrist finally arrives, there may have been so many cries of wolf that no one will be listening.

---

48   1 Pet. 4:7.
49   Luke 21:8.

CHAPTER 8

THE GLOBALIZATION OF RELIGION

> I can see ... the world on the verge of the first global civilization, spiritual refugees wandering the earth seeking a symbol of hope. I do believe that at the bottom of religions there is a treasure chest of hope which the world yearns for.... I can see the day of a United Religions.
>
> William E. Swing, Episcopal Bishop of California
> Founder of the United Religions Initiative
> October 19, 1996[1]

In the previous chapters, we have examined the major economic and political aspects of globalization that are helping to set the stage for the global reception of Antichrist as a world leader and master of global exchange. Globalization, however, is not confined to the economic and political spheres but also contains a powerful religious component that, in a way similar to the amalgamation of the world's economies and nation-states, is merging the world's religions into one.

We have seen in our discussion of the works of H. G. Wells (ch. 2) that the promise of building the new world order is fundamentally a religious undertaking, an act of faith. It is a modern error to regard the political and the religious as inherently

---

1 "Address to the 147th Diocesan Convention, the Episcopal Diocese of California." https://diocal.org/sites/default/files/media/PDF%20Docs/147th_Convention_Journal_1996.pdf. Accessed September 17, 2019.

separate, but there are important distinctions. Whereas economic and political globalization entails consolidating largely manmade organizational structures, the globalization of religion requires man to abandon or distort his deepest and most ancient form of identity: the nature and orientation of his worship. It is the figure of Antichrist which sheds light on modern efforts to merge religious systems that have been distinct for centuries. Antichrist will come not only as ruler of a new global, temporal order, he will come as the high priest and messiah of a new "church," a mystical society of believers, and preside from Jerusalem over a unified "religion of the future."

"Christian" Ecumenism

The globalization of religion may be seen most clearly in what has come to be known as "ecumenism", which posits that differing Christian denominations should be united and, sometimes beyond that, that Christianity itself may be beneficially merged with non-Christian religions. Ecumenism discounts dogmatic differences and engages in what amounts to moralism: the idea that the ethical teachings of religions are essentially the same and that their doctrinal incompatibilities are the product of historical accretions that may be acceptably discarded. By emphasizing morality, and papering over differences of historical fact and dogma, the world's religions can thus be portrayed as variations on a theme, as reflections of the same cosmic principle or "god," which have been artificially and deleteriously separated through history. Recombining them under some new banner, then, is only a reflection of the universal truth they supposedly share[2].

---

2   See "perennialism" or "perennial philosophy". Wikipedia, https://en.wikipedia.org/wiki/Perennial_philosophy. Accessed September 21, 2021

The religious aspect of globalization was incisively diagnosed by Hieromonk Seraphim Rose (+1982) even before the term globalization had gained popular usage. American-born Father Seraphim—widely regarded as a saint by Orthodox Christians in America and Russia—converted to Orthodoxy following a tortuous search that took him from Western Christianity through ancient Chinese philosophy, Oriental mysticism, and finally to Orthodoxy under the guidance of St. John Maximovich of San Francisco (+1966). Father Seraphim's path gave him insight into the attraction that Buddhism, Hinduism, and their variants held for many modern Westerners and where the increasingly ecumenistic tendencies of Western Christianity were leading. A brilliant scholar, linguist, and observer of history, and a true Orthodox monastic of the ancient ascetic tradition, Father Seraphim perceived that humanity had reached the advanced stages of the great "falling away"[3] prophesied by St. Paul and was busily giving itself over to a global pseudo-religion that would pave the way for the appearance of the Antichrist. Father Seraphim's seminal work, *Orthodoxy and the Religion of the Future*, cogently lays out the religious component of antichristian globalization.

Christian ecumenism generally implies acceptance of the "branch theory" of the Church, which posits that the differences among the Christian denominations of today are cosmetic and not substantive, that they are historical relics that may be beneficially discarded such that the prior unity of the Church may be regained. What proponents of branch theory cannot agree on, however, is when the unified "Church" became merely fragmented "Christianity." The twentieth century? The "age of reason"? The Protestant Reformation? Some hypothesize that the conversion of the Roman Empire and legalization of the Church in the fourth century, which ended centuries of bloody persecution, wrecked the "real" Church by mingling her with

---

3   2 Thes. 2:3.

the Roman imperial state. Some even blame the Apostle Paul for distorting Christ's "pure" message and setting the stage for two millennia of error. There is, of course, no general agreement, but the ecumenistic urge—to gather all ostensible Christians into one—can be felt throughout the Western Christian denominations and even among some Orthodox.

Ecumenism, far from promoting the Church as ecumenical, in fact denies the existence of the Church as universal and united. "The ideology behind ecumenism . . . is an already well-defined heresy: the Church of Christ does not exist, no one has the Truth, the Church is only now being built."[4] Ecumenism denies the Lord's promise that there should be "one flock and one shepherd."[5] The Lord prayed to His Father shortly before His Crucifixion that He would "keep through Your name those whom You have given Me, that they may be one as We are . . . that they all may be one, as You, Father, are in Me, and I in You."[6] An implicit assumption to ecumenism is that through the centuries the Father failed to keep the promise of maintaining the Church as *one*.

> He [St. Paul] calls it the Church "of God," showing that it ought to be united.... For if it be "of God," it is united, and it is one, not only in Corinth, but also in all the world: for the Church's name (*ecclesia*: properly, an assembly) is not a name of separation, but of unity and concord.[7]

It is not the case that the Church exists in fragments; the True Church is and has always been one; but it is the case, however politically incorrect it may be to say so, that the non-Orthodox have cut themselves off from her. "Christian ecumenism at its

---

4   Rose, *Orthodoxy and the Religion of the Future*, xxv.
5   John 10:16.
6   John 17:11, 21.
7   St. John Chrysostom, *Homily I on I Corinthians 1*, 1. B#56, p. 3 as quoted in Manley, *The Bible and the Holy Fathers*, 221.

best may be seen to represent a sincere and understandable error on the part of Protestants and Roman Catholics—the error of failing to recognize that the visible Church of Christ already exists, and that they are outside of it."[8]

Because, to Western Christians, the Church appears fragmented, the tendency is to fall back on emphasizing "Christianity" as the body of Christ rather than the Church, which implies a level of unity that "Christianity" alone clearly does not possess. Yet it is a central error of modern Western Christianity to suppose that the true Christian life can be lived apart from the True Church. Indeed, the idea of "Christianity" itself, while talked about freely by Protestants and others who pride themselves on their adherence to Scripture, possesses no Scriptural basis whatsoever.

> Before anything else, the [early] Christians became con-scious of themselves as members of the Church. The Christian community referred to itself as a "Church" in preference to all other names. The word "Church" (*ecclesia*) appears one hundred and ten times in the New Testa-ment, while such words as "Christianity" and similar words with the same ending are completely unknown in the New Testament. After the descent of the Holy Spirit on Christ's disciples and apostles, the Church came into being as a visible community with a spiritual interrelation among its members.[9]

It is only in the Church—not in some disembodied "Christianity"—that the mystical union of believers with God and with each other exists. Contrary to Orthodox ecclesiology, branch theory argues that it is possible to be a Christian apart

---

8   Rose, *Orthodoxy and the Religion of the Future*, xxix.
9   St. Ilarion Troitsky, *Christianity or the Church?* 17.

from the Church; that Roman Catholics, Orthodox, and the myriad kinds of Protestants are "Christians" even while the "Church" remains fragmented and disconnected. A variation on the theme is that all "Christians" are actually members of the same Church, but the Church is invisible, hidden behind the outward manifestations of denominational disunity. In contrast, Orthodoxy affirms that

> Christianity is not some sort of abstract teaching which is accepted by the mind and *found by each person separately. To the contrary, Christianity is a life* in which separate persons are so united among themselves that their unity can be likened to the unity of the Persons of the Holy Trinity. Christ did not pray only that His teaching be preserved so that it would spread throughout all the universe. He prayed for the unification of all those believing in Him.[10]

Contrary to the Lord's promise that the "gates of hell will not prevail" against His Church,[11] ecumenism supposes that Christ's Church does not now exist and must be built or rebuilt through the amalgamation of the different self-identified Christian sects. Even some Orthodox hierarchs have voiced this idea.

> In the movement for union [between Orthodoxy and Roman Catholicism], it is not a question of one Church moving towards the other; rather let us all together re-found the One, Holy, Catholic, and Apostolic Church, coexisting in the East and West.[12]

---

10   Ibid., 8. Emphasis in original.
11   Matt. 16:18.
12   Patriarch Athenagoras as quoted in Damascene, *Father Seraphim Rose*, 397.

Genuine Orthodox consciousness, in contrast, affirms that the Church by nature cannot be "refounded" because it is a divine institution of an eternal, unchanging essence, which reflects the eternal, unchanging nature of God, and which, regardless of historical circumstances, exists now on earth, now in Heaven, and will exist for all time in the age to come.

> Now I plead with you, brethren, by the name of our Lord Jesus Christ, that you all speak the same thing, and that there be no divisions among you, but that you be perfectly joined together in the same mind and in the same judgment.... Is Christ divided? Was Paul crucified for you? Or were you baptized in the name of Paul?[13]

> For the Apostle [Paul], the Church is not only *a single body*, but also *a single Spirit* (1 Cor. 12:11, 13; Eph. 4:3-4, 7; et al.). Here we understand, not a conformity of ideas or a unity of religious convictions, as certain Western thinkers wish to believe, but a single Spirit of God which penetrates the entire body of the Church, as the holy fathers and teachers of the Church testify.[14]

EXTRA-CHRISTIAN ECUMENISM

At the core of ecumenism's tendency to ignore doctrinal differences for the sake of an ersatz unity is the idea that the different Christian sects, and even non-Christian religions, are all legitimate paths to God; that "all roads lead to the same destination."

---

13   1 Cor. 1:10, 13.
14   St. Ilarion Troitsky, *Christianity or the Church?* 13.

[But] if all Christian bodies are relative to each other, then all of them together are relative to other "religious" bodies, and "Christian" ecumenism can only end in a syncretic world religion.

This is indeed the undisguised aim of the masonic ideology which has now inspired the Ecumenical Movement, and this ideology has now taken such possession of those who participate in the Ecumenical Movement that "dialogue" and eventual union with the non-Christian religions have come to the next logical step for today's denatured Christianity.[15]

As Father Seraphim demonstrates with great cogency, ecumenism is not a new idea at all but one of ancient pagan origin. It is, in effect, the old polytheism in which numerous gods were all considered legitimately divine and worthy of worship. This pagan idea seems to have gained steam in the West by way of Hinduism and in particular by the teachings of Swami Vivekananda, who attended the first "Parliament of Religions" in Chicago in 1893.

Father Seraphim identifies the basic message of Hinduism as being that "there is no such thing as difference. All is one. All differences are just on the surface; they are apparent or relative, not real."[16] "All religions are true, but Vedanta [the core teachings of Hinduism] is the ultimate truth. Differences are only matters of 'levels of truth.' "[17] The utility of such a message in the globalization of religion is plain. In such a paradigm, with all meaningful differences among religious traditions denied, the religious path one chooses becomes a question of mere personal preference. The search for truth, of discriminating between the true and the false, between good and evil, of "test[ing] the

---

15   Rose, *Orthodoxy and the Religion of the Future*, xxv.
16   Ibid., 13.
17   Ibid., 22.

spirits, whether they are of God, because many false prophets have gone out into the world,"[18] is implicitly abandoned.

Significantly, in Hinduism, differences between men and gods are also only apparent. Man, in short, *is* God, and so the search for God, for the ultimate reality, may be considered over as soon as it is begun. Searching and finding ultimate truth as distinct from error is fundamentally unnecessary.

> In Vivekananda's words: "Man is not traveling from error to truth, but climbing up from truth to truth, from truth that is lower to truth that is higher. The matter of today is the spirit of tomorrow. The worm of today—the God of tomorrow." The Vedanta rests on this: that man is God. So it is for man to work out his own salvation. Vivekananda put it this way: "Who can help the Infinite? Even the hand that comes to you through the darkness will have to be your own."
>
> Vivekananda was canny enough to know that straight Vedanta would be too much for Christians to follow, right off the bat. But "levels of truth" provided a nice bridge to perfect ecumenism—where there is no conflict because everyone is right.[19]

Questions of right and wrong, of dogma, of truth and falsity—and certainly of apostasy, heresy, blasphemy, and damnation—are scorned or simply left unasked. Any question that could prove divisive, that could shed light on the fundamental distinctions among religions, foster a genuine search for truth, and thereby impair globalization's program of general amalgamation and confusion, is off limits. And certainly Antichrist will not hesitate to avail himself of Hinduism's teaching that "man is God."

---

18   1 John 4:1.
19   Rose, *Orthodoxy and the Religion of the Future*, 22.

The inclusiveness of Hinduism extends to outright evil as well. The goddess Kali, one of the most popular in the Hindu pantheon, is customarily portrayed "in the midst of a riot of blood and carnage, skulls and severed heads hanging from her neck, her tongue grotesquely protruding from her mouth thirsting for more blood; she is appeased in Hindu temples by bloody offering of goats."[20] Of her, Swami Vivekananda says: "'I worship the Terrible! . . . Let us worship the Terror for Its own sake. How few have dared to worship Death, or Kali! Let us worship Death! Who cannot say that God manifests Himself as evil as well as Good? But only the Hindu dares worship Him as evil.'"[21] Father Seraphim relates the experience of a former Hindu and convert to Orthodoxy, that worshipping the ice image of Shiva in the Cave of Amarnath in the Himalayas, after entering with "tears of devotion," made her physically sick. She was "[s]tunned to find it a place of inexplicable wrongness," which reminded her of the bloody ceremonies of ritual magic performed by the Ifugao headhunters in the Philippines, which she had personally witnessed.[22] Ecumenism-minded Christians would do well to recall St. Paul's admonition: "Do not be unequally yoked together with unbelievers. For what fellowship has righteousness with lawlessness? And what communion has light with darkness?"[23]

Modern ecumenism, both within Christianity and between Christianity and non-Christian religions, has thus been largely inspired by one of the most ancient pagan belief systems, Hinduism. For any true-blooded Christian, this fact should be enough to condemn ecumenism outright. A tendency, however, is to see ecumenism as an extension of the Church's great commission to make disciples of all nations and the mandate

---

20   Ibid., 22.
21   Ibid., 19–20.
22   Ibid., 17.
23   2 Cor. 6:14.

to love one's neighbor. Forgotten is the indispensability of witnessing to the truth as a component of both. Forgotten is the bloody history of the Church, in which countless martyrs gave their lives because they refused to make precisely the sorts of compromises that ecumenism now advocates for the sake of unity. Under the polytheistic early Roman Empire, Christians suffered martyrdom not so much for confessing Christ but for refusing to recognize or worship other gods. It was the spiritual exclusivity of the Church that pagan Rome—and the world generally—found so offensive, and it is exactly that exclusivity that ecumenism is struggling to get the Orthodox to relinquish. As God instructed the Israelites, and St. Paul instructed the early Church, "'Come out from among them and be separate, says the Lord. Do not touch what is unclean, and I will receive you.' And, 'I will be a Father to you, and you shall be My sons and daughters, says the LORD Almighty.'"[24] The terrible, pitiful irony is that, what the Roman legions, Muslim hordes, and Communist secret police with all their instruments of torture and death were unable to achieve through the centuries, smiling "Christian" ecumenists now are.

It is not hard to see that the advancement of ecumenism perfectly fits the larger antichristian program: Antichrist will come and crown the new, syncretic world religion that ecumenism is building as its high priest, messiah, and, indeed, god. Antichrist will complete the "unification" of the "Church" that so many misguided Christians are laboring for. Ecumenism seeks first to fragment the Christian denominations by inducing them to jettison their remaining traditions and then recon-stitute them into a new global mass that may be swayed from the top. The only way for ecumenism to succeed is by paper-ing over the theological and ecclesiological differences among Christians and especially the notion that any one Christian

---

24   2 Cor. 6:17-18 (Is. 52:11; Ezek. 30:34, 41; 2 Sam. 7:14).

"denomination"—such as Orthodoxy—may itself rightly be considered the True Church of Christ already in existence. Ecumenism is, in the minds of some of its devotees, busily "transforming the modern world into the Kingdom of God in preparation for His return."[25] Any such god "returning" to the contemporary world could have only one identity.

THE GLOBAL VISION OF FATHER PIERRE TEILHARD DE CHARDIN, S. J.

Much of ecumenism's success in our time seems the result of intellectual laziness in not differentiating the truth claims among the variants of Christianity and non-Christian religions. There are some, however, who have very consciously made the merging of the world's religions a paramount goal and have gone to the trouble of expounding a theoretical basis for it and providing it with a pseudo-Christian justification. One such man was the Jesuit Pierre Teilhard de Chardin (1881–1955), "an internationally known scientist and prolific religious writer,"[26] who devoted much of his intellectual life to fusing Christianity with modern ideas of evolution in order to weld "together science, religion, and mysticism in one unifying synthesis."[27] The search for such a "unifying synthesis" implies, of course, that such a synthesis, e.g., Orthodox Christianity, does not now exist and has to be found or constructed—the central assumption of the Gnostic enterprises that we have examined. As in the case of Wells, Teilhard's writing is a good example of a much broader stream of thought among contemporary philosophers and theologians that eagerly anticipates the merging of the

25   Roman Catholic Archbishop Thomas Connelly as quoted in Rose, *Orthodoxy and the Religion of the Future*, 177.
26   Ursula King, *Pierre Teilhard de Chardin* (Maryknoll, Orbis, 2004), 9.
27   Ibid., 10.

world's religions into a single, global "religion of the future." What Wells anticipated in the political dimension, Teilhard hoped to accomplish in the religious.

As a prologue to his essay, *How I Believe,* Teilhard states:

> I believe that the universe is an evolution.
> I believe that evolution proceeds toward spirit.
> I believe that the spirit is fully realized in a form of personality.
> I believe that the supremely personal is the universal Christ.[28]

At first pass it is hard to know what to make of that, and indeed much of Teilhard's writing is seriously opaque (e.g., the "oneness of *unicity*").[29] Certainly, however, the progressive idea of evolution figures centrally in his writing and the particular idea that human evolution is not merely occurring biologically but socially and culturally as well.

> Natural evolution ... seems now to be fully occupied with what concerns the soul. From being organic and predominantly determined it has become predominantly psychological and conscious; but it is not dead, nor has its reach even been shortened.... Who knows *what astonishing species and natural gradations* of soul are even now being produced by the persevering effort of science, of moral and social systems—without which the beauty and perfection of the mystical body would never be realized?[30]

According to Teilhard, the world is evolving, beneficially, not only through a natural or biological process but through the

---

28   Teilhard, *Christianity and Evolution,* 96 as quoted in King, *Teilhard,* 21.
29   Teilhard, *The Heart of Matter,* 29–33 as quoted in King, *Teilhard,* 60. All emphases in original.
30   Teilhard, *Writings in Time of War,* 64-5 as quoted in King, *Teilhard,* 52.

"persevering effort of science," i.e., through Gnostic activism. This process of human-assisted evolution, which is increasing intellectual and cultural interconnectedness on a global level, in turn is giving birth to what Teilhard calls the "noosphere," a collective consciousness that is the penultimate stage in human evolution. The final stage will occur when the evolving noosphere reaches the "Omega Point," an end of history when all mankind will become one with each other and with God. Within this cosmic evolutionary process, Teilhard sees an "*evolutionary role* of religions,"[31] in which a convergence of the world's religions assists in the general movement of humanity toward a final oneness.

> A sifting and general convergence of religions, governed by and based on their great value as an evolutionary stimulus— that, in short, is the great phenomenon of which we would appear to be at this moment both the agents and the witnesses.[32]

This convergence leads, in time, to a "universal communion,"[33] "a total terrestrial religious consciousness,"[34] a single, global religion of the future. From our earlier analysis of heresies in the post-schism West, we can readily identify Teilhard's thinking as an antichristian Gnostic teleology *par excellence*. An "ultimate belief" in "*an absolute direction of growth*" abetted by science, all masquerading under the banner of Christianity, fills the bill to the letter.

A particularly remarkable aspect of Teilhard's system is that, while claiming to be Christian, it is so self-consciously Gnostic and "evolutionary." For years, champions of naturalistic

---

31   Teilhard, *Activation of Energy*, 238 as quoted in King, *Teilhard*, 132.
32   Ibid., 238-42 as quoted in King, *Teilhard*, 142.
33   Teilhard, *Heart of Matter*, 93–96 as quoted in King, *Teilhard*, 115.
34   Teilhard, *Activation of Energy*, 238-42 as quoted in King, *Teilhard*, 142.

evolution from Thomas Huxley (1825-95) to our own time have deployed their hypothesis to denigrate religion and, in particular, Christianity. One of the most prominent and enthusiastic evolutionists of the twenty-first century, Richard Dawkins (b. 1941), has built a global following with such books as *The God Delusion*, *A Devil's Chaplain*, and *The Blind Watchmaker: Why the Evidence of Evolution Reveals a Universe without Design*. Dawkins has become a leading celebrity among the "new atheists" who ridicule, belittle, and besmirch what publicly remains of Christianity in fulfillment of the teaching of the Apostle Jude:

> These are grumblers, complainers, walking according to their own lusts; and they mouth great swelling words, flattering people to gain advantage. But you, beloved, remember the words which were spoken before by the apostles of our Lord Jesus Christ: how they told you that there would be mockers in the last time who would walk according to their own ungodly lusts.[35]

Like many evolutionists, Dawkins makes no bones about his theory's implications for theistic religion. "The universe we observe has precisely the properties we should expect if there is, at bottom, no design, no purpose, no evil, no good, nothing but blind, pitiless indifference."[36]

> What has theology ever said that is of the smallest use to anybody? When has theology ever said anything that is demonstrably true and is not obvious? ... If all the achievements of theologians were wiped out tomorrow, would anyone notice the smallest difference? Even the

---

35   Jude 1:16-18.
36   Richard Dawkins, *River Out of Eden: A Darwinian View of Life*. https://www.goodreads.com/quotes/22201-the-total-amount-of-suffering-per-year-in-the-natural. Accessed September 16, 2019.

bad achievements of scientists, the bombs, and sonar-guided whaling vessels work! The achievements of theologians don't do anything, don't affect anything, don't mean anything. What makes anyone think that "theology" is a subject at all?[37]

It is this sort of virulent, God-hating, Gnostic pride that Teilhard's "evolutionary synthesis" tries to reconcile, strangely and illogically, with something he calls "Christianity". After years of resisting the encroachment of naturalistic evolution into what remains of Western Christian consciousness, the Latin church produced in Teilhard a bold champion of evolution who confused it with his own disordered understanding of Christianity into a truly bizarre antichristian synthesis.

What, we now see, we have to do is not simply to forward a human task but, in some way, to bring Christ to completion; we must, therefore, devote ourselves with still more ardor, even in the natural domain, to the cultivation of the world.[38]

[T]here is indeed an *absolute* fuller-being and an *absolute* better-being, and they are rightly to be described as a progress in consciousness, in freedom, and in moral sense. Moreover, these higher degrees of being are to be attained by concentration, purification, and maximum effort...
    The true summons of the cosmos is a call consciously to share in the great work that goes on within it...

---

37   Richard Dawkins, "The Emptiness of Theology," *Free Inquiry Magazine*, v. 18, no. 2. https://www.rzim.org/read/a-slice-of-infinity/theology-as-a-subject. Accessed September 16, 2019.
38   Teilhard, *Writings in Time of War*, 64-5 as quoted in King, *Teilhard*, 51.

"The world is still being created, and it is Christ who is reaching his fulfillment in it."[39]

Teilhard's thinking is a salient example of the antichristian Gnosticism identified by Voegelin, which ascribes "to intramundane activity... the premium of salvation,"[40] and which has driven mankind's futile efforts of ending history and establishing the Kingdom of God on earth. Teilhard's formula, while full of references to Christ, in fact constitutes an utter denial of the Lord's kingship and divinity, the fallenness of the world and its tendency apart from God to grow ever more sinful, and the Lord's words on the Cross that "It is finished,"[41] i.e., that through His sacrifice He has accomplished the salvation of man. Yet Teilhard insists on calling his system of thought, dressed up in pseudo-scientific verbiage, "Christian", just as the man himself remained self-consciously Roman Catholic. While the Vatican repressed Teilhard's writings during his lifetime—suspecting even then that something was wrong—yet has the fame of this scholar, a product of Latin scholasticism in the vein of Joachim of Fiore, grown to make him one of our time's leading "Christian" prophets of the global religion of the future.

While professing Roman Catholicism, Teilhard, like other Gnostics, rejects past and present forms of Christianity and looks to some imaginary future formulation. "[T]he sort of faith that is needed, in terms of energy, for the correct functioning of a totalized human world has not yet been satisfactorily formulated in any quarter at all."[42]

As I said before, it is still, and will always be, Christianity: but a "reborn" Christianity, as assured of victory tomor-

---

39   Teilhard, *Writings in Time of War*, 28-32, 60 as quoted in King, *Teilhard*, 49.

40   Voegelin, *The New Science of Politics*, 130.

41   John 19:30.

42   Teilhard, *Heart of Matter*, 97 as quoted in King, *Teilhard*, 167.

row as it was in its infancy—because it alone (through the double power, *at last fully understood*, of its cross and resurrection) is capable of becoming the religion whose specific property is to provide the driving force in evolution.[43]

Lost in his Gnostic fantasy, Teilhard cannot understand that it is Holy Orthodoxy that is still the same Christianity "assured of victory tomorrow as it was in its infancy" not some "reborn" variation that, thanks to some novel insight, will be *"at last fully understood."* The Church has been fully understood by her saints since the descent of the Holy Spirit at Pentecost.

What is so profoundly antichristian about Teilhard's Gnostic system is his insistence that it is Christ Who is this "driving force in evolution" and it is in Christ that the process will end when it reaches the Omega Point. In moving toward a "harmony between a religion that is christic and an evolution that is convergent in type,"[44]

> It is not, I insist, another Christ: it is the same Christ, still and always the same, and even more so in that it is precisely in order to retain for him his essential property of being *coextensive with the world* that we are obliged to make him undergo this colossal magnification.
>
> Christ-Omega: the Christ, therefore, who animates and gathers up all the biological and spiritual energies developed by the universe. Finally, then, Christ the evolver.[45]

In a flagrant inversion of the Lord's words that "I am not of this world,"[46] Teilhard makes him "coextensive with the

---

43   Ibid., 97-8 as quoted in King, *Teilhard*, 167-8.

44   Ibid., 93 as quoted in King, *Teilhard*, 114.

45   Teilhard, *Science of Christ*, 167 as quoted in King, *Teilhard*, 94-5.

46   John 17:16.

world." Teilhard sees the whole, great, christic evolution of the universe finally taking on "the quality of a person,"[47] i.e., finding an incarnation in human history. In time, Teilhard's "evolved" form of Christianity must reach the logical conclusion identified by Orthodoxy.

> A general convergence of religions on a universal Christ who fundamentally satisfies them all: that seems to me the only possible conversion of the world, and the only form in which a religion of the future can be conceived.[48]

> It is toward him and through him, the inner life and light of the world, that the universal convergence of all created spirit is effected in sweat and tears. He is the single center, precious and consistent, who glitters at the summit that is to crown the world...[49]

"He," of course, is readily identifiable as Antichrist. While it arrogates to itself the epithet "Christian", this endpoint of history, the crown of this universal convergence in Teilhard's vision is not divine but Satanic. In contrast, Orthodoxy affirms that,

> The Kingdom of God does not evolve. It undergoes no development. It is utterly Divine in its origin and trans- formative in its coming. It cannot be brought about through political or economic efforts. Instead, the heresy of "advancing the Kingdom," has simply been the ex- cuse to abandon the teaching of the faith and trust in the secular works of man. It has also been among the many modern motives for killing millions of people.... There is

---

47   Teilhard, *Human Energy*, 42-7 as quoted in King, *Teilhard*, 135.
48   Teilhard, *How I Believe*, 41 as quoted in Damascene, *Father Seraphim Rose*, 536.
49   Teilhard, *Science and Christ*, 34 as quoted in King, *Teilhard*, 91.

no greater danger in our present age than the concept of "advancing the Kingdom."... In time, it will be the slogan of the anti-Christ...[50]

In Teilhardism, Roman Catholicism has come virtually to the farthest limit of its blasphemy against the true teachings of the Church of Christ. That which is called "Christ" in this philosophy is precisely what the Orthodox Church knows as *Antichrist:* the "emerging" pseudo-Christ who promises mankind a "spiritual" *kingdom of this world.* In this philosophy the concept and taste for the *other world,* the possession of which distinguishes Orthodox Christians from other men, is totally obliterated.[51]

Of all the deceived and deceiving prophets who have labored to bring into history its great and final king, the worldly "savior" and capstone of history's "universal convergence," Father Pierre Teilhard de Chardin, S. J., surely ranks among the most deceived of our time.[52] Even so, the globalist urge among the Roman Catholic Church continues apace under the leadership of another Jesuit, Pope Francis, who has called for "a supranational, legally constituted body to enforce United Nations Sustainable Development Goals and implement 'climate change' policies," which in turn echoed his predecessor, Pope Benedict XVI, who called for a "true world political authority" to "manage the global economy," "guarantee the protection of

---

50   Fr. Stephen Freeman, "Brief Notes on the Kingdom – You Are Not Advancing It." https://blogs.ancientfaith.com/glory2godforallthings/2015/12/08/brief-notes-on-the-kingdom-you-are-not-advancing-it/. Accessed September 16, 2019.

51   Fr. Seraphim Rose, *Genesis, Creation, and Early Man: The Orthodox Christian Vision* (Platina, St. Herman of Alaska Brotherhood, 2000), 370-1.

52   And yet, despite the depth of Teilhard's deception, it seems that some genuinely Christian element of his personality remained. He wondered: "Or am I, after all, simply the dupe of a mirage of my own mind? I often ask myself that question." (*Heart of Matter,* 97-102 as quoted in King, *Teilhard,* 168.)

the environment," "regulate migration," "bring about integral and timely disarmament," and work for the "common good."[53]

THE CHURCH OF ANTICHRIST

Because Antichrist will style himself "Christ" it is reasonable to expect that the religious body that he will head will call itself "Christian" and a "church". Such a "church" of Antichrist will be filled with "Christians" whose resemblance to the Apostles, martyrs, and saints of the historical Church will be strictly nominal. As we have seen in our analysis of the rise of many Protestant movements, such antichristian "churches" are plentiful in the history of the West. Such "Christians" look to a false christ even while the name of Jesus is on their lips. The vagueness, confusion, and cultishness that so define modern Western Christianity are trappings not of the Church of Christ but of the coming church of Antichrist. While Christ's Orthodox Church labors to give birth to Christ in each of her members, the antichristian church is laboring with ever greater vigor to give birth to its own christ, its own messiah, who will fulfill and embody all of its distorted hopes. As the prophets of the Old Testament paved the way for the coming of the True Christ, so today's' antichristian prophets, priests, and theologians—consciously or not—are doing for the global reception of Antichrist.

The worldly Christianity of today would be unrecognizable to the Orthodox of the early Church or even to tradition-minded Western Christians of just a few lifetimes ago. In our time, "Christian" demagogues preach a gospel of wealth and self-fulfillment to gigantic arena-style congregations in fulfillment of

---

53   "Pope Francis Calls for New 'Supranational' Authorities to Enforce UN Goals," May 2, 2019. https://www.lifesitenews.com/news/pope-francis-calls-for-new-supranational-authorities-to-enforce-UN-goals. Accessed September 17, 2019.

St. Paul's prophecy that "the time will come when they will not endure sound doctrine, but according to their own desires, because they have itching ears, they will heap up for themselves teachers; and they will turn their ears away from the truth, and be turned aside to fables."[54] In these mass gatherings in which reason and the senses are overwhelmed by huge electronic displays and Dionysian pop music, aesthetically indistinguishable from so much modern entertainment, the individual soul becomes carried away in a torrent of contrived mass emotion suggestive of the mass rallies of Communism and National Socialism.

Perhaps most ironically, many of today's "Bible" churches, which ostensibly draw their inspiration *sola scriptura*, have almost entirely abandoned the teachings of the Bible. Whereas the services of the Orthodox Church are based on the Psalms and her divine liturgy recapitulates the earthly life of Christ, many "Bible" churches have chosen entertainment-based curricula designed for fleeting modern attention spans that have only the most superficial basis in Scripture. Their Biblical component—everywhere present in Orthodox services—is seen almost exclusively in preaching, often from a modern, bowdlerized version of the Bible. Such homilies lack grounding in the wisdom of the historical Church and instead draw on changing modern opinions divorced from original context by huge barriers of time, language, and culture. Nothing prevents the latest hot-shot preacher who "discovers" some "new" twist on Scripture from setting up his own "church" and employing the best in modern salesmanship to win devotees.

> For such are false apostles, deceitful workers, transforming themselves into apostles of Christ. And no wonder! For Satan himself transforms himself into an angel of light.

---

54   2 Tim. 4:3-4.

Therefore it is no great thing if his ministers also transform themselves into ministers of righteousness, whose end will be according to their works.[55]

But there were also false prophets among the people, even as there will be false teachers among you, who will secretly bring in destructive heresies, even denying the Lord who bought them, and bring on themselves swift destruction. And many will follow their destructive ways, because of whom the way of truth will be blasphemed. By covetousness they will exploit you with deceptive words; for a long time, their judgment has not been idle, and their destruction does not slumber.[56]

As we have seen in our earlier discussion of early Protestantism (ch. 5), *sola scriptura* is an identifiably Gnostic principle which bears more likeness to the Judaic treatment of the Talmud and the Islamic treatment of the Qur'an than to the actual role Scripture played in the life of the early Church. "By Scripture alone" means, in practice, that there can be as many conflicting interpretations of Scripture as individuals who try to interpret it. Reading the Bible literally, as affirmed in many "Bible" churches, fails on a variety of levels, not least of which is that the Bible is not a technical document but a "library" consisting of history, prophecy, poetry, correspondence, parables, etc., which, to read literally and without discernment, is by nature to misunderstand.[57]

---

55   2 Cor. 11:13-15.

56   2 Pet. 2:1-3.

57   One might further add, in brief, that very few can read Scripture in its original language and that, as a matter of historical record, it was the Church that gave the world the Bible – not the other way around. The Orthodox Church has always taught that merely reading Holy Scripture according to one's own lights is spiritually hazardous. Bishop St. Ignatius Brianchaninov (+1867) warns us, "Do not think it is enough for you to read only the Gospels, without the writings of the Holy Fathers! This is a proud thought, a dangerous thought. It would be better if the Fathers lead

Having abandoned iconography and the divine liturgy, modern "Bible" churches incline toward other forms of spectacle. One such prominent example is the phenomenon of "faith healing", in which preachers appear to heal in spectacular fashion those with physical disease or demonic possession. This betokens not a genuine outpouring of the Holy Spirit as witnessed in the lives of the Apostles but *prelest*, an Orthodox term connoting pride and spiritual deception.[58]

> St. John Cassian, the great 5th-century Orthodox father of the West, who wrote with great discernment on the working of the Holy Spirit in his Conference on "Divine Gifts," notes that "sometimes the demons [work miracles] in order to lift into pride the man who believes himself to possess the miraculous gift, and so prepare him for a more miraculous fall. They pretend that they are being burnt up and driven out from the bodies where they were dwelling through the holiness of people whom truly they know to be unholy.... In the Gospel we read: *There shall arise false Christs and false prophets....*"[59]

Great spiritual gifts are given to a rare few blessed with the extraordinary humility to handle them; on the contrary, the

---

you to the Gospels, as though you were their beloved child whom they raise and educate through their writings. All who foolishly and proudly reject the Holy Fathers, who approach the Gospels with foolish brazenness and unclean mind and heart, fall into a lethal self-deception. The Gospel has rejected them, for it only accepts those who are humble." (*The Field: Cultivating Salvation*, [Jordanville, Holy Trinity], 27)

58   "The term *prelest* (Russian прелесть) has come into English usage for lack of a precise equivalent, although it is often translated as 'spiritual delusion,' 'spiritual deception,' or 'illusion,' accepting a delusion for reality in contrast to spiritual sobriety. Prelest carries a connotation of allurement in the sense that the serpent beguiled Eve by means of the forbidden fruit." (*Orthodox America*. https://frmilovan.wordpress.com/page/258/. Accessed September 16, 2019.)

59   Conference XV:2, in Owen Chadwick, *Western Asceticism* (Philadelphia, Westminster, 1958), 258 as quoted in Rose, *Orthodoxy and the Religion of the Future*, 146-7.

"wonder-workers" of today evince all manner of pride and conceit, often lavishing upon themselves the material largesse of their beguiled congregations, while promising their devotees a life of worldly delights. Such men, devoid of understanding of the True Church and under obedience to no true Christian authority who might check their excesses, fancy themselves self-appointed apostles to the contemporary world.

> According to Bishop Ignatius [Brianchaninov], the deception known as *fancy* "is satisfied with the invention of counterfeit feelings and states of grace, from which there is born a false, wrong conception of the whole spiritual undertaking.... It constantly invents pseudo-spiritual states, an intimate companionship with Jesus, an inward conversation with him, mystical revelations, voices, enjoyments.".... "Fancying of himself . . . that he is filled with grace, he will never receive grace.... He who ascribes to himself gifts of grace fences off from himself by this 'fancy' the entrance into himself of Divine grace, and opens wide the door to the infection of sin and to demons." *Thou sayest, I am rich, and increased with goods, and have need of nothing; and knowest not that thou art wretched, and miserable, and poor, and blind, and naked* (Rev. 3:17).[60]

Genuine miracle-working gifts of the Holy Spirit "are given to Saints of God solely at God's good will and God's action, and not by the will of men and nor by one's own power. They are given unexpectedly, extremely rarely, in cases of extreme need, by God's wondrous providence, and not just at random."[61]

---

60   Rose, *Orthodoxy and the Religion of the Future*, 165-6.
61   St. Isaac the Syrian (+700) as quoted in Rose, *Orthodoxy and the Religion of the Future*, 166.

Perhaps the most egregious example of how far Western Christianity has strayed is that of modern-day "charismatics," who claim to speak in tongues, but who in fact take leave of their God-given rationality and debase themselves in a riot of senseless hysterics suggestive of the demoniacs of the Gospels. The charismatic movement, which evolved out of the Pentecostal church founded in 1900, has found receptive audiences in numerous Western Christian denominations, including Roman Catholicism, and has even attempted to insinuate itself into some corners of Orthodoxy. St. Paul, while validating speaking in tongues, nonetheless warned against them being taken to excess.

> But now, brethren, if I come to you speaking with tongues, what shall I profit you unless I speak to you either by revelation, by knowledge, by prophesying, or by teaching?… [I]f the whole church comes together in one place, and all speak with tongues, and there come in those who are uninformed or unbelievers, will they not say that you are out of your mind?[62]

Far from "outpourings of the Holy Spirit," contemporary charismatic gatherings in which participants supposedly "speak in tongues" are scenes of histrionic gibberish or worse: genuine demonic inspiration. St. Gregory Palamas (+1359) warned against "demonic tongues" masquerading as sanctity. Nowhere outside the Apostolic era has the Church recognized authentic speaking in tongues.[63] St. Augustine, writing at the turn of the fifth century, affirmed that speaking in tongues during the Apostolic era

---

62   1 Cor. 14:6, 23.
63   See Rose, *Orthodoxy and the Religion of the Future*, 137.

were signs adapted to the time. For it was fitting that there
be given this sign of the Holy Spirit in all tongues to show
that the Gospel of God was to run through all tongues
over the whole earth. That was done for a sign, and it
passed away.[64]

As Father Seraphim Rose cogently demonstrated, the charismatic practice of "laying on of hands"—a distortion of the
Apostolic laying on of hands that occurs during the Orthodox
ordination of clergy and consecration of hierarchs[65]—which
often precedes episodes of "glossolalia," constitutes a psy-
cho-spiritual technique that opens participants to demonic
influence in the manner of eastern pagan practices.[66] The
so-called charismatic "baptism" of the Holy Spirit, in which
the newly "baptized" supposedly speak in tongues, amounts
to a *"mediumistic initiation,"*[67] a form of channeling as practiced
by pagan mystics, spiritists, and psychics who actively seek out
communion with fallen spirits for worldly purposes.

Summarizing the situation in the United States, some have
gone so far as to argue that "the American Religion" is not
really Christian anymore, that it shares more in common with
the Gnostic heresies that plagued the early Church than with
anything authentically Christian.

A new religion has been slowly replacing European Christianity
in the United States since the country's founding. Sometimes
it has manifested itself in fresh and ecstatic revelations, as
with the Mormons and the Adventists.... In other instances, the American Religion has adopted older Protestant

---

64   St. Augustine, *Homilies on John*, VI:10 as quoted in Rose, *Orthodoxy and the Religion of the Future*, 125.

65   See 2 Tim. 1:6.

66   See Rose, *Orthodoxy and the Religion of the Future*, ch. 7, "The Charismatic Revival."

67   Ibid., 136.

identities, like the Baptists, but replaced those faiths with
an apparent creedlessness that conceals archaic shamanisms,
together with 17th and 18th century enthusiastic revivals
of Gnostic heresies prevalent in the early Christian period...
Though it mostly calls itself by the name of one Protestantism
or another, this American Religion is post-Protestant,
indeed post-Christian.[68]

Of course, not all contemporary heterodoxy is confined to
the "low" Protestant mega-churches filled with Orwellian television screens, laser lightshows, and pop music. There remain
the "high" Protestant churches, which today proudly flaunt the
sin of Sodom in the form of homosexual clergy and "gay marriage." And there is modern-day Roman Catholicism, afflicted
by the abominable scourge of pederasty and cover-up, and
which, not unlike the mega-churches, cultivates a clamoring,
rock-star adoration of the "infallible" Pope. Such "Christianity,"
concerned not with the correct worship of God and the transformation of the heart into a dwelling fit for Him, but with social
work, public posturing, and the quantity rather than quality of
the faithful, is a religion of this world, not of the next. However
well-intended many of the devotees of such "churches" may be,
the primary characteristic of such bodies is not Christian but
antichristian. It is only Holy Orthodoxy, beaten and bloodied
through the centuries by heretics, jihadists, barbarians, fascists,
Communists, and, most sadly, Western Christians of various
stripes, that alone retains the purity of Christ's doctrines and
"the Spirit of truth," which alone can "guide us into all truth."[69]
    Probably the most widespread heretical notion that pervades
Western Christianity is the idea that the form that prayer and

---

68   Harold Bloom, "The New Heyday of Gnostic Heresies." *The New York Times*.
April 26, 1992. https://www.nytimes.com/1992/04/26/opinion/new-heyday-
of-gnostic-heresies.html. Accessed September 16, 2019.
69   John 16:13.

worship should take lie in the eye of the beholder, that they are a question of personal preference. Ex-Muslim Archimandrite Daniel Byantoro of Indonesia has put it aptly when he affirms that Orthodox Christians are the true Muslims, i.e., those who truly submit (in Arabic الاسلام *islam* means submission) to the will of God. Western Christians are invariably trying to make up their own minds about matters of doctrine, how to pray, what sort of worship they prefer, which preacher to listen to, etc. without submitting to the Holy Traditions established by God in His One Church and taking their own will out of it.

Worship of God is not something to be decided by the fallible reason of the individual; rather it is the highest and most important aspect of the relationship between God and man and can only properly take place in accordance with God's own statutes. It defies reason that God should have specified so exactly the form that worship was to take in ancient Israel—the type of sacrifices to be offered, the color of vestments to be worn by the priests, even the flavor of incense to be offered—and then leave it up to individual whim in the Christian era with the predictable result of liturgical anarchy.

> Then [the priests] Nadab and Abihu, the sons of Aaron, each took his censer and put fire in it, put incense on it, and offered profane fire before the LORD, which He had not commanded them. So fire went out from the LORD and devoured them, and they died before the LORD.[70]

As improper worship, even among ordained temple priests, could lead to physical death in the Old Testament dispensation, so in the New Testament can it lead to spiritual death. With his expulsion from Paradise, man lost his reliable intuition as to how God ought to be worshipped. It is only through the

---

70   Lev. 1:1-3.

received wisdom of Christ's Church, conserved and handed down through the centuries from the time of the Lord Himself, that the correct worship of God can take place.

> Enter by the narrow gate; for wide is the gate and broad is the way that leads to destruction, and there are many who go in by it. Because narrow is the gate and difficult is the way which leads to life, and there are few who find it…. Beware of false prophets, who come to you in sheep's clothing, but inwardly they are ravenous wolves. You will know them by their fruits…. Not everyone who says to Me, "Lord, Lord," shall enter the kingdom of heaven, but he who does the will of My Father in heaven. Many will say to Me in that day, "Lord, Lord, have we not prophesied in Your name, cast out demons in Your name, and done many wonders in Your name?" And then I will declare to them, "I never knew you; depart from Me, you who practice lawlessness!"[71]

It is increasingly apparent what are the fruits of a millennium of Western heresy and apostasy: the Crusades, simony and indulgences, the sack of Constantinople, the distortions of the Reformation, the bloody European Wars of Religion of the sixteenth and seventeenth centuries, the fantastically destructive revolutions of the modern era and their attendant genocides; to that, add subtler—but similarly destructive—revolutions such as the sexual revolution, two World Wars, the open debasement of Western Christianity by mammon, sexual immorality, and pagan syncretism, and now the burgeoning heresy of ecumenism. Many people's rejection of God in our time may be a natural reaction to what they now see pass for Christianity. Never having encountered Christ's True Church, but only the distortions and

---

71   Matt. 7:13-16; 21-3.

counterdistortions of the West in which "lawlessness abounds" and "the love of many" has "grown cold,"[72] one can hardly blame them.

Our own time attests that there is no apparent limit to the sheer weirdness of the variations on modern antichristianity. A few examples are sufficient for purposes of illustration; we cannot attempt even a cursory survey in the space afforded here. One of the more prominent, self-consciously "Christian" examples of recent memory, was that of the Reverend Sun Myung Moon (1920–2012), founder of the Unification Church. As well as a religious figure and self-proclaimed messiah, Moon was a self-made billionaire and media baron.

> In his personal manifesto, *Divine Principle* (1957), Moon argued that, had He lived, Jesus would have married the ideal wife and begotten the perfect "pure" family. Moon would complete the task with the aim of unifying all religions and societies under his personal rule, liberating them from the sinful condition caused (Moon claimed) by Eve's illicit sex with Satan.... Moon's critics often claimed that the Moonies were less a religious movement than a vehicle for Moon's own global ambitions. "God is living in me and I am the incarnation of Himself," he once told Time magazine. "The whole world is in my hand and I will conquer and subjugate the world."[73]

By contemporary standards, Moon's illusions of grandeur, while enormous, are almost unremarkable. Moon died in 2012 leaving an unsubjugated world behind him. His pretense to being the incarnation of God who would unify all religions marks

---

72   Matt. 24:12.
73   "Obituary: The Reverend Sun Myung Moon," *The Telegraph*. http://www. telegraph.co.uk/news/obituaries/9517193/The-Rev-Sun-Myung-Moon. html. Accessed September 16, 2019.

him as a clear, if unsuccessful, candidate to be the Antichrist. Another, less well-known, but even more unusual, example of a contemporary antichrist is that of Jose Luis de Jesus Miranda (b. 1946), who started his own "church" in Miami, Florida, and who claims that he is both Jesus Christ and Antichrist together.

> "Antichrist is the best person in the world," he says. "Antichrist means don't put your eyes on Jesus because Jesus of Nazareth wasn't a Christian. Antichrist means do not put your eyes on Jesus Christ of Nazareth. Put it on Jesus after the cross." And de Jesus says that means him. So far, de Jesus says that his flock hasn't been scared off by his claims of being the Antichrist. In a show of the sway he holds over the group, 30 members of his congregation Tuesday went to a tattoo parlor to have 666 also permanently etched onto their skin…. Followers have protested Christian churches in Miami and Latin America, disrupting services and smashing crosses and statues of Jesus. De Jesus preaches there is no devil and no sin. His followers, he says, literally can do no wrong in God's eyes. The church calls itself the "Government of God on Earth" and uses a seal similar to the United States.[74]

It is probably difficult to overestimate the extent to which the spirit of antichrist permeates contemporary Western society. Modernity has transformed, and even inverted, the traditional conception of religion as a means of orienting oneself towards God. Distinctively modern rituals such as watching television and other forms of mass electronic entertainment, almost regardless of the content they carry, fairly qualify as religious

---

74   "Pastor with 666 tattoo claims to be divine," *CNN.com*. http://www.cnn.com/2007/US/02/16/miami.preacher/index.html. Accessed September 16, 2019.

in nature. Marshall McLuhan's dictum that "the medium is the message" is continually born out. While various Christian and other commentators have observed the deleterious effects of modern mass media, it is illuminating to note the observations of the Church's avowed enemies, which tend to confirm, sometimes uncannily, one's worst fears. The writings of our time's leading Satanist, for example, read like the trenchant insights of a serious Orthodox commentator with the value system turned upside-down. They are worth quoting at some length:

> Many of you have already read my writings identifying TV as the new God. There is a little thing I neglected to mention up until now—television is the major mainstream infiltration of the New Satanic religion.
>
> The birth of TV was a magical event foreshadowing its Satanic significance.... The TV set, or Satanic family altar, has grown more elaborate since the early '50s, from the tiny, fuzzy screen to huge "entertainment centers" covering entire walls with several TV monitors. What started as an innocent respite from everyday life has become in itself a replacement for real life for millions, a major religion of the masses.
>
> The consumer society in which we now live is an extension of the society once governed by religion for many centuries. Instead of obeying the holy bible, right or wrong, TV advertising now instructs what to buy and what not to buy.... [M]odern heresy—not conforming to a television lifestyle, not accepting television truths—is liable to be punished with as much righteous enthusiasm as ever.
>
> The clergy of the TV religion are those entertainers, newscasters in particular, who nightly spread the Word from their cathode-ray pulpit. The network newscasters are the High Priests and High Priestesses of Satanism,

bending the minds of viewers to the requirements of con-
sumer marketing. The local newscasters are the parish
priests, yawking, ribbing and emoting over the latest local
tragedies. Celebrities, whether local or national, are all
part of the hierarchy of the church, men of the cloth...

There is no way a person can escape religion as long
as he is living in a religious environment. Situation
comedies, dramatic series and soap operas are broadcast
day and night seven days a week to activate and sustain
the lifestyles of the parishioners, where before only fa-
natics practiced daily devotions. The masses committed
only one day, Sunday, to the Christian God. As I've said
before, the TV Guide is the new concordance. Tabloids
and news magazines supply the instructions for pious
living.[75]

Anton LeVay (1930-97) by no means lamented the burgeoning
"Satanic infiltration" of modern culture; he wrote not to bemoan
the rise of television as the Satanic religion of the masses but to
rejoice in it. Even so, he was careful to limit his own children's
exposure to "demon TV."

While recognizing the present state of anarchy and superficial-
ity among the Western sects, the illogic and antichristian nature
of the ecumenical movement, and the truly devilish inspiration
of much modern culture, we must not imagine that the coming
"church" of Antichrist will be easy to recognize or to resist.

Non-Christian "spirituality" is no longer a foreign im-
portation in the West; it has become a native American
religion putting down deep roots into the consciousness

---

75   Anton Szandor LeVey, "Some Evidence of a New Satanic Age, Part 2," in *The Devil's Notebook*. https://answersingenesis.org/theory-of-evolution/quotes/99-quotable-quotes/. Accessed October 5, 2019.

of the West. Let us be warned from this: the religion of the future will not be a mere cult or sect, but a powerful and profound religious orientation which will be absolutely convincing to the mind and heart of modern man.[76]

Indeed, for those who have rejected Christ, Antichrist will appear to bring an unprecedented flowering of spirituality.

> The Messianic Era [sic] will usher in the rebirth of virtue, a renaissance of spirituality and an understanding of God's will. The world will experience a spiritual revival that will result in the perfection of the human condition. Man will achieve the same state of godliness as on the day he was created. "The wolf shall dwell with the lamb."[77]

> The Antichrist must be understood as a spiritual phenomenon. Why will everyone in the world want to bow down to him? Obviously, it is because there is something in him which responds to something in us—that something being a lack of Christ in us. If we will bow down to him (God forbid that we do so!), it will be because we will feel an attraction to some kind of external thing, which might even look like Christianity, since "Antichrist" means the one who is "in place of Christ" or looks like Christ.[78]

As St. Ignatius Brianchaninov has already told us, "The Antichrist will be the logical, just, and natural result of the general moral and spiritual direction of mankind."[79] We do not know when Antichrist will make his appearance, perhaps soon,

---

76   Rose, *Orthodoxy and the Religion of the Future*, 67.

77   Leibel Reznick, *The Mystery of Bar Kokhba: An Historical and Theological Investigations of the Last King of the Jews*, 137-8 as quoted in Jones, 52.

78   Damascene, *Father Seraphim Rose*, 829.

79   St. Ignatius Brianchaninov as quoted in Damascene, *Father Seraphim Rose*, 731.

perhaps not for many generations, but Orthodox Christians must resist today the "spirit of the times" that is setting the stage for his arrival. It is to the positive nature of what the "religion of the future" may look like that we will now turn.

CHAPTER 9

THE EMPIRE OF THE PHARISEES

"Woe to you, scribes and Pharisees, hypocrites! Because you build the tombs of the prophets and adorn the monuments of the righteous, and say, 'If we had lived in the days of our fathers, we would not have been partakers with them in the blood of the prophets.' Therefore you are witnesses against yourselves that you are sons of those who murdered the prophets. Fill up, then, the measure of your fathers. Serpents! Brood of vipers! How can you escape the damnation of hell?"

Matthew 23: 29-33

In the first centuries of the Christian era, two groups of men set out from the Holy Land with a common objective: to conquer the world. One group was the Holy Apostles. In short order, they set the world afire with the Gospel of Jesus Christ and built the most enduring and influential institution in world history, the Church of Christ. Their work, inspired by God, stands to this day and will continue eternally in the age to come. The other group was their antagonists, the Pharisees, the anti-Apostles, who sought to remake the world in their own, very different, image. These two bodies of men—the first "as men condemned to death… poorly clothed, and beaten, and homeless… made as the filth of the world, the offscouring of all things"[1]—the other who "love the uppermost rooms at feasts, and the chief seats in the synagogues, and greetings in the market, and to be called by men, 'Rabbi, Rabbi' "[2]—both claiming to represent the tradition of the God of Israel, yet utterly antithetical in their interpretations of it, represent in plainest fashion the two forces that struggle in history for the hearts of men.

God became incarnate and shed His blood to save mankind from their sins and from death. He inspired His Apostles with His Holy Spirit that they might make disciples of all nations and carry the message of His Gospel to the far reaches of the earth. And the enemy of mankind, Satan, inspired his disciples, the unrepentant Pharisees, who thought themselves righteous because they had "Abraham" as their "father,"[3] but whose "father" is in fact "the devil,"[4] to build their own "church," "the synagogue of Satan,"[5] which was to transform the world into the image of their master.

For centuries, the apostolic mission, the building of the Church, carried the day. Later, through heresy and schism, the Church's ascendancy began to wane. Formerly Orthodox peoples turned away from the fullness of God's revelation and adulterated its pure doctrine with "traditions of men"[6] and "fables."[7] As civil society separated itself from the Church, the latter was progressively shorn of her outer defenses, and slowly, over the centuries, the spirit of the Pharisees was able to gather force in the world.

---

1   1 Cor. 4:9-13.
2   Matt. 23:6-7.
3   John 8:39.
4   John 8:44.
5   Rev. 2:9; 3:9.
6   Mark 7:8.
7   2 Tim. 4:4.

The corrupt ruling classes that the Lord denounced in His day—the money-changers,[8] scribes, lawyers,[9] and Pharisees—have direct analogues in today's financial sharks, ivory-tower academics, "experts," bureaucratic busybodies, and religious charlatans who thrive in modern society. The Orthodox empires of yesteryear, governed however imperfectly by fallible men according to the principles of Christian justice, mercy, and truth, have given way to the global Empire of the Pharisees, which awaits the coming of its prince.

While the original Apostles and Pharisees have long since passed on to eternity, their spiritual heirs continue in their divergent legacies. The Church and the "synagogue of Satan" continue to vie for the hearts and minds of men even if only the former declares herself openly. While the worldly principles embodied by the Pharisees have always been at war with Christ and His Church, it was not until the modern era that they discernibly gained the upper hand. From the first centuries in the life of the Church, when she won over the Roman Empire and showed herself as the pre-eminent cultural force in the world, she is now seen as but one choice among many at the bizarre bazaar of world religions that features everything from myriad variations of pseudo-Christianity to "new atheism" to paganism to witchcraft to "UFOs and their spiritual mission."[10] No longer do Orthodox monarchs rally their subjects to resist heresy and injustice, to raise the banner of the Cross against alien creeds and the subversion of Christian society; now the great nations of the world have been reduced to chaotic secular "democracies"—oligarchies as we have seen—in which

---

8   Matt. 21:12-13.

9   See Luke 11:46-52.

10   See Benjamin Creme's *The Gathering of the Forces of Light: UFOs and their Spiritual Mission*. Creme argues that UFOs are assisting in the eventual emergence of "Maitreya," the Buddhist "World Teacher," who Creme believes will in time unite and consummate the world's religions. Yet another variation on Antichrist.

antichristian demagogues outbid each other to heap the blessings of mammon upon their people. The principles and methods of the Pharisees—intrigue, deceit, legalism, hypocrisy, false piety, the seeking after "signs and wonders"[11]—are the dominant principles of the world today and, tragically, of what masquerades as so much "Christianity".

The Façade of "Judeo-Christianity"

As discussed in the preceding chapter, ecumenism is the principal negative force eroding the traditional differences among religions and confusing them into a single, amorphous mass that can be shaped into a global "religion of the future." We have, however, intimations as to what the positive character of this coming "religion" may look like. While it is unclear now, like other aspects of globalization, it is slowly coming into focus, while its ultimate form is elucidated by the figure of the coming Antichrist.

From our earlier study, we know that Antichrist will not merely be the archenemy of Christ, but he will actually appear to be Christ come again, which is the essence of his great deception. Thus, it is logical to expect that many of his followers will identify as Christians, imagining that they are beholding Jesus Christ in His second advent. Furthermore, Scripture and the Holy Fathers also tell us that Antichrist will be received by the mass of the world but especially by many self-proclaimed Jews who will see in him their promised messiah. As St. Cyril has told us, "[B]y the lying signs and wonders of his magical deceit having beguiled the Jews, as though he were the expected Christ, he shall afterwards be characterized by all kinds of crimes of

---

11   John 4:48; see also Matt. 8:38.

inhumanity and lawlessness."[12] St. Hippolytus agrees, "Above all, moreover, [Antichrist] will love the nation of the Jews. And with all these he will work signs and terrible wonders, false wonders and not true... And after that he will build the temple in Jerusalem and will restore it again speedily and give it over to the Jews."[13] Modern commentators have similarly observed that Antichrist will ally himself with a significant movement of Jews.[14]

By "Jews" we have in mind those who continue to identify as the Israelite people but who do not accept Jesus of Nazareth as the prophesied Messiah. Because of their rejection of Jesus as the Christ, many Jews continue to anticipate their promised messiah. Indeed, there have been many false alarms through history in which Jews worldwide believed they had found their savior. The leader of the disastrous Third Jewish-Roman War of 132-5 AD, Simon Bar Kochba, later executed by the Romans, was proclaimed messiah by the rabbinical authorities of his day. The most famous example in more recent times was that of Sabbatai Zevi (1626-76), who enflamed much of European Jewry by claiming to be the messiah, and who set up a community devoted to himself in Smyrna, Turkey. He hugely disappointed, however, when he was imprisoned by the Turks and converted to Islam.

The memories of Bar Kochba and Zevi have bestowed a note of circumspection among later generations in recognizing any claimant to the messianic throne. Nevertheless, the Lord Himself prophesied that those who rejected Him would one day receive another in His place: "I have come in My Father's name, and you do not receive Me; if another comes in his own

---

12   Lecture XV, no. 12.

13   St. Hippolytus of Rome, *Discourse on the End of the World*, sections 23, 25. https://www.ccel.org/ccel/schaff/anf05.iii.v.i.xxiii.html; https://www.ccel.org/ccel/schaff/anf05.iii.v.i.xxv.html. Accessed September 17, 2019.

14   See, for example, Chris White's *False Christ: Will the Antichrist Claim to be the Jewish Messiah?* (Ducktown, CWM, 2014).

name, him you will receive."[15] The other who will come "in his own name" whom the spiritual descendants of the Pharisees will receive is Antichrist. Antichrist will be the messiah of the "synagogue of Satan," the worldly redeemer whom many Jews and heterodox Christians will receive as their king. It will be such a peculiar alliance of Jews and deluded Christians that will make up the core of the faithful of the religion of Antichrist. It is not wrong, then, to describe this coming religion of Antichrist as self-consciously "Judeo-Christian", a term that is already current. Antichrist will unite those Jews who are looking for the messiah and "Christians" who are anticipating an earthly reign of Jesus Christ.

In coming to understand what is meant by Judeo-Christianity, an important distinction must be made between "Judaism," a religion and cultural worldview whose principles are open to analysis, and "Jews," who identify as the descendants of the tribes of Israel and Judah notwithstanding adherence to some form of religious Judaism. In modern circumstances, self-identified Jews may or may not be biologically descended from ancient Israel and Judah and they may or may not accept the tenets of Judaism.

> The ethnic group does not define the religious system... All Judaists—those who practice the religion, Judaism— are Jews, but not all Jews are Judaists. That is to say, all those who practice the religion, Judaism, by definition fall into the ethnic group, the Jews, but not all members of the ethnic group practice Judaism.[16]

---

15   John 5:43.
16   Jacob Neusner, "Defining Judaism" in *The Blackwell Companion to Judaism* (Malden, Blackwell, 2000, 2003), 5.

For the sake of clarity, it is better to refer to "Judaists," adherents of Judaism and others who accept Judaism's central tenets, following the work of Rabbi Jacob Neusner. As Rabbi Neusner points out, there are plenty of self-identified Jews who reject religious Judaism. The confusion can only be cleared up by emphasizing that we are here examining the basic tenets of Judaism in its traditional, orthodox form, which pertains to Jews only insofar as they retain a Judaic religious orientation. Indeed, the question of what it means to be a Jew is a question addressed by the greatest Christian evangelist, St. Paul:

> For he is not a Jew who is one outwardly, nor is circumcision that which is outward in the flesh; but he is a Jew who is one inwardly; and circumcision is that of the heart, in the Spirit, not in the letter; whose praise is not from men but from God.[17]

True Jews are those who love God and keep His commandments regardless of biological descent, i.e., the faithful Church. However, since the time of the early Church, the term "Jews" has connoted those who, while identifying as tribal Israel, have rejected Jesus as the Messiah.

> What does St. John [the Apostle and Theologian] mean when he refers to "Jews"? When St. John uses the words "*oi Ioudaoi* [οι Ιουδαίοι]," he is referring to a group that has rejected Christ. The coming of Christ changed Jewish identity forever, something the Jews at His time comprehended only with difficulty. From then, the terms "Israelite" and "Jew" were no longer synonyms, because ..."the 'true Israelites' " from the Christian perspective

---

17   Rom. 2:28-9.

"are precisely those who, like [the Apostle] Nathaniel, recognize in Jesus the Messiah."[18]

Significantly, modern Judaists agree that Jewish identity, while generally flexible in its religious orientation, absolutely precludes Christianity, i.e., a Jew who embraces Christianity—certainly Orthodoxy—becomes excluded from the group.

> While not all Jews practice Judaism, in the iron-consensus among contemporary Jews, Jews who practice Christianity cease to be part of the ethnic Jewish community, while those who practice Buddhism remain within. The upshot is that the ethnic and the religious in the world of the Jews present confusion.[19]

There is no room in Judaism, in other words, for Christianized Jews; such "Jews" are seen as Christians; "Jews for Jesus" is an oxymoron.[20]

Thus, "Judeo-Christianity" presents a fundamental contradiction, but it finds justification in a variety of ways. In the contemporary West, Judeo-Christian is often used to imply a recognition of the validity of both the Old and New Testaments and a common basis to Judaism and Christianity. Indeed, the Orthodox Christian tradition affirms the canonicity of the entire Bible, but no seriously minded Judaist or Christian could accept the notion that Judaism and Christianity are both valid understandings of Holy Scripture. "St. Justin rejects the suggestion

---

18   Jones, *The Jewish Revolutionary Spirit*, 33-4.

19   Neusner, "Defining Judaism" in *The Blackwell Companion to Judaism*, 6.

20   "Jewish theology is built on the observance of mitzvot (commandments) in order to hasten the arrival of the messiah—who has not yet arrived. Judaism simply doesn't recognize Jesus as the messiah. Jews for Jesus, even if they speak Hebrew, pray out of a *siddur*, or observe Shabbat, believe in a theology that is in opposition to Judaism." *My Jewish Learning*. https://www.myjewishlearning.com/article/ask-the-expert-jews-for-jesus/. Accessed September 17, 2019.

that the Old Testament is a link holding together the Church and the Synagogue. For him quite the opposite is true."[21] While the Old Testament is nominally common to both, Orthodox Judaism and Orthodox Christianity comprise antithetical interpretations thereof—reflecting, in fact, the same fundamental disagreement between Jesus and the Pharisees of two thousand years ago. Then and now, somebody was right and somebody was wrong: either Jesus of Nazareth is the Messiah prophesied by the Old Testament or He is not. If He is, then Judaists who persist in their unbelief are guilty of rejecting their Messiah; if not, Christians are guilty of following a charlatan or a madman who claimed "that God was his Father, making himself equal with God."[22] One cannot have it both ways. Trying to see Jesus Christ as merely a philosopher, prophet, or moral teacher is logically unacceptable. As C. S. Lewis put it, there are only three possibilities: liar, lunatic, or Lord. No man who claims to be one with God can possibly be considered in a positive light unless he is in fact one with God; otherwise he can only be regarded as a deceiver and a megalomaniac.

> Then the Jews surrounded Him and said to Him, "How long do You keep us in doubt? If You are the Christ, tell us plainly." Jesus answered them, "I told you, and you do not believe. The works that I do in My Father's name, they bear witness of Me.... I and My Father are one." Then the Jews took up stones again to stone Him. Jesus answered them, "Many good works I have shown you from My Father. For which of those works do you stone Me?" The Jews answered Him, saying, "For a good work

---

21 Florovsky, *Collected Works*, v. 4, 31. https://www.bulgarian-orthodox-church. org/rr/lode/florovsky4.pdf. Accessed September 17, 2019.
22 John 5:18.

we do not stone You, but for blasphemy, and because You, being a Man, make Yourself God."[23]

A commonly held belief among many Western Christians today of the Judeo-Christian variety is that self-identified Jews need not accept Jesus as the Messiah because they remain a "covenant people." This idea affirms that Jews, by virtue of their tribal descent and/or adherence to the Judaic religion, maintain the Old Covenant with God and may therefore acceptably continue to deny Jesus of Nazareth as the Christ. Lost is the fact that Jesus could only be the Christ if He fulfills the promises of the Old Covenant, and therefore to reject the New Covenant is to reject the Old as well. "The Father loves the Son, and has given all things into His hand. He who believes in the Son has everlasting life; and he who does not believe the Son shall not see life, but the wrath of God abides on him."[24] Jesus' claim that "I am the way, the truth, and the life. No one comes to the Father except through Me"[25] does not allow for "special access" to God apart from Christ Himself, Who indeed is God come in the flesh. To reject Jesus as the Christ is to reject the God of the Old Testament as well as of the New.

The related idea that Judaism today is the religion of the Old Testament while Christianity is that of the New is similarly insupportable. If the New Covenant is to have any validity, it must be considered the extension and fulfillment of the Old, as Jesus Himself said it was. During the time of the Lord's ministry, there were no New Testament Scriptures; the disagreements between Him and the Pharisees, and later between the Apostles and the Pharisees, were exclusively with respect to the Old Testament.

---

23   John 10:24-33.
24   John 3:35-6. See Jn 8:23-4.
25   John 14:6.

You search the Scriptures, for in them you think you have eternal life; and these are they which testify of Me.... Do not think that I shall accuse you to the Father; there is one who accuses you—Moses, in whom you trust. For if you believed Moses, you would believe Me; for he wrote about Me. But if you do not believe his writings, how will you believe My words?[26]

The famous phrase of St. Augustine can be taken as typical of the whole Patristic attitude towards the Old Dispensation. *Novum Testamentum in Vetere latet. Vetus Testamentum in Novo patet.* (The New Testament was latent in the Old Testament; the Old Testament becomes patent in the New Testament.) The New Testament is an accomplishment, or a consummation, of the Old. Christ Jesus is the Messiah spoken of by the prophets. In Him all promises and expectations are fulfilled. The Law and the Gospel belong together. And nobody can claim to be a true follower of Moses unless he believes that Jesus is the Lord.[27]

Either the Messiah came as the "despised and rejected Man of sorrows"[28] prophesied by Moses and the prophets, Who died on the Cross and rose again, or he will come as the latter-day conqueror who will reign in Jerusalem as king of the world. God's promise to Abraham that "in thy seed shall all the nations of the earth be blessed"[29] was either fulfilled in Jesus Christ and the Church or it will be fulfilled by the ephemeral harmony and prosperity that Antichrist will bring at the end of history.

---

26   John 5:39, 45-7.
27   Fr. George Florovsky. *Collected Works*, v. 4. 1975. 31-2. https://www.bulgarian-orthodox-church.org/rr/lode/florovsky4.pdf. Accessed September 17, 2019.
28   Is. 53:3.
29   Gen. 22:18.

In trying to understand the contradictory nature of Judeo-Christianity, it is imperative to bear in mind that it is the Talmud—not the Torah of the Old Testament—that is the highest scriptural authority in Judaism. The Talmud—specifically the Babylonian Talmud, which is considered more authoritative than the Jerusalem or Palestinian Talmud—is a compendium of commentaries on Judaic law and Scripture believed to have existed for centuries in oral form from the time of Moses. This oral tradition was put down in writing during exile from the Holy Land in the first centuries of the Christian era and became the first part of the Talmud, the Mishnah; the Gemara, the second part, consists of further glosses, debates, and commentary on the transcribed "oral tradition." While the schools of Talmudic analysis, Hillel and Shammai, sometimes differ in their interpretations, there is consensus that the decrees of both speak with the authority of the word of God—even when they disagree.[30] The Talmud, which runs to more than six thousand pages, is the central and final authority in all of Judaism.

The Talmud is the prism, receiving, refracting all light. To state the proposition in academic language: into that writing all prior canonical writings emerged; to it, all appeal is directed; upon it, all conclusions ultimately rest. In the language of Torah itself: study of the Torah begins, as a matter of simple, ubiquitous fact, in the Talmud.... In all decisions of law that express theology in everyday action, the Talmud forms the final statement of the Torah, mediating Scripture's rules. Innovations of every kind, whether in the character of the spiritual life or in

---

30   Michael Hoffman, *Judaism Discovered* (Coeur d'Alene, Independent History and Research, 2008), 344.

the practice of the faith in accord with its norms, must find justification in the Talmud.[31]

The foregoing "innovations of every kind" is significant, and speaks volumes about the differences between the holy texts of Orthodox Christianity and Judaism. While, in the former, Holy Tradition conserves and protects the Word of God from the errors of innovation, in the latter, the Talmud facilitates them. It was exactly such innovations that Christ challenged when He confronted the Pharisees for annulling the Word of God with "the commandments of men"[32]—the same oral tradition that would later find written expression as the Talmud.

> Judaic theologians claim that "… ancient rabbis taught that the revelation granted to Moses had been delivered in two forms, a smaller revelation in writing and the larger one kept oral. This 'Oral Torah' had been transmitted faithfully by the leaders of each generation to their successors, by Moses to Joshua, and then to the elders, then to the prophets, to the men of the Great Assembly, to the leaders of the Pharisees, and finally to the earliest rabbis. The earliest rabbis saw themselves… as heirs to the Pharisees."[33] This supposed transmission of the "Oral Torah," the tradition of the elders, from Moses to Joshua, to the prophets, was challenged by Jesus Christ who termed it not Torah, but the commandments of men which nullify irrevocably the word and doctrine of God, making the tale of the transmission itself a fraud.[34]

---

31   Neusner, *Rabbinic Judaism*, 205 as quoted in Hoffman, *Judaism Discovered*, 27.
32   Mark 7:7.
33   Goldenburg, *Talmud*, 130 as quoted in Hoffman, *Judaism Discovered*, 187.
34   Hoffman, *Judaism Discovered*, 187.

[Jesus] answered and said to them, "Well did Isaiah prophesy of you hypocrites, as it is written: 'This people honors Me with their lips, but their heart is far from Me. And in vain they worship Me, teaching as doctrines the commandments of men.' For laying aside the commandment of God, you hold the tradition of men—the washing of pitchers and cups, and many other such things you do."[35]

As the Talmud, these "commandments of men", which Christ censured for suffocating ordinary Jews and twisting the Word of God, eventually came to be nothing short of divinized in Orthodox Judaism. Whereas in Orthodox Christianity, God became flesh in Jesus Christ, in Orthodox Judaism, " ... the Babylonian Talmud represents God in the flesh,"[36] not unlike the Qur'an in Islam, which orthodox Muslims regard as uncreated and pre-eternal.[37] The Talmud, the innovations of men amassed over centuries in contravention to the tradition of Holy Scripture, is Judaism's greatest idol, something no Christian can accept.

Technically accurate but misleading notions such as "Christ was a Jew" serve to muddy the waters of Judeo-Christianity further. Indeed, Christ was a Jew, i.e., descended from Abraham, Jacob, and Judah, and, in His own words, "Salvation is of the Jews,"[38] but He in no way was a practitioner of the Judaic religion, the centerpiece of which is the rejection of Him as the Christ. The question then and now is, which tradition faithfully represents God's revelation to mankind? Who today composes the true Israel?

---

35   Mark 7:6-12.
36   Jacob Neusner and Bruce D. Chilton, *God in the World* (Eugene, Wipf and Stock, 1997), 9. books.google.fr/books?id=KQ5LAwAAQBAJ
37   See H. Lammens, *Islam: Beliefs and Institutions, translated by Sir E. Denison Ross* (London, Frank Cass and Co. Ltd., 1929, 1968), esp. 37-8.
38   John 4:22.

Does this blessedness then come upon the circumcised only, or upon the uncircumcised also? For we say that faith was accounted to Abraham for righteousness. How then was it accounted? While he was circumcised, or uncircumcised? Not while circumcised, but while uncircumcised. And he received the sign of circumcision, a seal of the righteousness of the faith which he had while still uncircumcised, that he might be the father of all those who believe, though they are uncircumcised, that righteousness might be imputed to them also, and the father of circumcision to those who not only are of the circumcision, but who also walk in the steps of the faith which our father Abraham had while still uncircumcised.[39]

The ancient faith which our father Abraham had while still uncircumcised is the faith of the Lord's Church today. The heirs of Abraham are those who keep the commandments of God rather than those necessarily descended from his flesh.

For they are not all Israel who are of Israel, nor are they all children because they are the seed of Abraham; but, "In Isaac your seed shall be called." That is, those who are the children of the flesh, these are not the children of God; but the children of the promise are counted as the seed.[40]

Therefore know that only those who are of faith are sons of Abraham. And the Scripture, foreseeing that God would justify the Gentiles by faith, preached the gospel to Abraham beforehand, saying, "In you all the nations shall

---

39   Rom. 4:9-12.
40   Rom. 9:6-8.

be blessed." So then those who are of faith are blessed with believing Abraham.[41]

In Christ, social and ethnic distinctions are sublimated into the Church, the Body of Christ. "For we are members of His body, of His flesh and of His bones."[42]

> For as many of you as were baptized into Christ have put on Christ. There is neither Jew nor Greek, there is neither slave nor free, there is neither male nor female; for you are all one in Christ Jesus. And if you are Christ's, then you are Abraham's seed, and heirs according to the promise.[43]

> Judaism was not viewed [by the first-millennium Church] as the repository of the spiritual truths or knowledge of the Old Testament... True Israelites could only be Christians, not followers of Judaism. The followers of Judaism are anti-Biblical; they had to violate the Old Testament in order to reject Jesus, for the "Scriptures testify of me."[44]

Judaism's own depictions of Jesus of Nazareth should dispel any notion that Judeo-Christianity can be considered as anything other than an oxymoron. The Talmud alternatively refers to Jesus pejoratively as *otho isch* ("that man"), *peloni* ("a certain one"), *naggar bar naggar* ("the carpenter son of a carpenter") and *ben charsch etaim* ("the son of a wood worker"), *talui* ("the one who was hanged [on a tree]"), and categorically rejects the Christian

---

41   Gal. 3:7-9.
42   Eph. 5:30.
43   Gal. 3:27-9.
44   Hoffman, *Judaism Discovered*, 144.

affirmation of Jesus as the Christ.[45] The awkward reality for Judeo-Christians is that Jesus of Nazareth, the Messiah and God of Christianity, is depicted in the Talmud as a magician and a fraud, a charlatan who was rightly killed and who is condemned to an eternity of torment.[46] It is a sign of the extreme confusion of our age that Judeo-Christianity can enjoy such widespread acceptance and, indeed, that the age of Antichrist approaches.

THE ISRAEL OF GOD

Modern Judeo-Christians would have been readily recognizable to the Apostles and early Church Fathers as Judaizers: those who would not accept the dispensation of grace brought by Christ and clung in varying degrees to the dispensation of the law, which was powerless to save.[47] The multiplication of judaizing errors in Western Christendom has progressed alongside the rise of Gnosticism that we have examined. Indeed, from the very first centuries of the Church, the two have been integrally connected.

> [St.] Irenaeus' work [*Against Heresies*, Ἔλεγχος καὶ ἀνατροπὴ τῆς ψευδωνύμου γνώσεως/*Adversus Haereses*], as its title implies, was written to combat heresy, specifically

---

45   I. B. Pranaitis, *The Talmud Unmasked* (New York, E. N. Sanctuary, 1892, 1939), 28-9.

46   Jones, *The Jewish Revolutionary Spirit*, 18, 90.

47   "We who are Jews by nature, and not sinners of the Gentiles, knowing that a man is not justified by the works of the law but by faith in Jesus Christ, even we have believed in Christ Jesus, that we might be justified by faith in Christ and not by the works of the law; for by the works of the law no flesh shall be justified…. Therefore He who supplies the Spirit to you and works miracles among you, does He do it by the works of the law, or by the hearing of faith?—just as Abraham 'believed God, and it was accounted to him for righteousness.' Therefore know that only those who are of faith are sons of Abraham." (Gal 2:15-16, 3:5-7)

Gnosticism, but in entering the fray he had to deal with the Jews, acknowledging "from the very beginning of the Gnostic attack on Christianity," that Gnosticism was associated with judaizing.[48]

"Gnostic heresy was the great opponent of Christianity in the early centuries," observes Eric Voegelin, but "Gnosis does not by inner necessity lead to the fallacious construction of history which characterizes modernity..."[49] The peculiar conception of history culminating in a realm of earthly perfection, which has been the bane of revolutions and political rebellion for the past two thousand years, was a Judaic contribution.[50] It perdures in our time through the widespread acceptance of Judeo-Christianity amidst the ongoing march of globalization. Indeed, a competent examination of the historical record testifies to the central role Judaic influences have had in the rise of schism, heresy, and revolution in the history of Christendom.[51]

The tendency among heterodox Western Christians today to confuse Judaism and Christianity replays the Judaizing heresies of the early Church that St. Paul, among others, fought so hard against. Then, as now, Judaizers caused great confusion as to the nature of God's covenant with His people. Contrary to those who continue to cling to the Law, Jesus Christ came to fulfill the Old Testament prophecies that God would one day make a New Covenant with His faithful that would break the rabbinical monopoly on the Mosaic Law.

"Behold, the days are coming," says the LORD, "when I will make a new covenant with the house of Israel and

---

48   Jones, *The Jewish Revolutionary Spirit*, 72.
49   Voegelin, *The New Science of Politics*, 126.
50   See Jones, *The Jewish Revolutionary Spirit*.
51   See Louis I. Newman, *Jewish Influence on Christian Reform Movements* (New York, Columbia University, 1925).

with the house of Judah—not according to the covenant that I made with their fathers in the day that I took them by the hand to lead them out of the land of Egypt, My covenant which they broke, though I was a husband to them, says the LORD. But this is the covenant that I will make with the house of Israel after those days, says the LORD: I will put My law in their minds, and write it on their hearts; and I will be their God, and they shall be My people."[52]

The faithful Israelites of Jesus' time became the Church and spread the message of the Gospel to the nations; the unbelieving remained at the temple in Jerusalem, soon to be destroyed. It is the Church that is the only "Israel of God."[53] Only by sweeping the divisive truth under the rug can such a self-contradictory idea as modern Judeo-Christianity maintain its currency.

> The Jews, many [early] Christian writers made clear, were different from the Hebrews. The Hebrew religion had a priesthood, a Temple, and sacrifice. After [the destruction of the Temple in] 70 AD, the Jews had none of these things, so the religion of the Jews could not be the same as that of the Hebrews. The only religion that had a priesthood, a Temple, and a sacrifice was the Catholic Church [sic], the New Israel. The Jews did not have a separate but equal covenant; the only real basis for fulfilling their covenant had been destroyed.[54]

---

52   Jer. 31:31-3.

53   Gal. 6:16. "Enter by the narrow gate; for wide is the gate and broad is the way that leads to destruction, and there are many who go in by it. Because narrow is the gate and difficult is the way which leads to life, and there are few who find it." (Matt. 7:13-14)

54   Jones, *The Jewish Revolutionary Spirit*, 66.

"Therefore I say to you, the kingdom of God will be taken from you and given to a nation bearing the fruits of it."[55]

The Orthodox doctrine that the Church is the Body of Christ, the people Israel, is often derogated under the heading of "supercessionism," "fulfillment" or "replacement" theology, i.e., that the Church replaced or superseded tribal Israel as the people of God. Indeed, Jesus Christ and the Church do fulfill God's promises to Abraham, Moses, and the prophets. "The early Church recognized Christianity as having been founded by Israelites and representing the only true religion of the Bible. It is Christians who are 'a chosen generation, a royal priesthood, a holy nation...' (1 Pet. 2:9)."[56] As always, "the Israel of God" are those faithful to His commands, whether nominally of tribal Israel in the Old Testament dispensation or of the Church in the New. "For in Christ Jesus neither circumcision nor uncircumcision avails anything, but a new creation."[57] While God's love is unchanging, the covenants that He makes with His people require their willing participation. Love implies freedom, and God's people are free to forsake Him and to choose the path of destruction. Such was God's promise to His people Israel, then and now.

> Behold, I set before you today a blessing and a curse: the blessing, if you obey the commandments of the LORD your God which I command you today; and the curse, if you do not obey the commandments of the LORD your God, but turn aside from the way which I command you today, to go after other gods which you have not known.[58]

> But if you turn away and forsake My statutes and My commandments which I have set before you, and go and

---

55   Matt. 21:43.
56   Hoffman, *Judaism Discovered*, 144.
57   Gal. 6:15.
58   Deut. 11:26-8.

serve other gods, and worship them, then I will uproot
them from My land which I have given them; and this
house which I have sanctified for My name I will cast out
of My sight, and will make it a proverb and a byword
among all peoples.[59]

To be among God's chosen people bestows both privilege
and responsibility and means being held to a higher standard.
"Chosenness" is a mark of God's generosity rather than an indication of one's worthiness or merit, a fact that ancient Israel
was inclined to forget.

Therefore understand that the LORD your God is not
giving you this good land to possess because of your righteousness, for you are a stiff-necked people. Remember!
Do not forget how you provoked the LORD your God to
wrath in the wilderness. From the day that you departed
from the land of Egypt until you came to this place, you
have been rebellious against the LORD.[60]

Lest some conclude that a critique of Judeo-Christianity, or
of Judaism itself, must amount to "anti-Semitism", it is worth
reflecting on what that term means. First, it certainly does not
connote prejudice against all Semitic peoples, which includes
Arabs; it specifically connotes Jews—and Jews defined broadly
without necessary reference to the Judaic religion. As we have
taken pains to point out, we are interested in the contradictions
between Orthodox Christianity and Judaism, a religion, not
the broader category of self-identified ethnic Jews. Prejudice
and hostility against Jews is as old as prejudice and hostility
against men and peoples in general, but anti-Semitism as we

59   2 Chr. 7:19-20.
60   Deut. 9:6-7.

understand it today developed in Germany in the latter half of the nineteenth century as a specifically racial theory, in which Jews as an ethnic group were systematically maligned, and had nothing to do with orthodox Christian thought.[61] Furthermore, it is nonsensical for any believing Christian to harbor animus against ethnic Jews, as it was precisely as an ethnic Jew that God Himself chose to become incarnate as Jesus Christ. The Orthodox Church has never had a beef with Jews per se, but she has been in tension with Judaism since the time of the Apostles over the perennial question: is Jesus the Christ or not?

In this study, we have endeavored to rely as much as possible on the most authoritative sources, namely, Holy Scripture, to guide us. The most reliable critique of Judeo-Christianity comes from those same sources, including the Old Testament, which both Judaism and the Church accept. From a reading of the Old Testament, we gain insight into the nature of God's covenant with man, both with ancient Israel and with the Church today. Contrary to the Pharisees of Christ's time, who believed that their salvation lay in having "Abraham as their father,"[62] God's covenants to His people, then and now, are contingent on their faithful obedience. God promised Abraham that "in your seed all the nations of the earth shall be blessed, because you have obeyed My voice";[63] God's blessing reflected Abraham's great obedience — "since you have not withheld your son, your only son, from Me"[64]—and, indeed, this same blessing may be lost through disobedience. Ancient Israel was free to reject God— as those of the Church are now—and many did so, repeatedly. Indeed, their rejection of God was incisively prophesied by their

61   "Antisemitism," *Wikipedia*. https://en.wikipedia.org/wiki/Antisemitism. Accessed September 17, 2019.

62   Matt. 3:9.

63   Gen. 22:18.

64   Gen. 10:16 pm. Prefiguring, of course, the sacrifice of God's only Son on the Cross for the sake of humanity, thus fulfilling God's promise.

greatest prophet, Moses, who foretold their history as wanderers among the nations, and who, far from remaining as God's chosen people, "would leave their name as a curse to My chosen,"[65] "an astonishment, a proverb, and a byword among all nations."[66]

> And the LORD said to Moses: "Behold, you will rest with your fathers; and this people will rise and play the harlot with the gods of the foreigners of the land, where they go to be among them, and they will forsake Me and break My covenant which I have made with them. Then My anger shall be aroused against them in that day, and I will forsake them, and I will hide My face from them, and they shall be devoured." [67]

In sharp contrast to the Hollywood view of Moses as the affectionate father of the Hebrews who blessed their hard-sought entry into the Promised Land, the great prophet testified against them that after his death they would persist in their disobedience and would forsake the Lord Who had delivered them.

> Take this Book of the Law and put it beside the ark of the covenant of the LORD your God, that it may be there as a witness against you; for I know your rebellion and your stiff neck. If today, while I am yet alive with you, you have been rebellious against the LORD, then how much more after my death? Gather to me all the elders of your tribes, and your officers, that I may speak these words in their hearing and call heaven and earth to witness against them. For I know that after my death you will become utterly corrupt, and turn aside from the way

---

65   Isa. 65:15.
66   Deut. 28:36.
67   Deut. 31:16-17.

which I have commanded you. And evil will befall you in the latter days, because you will do evil in the sight of the LORD, to provoke Him to anger through the work of your hands.[68]

Moses was not the only prophet to chastise Israel; indeed, the prophetic office seems primarily to have been a disciplinary one. Elijah lamented, "I have been very zealous for the LORD God of hosts; because the children of Israel have forsaken Your covenant, torn down Your altars, and killed Your prophets with the sword. I alone am left; and they seek to take my life."[69] Jeremiah compared Israel to a faithless wife, "'Surely, as a wife treacherously departs from her husband, so have you dealt treacherously with Me, O house of Israel,' says the Lord."[70] Isaiah, prefiguring the Lord Jesus' rebuke that "this people honors Me with their lips, but their heart is far from Me,"[71] upbraided Israel as a "sinful nation, a brood of evildoers [with] hands full of blood" and hypocrites who offer "futile sacrifices."[72] He addressed the Hebrews not as the people of God but as "you rulers of Sodom [and] you people of Gomorrah [who] draw near with their mouths and honor Me with their lips, but have removed their hearts far from Me."[73]

> "Hear, O heavens, and give ear, O earth! For the LORD has spoken: "I have nourished and brought up children, and they have rebelled against Me; the ox knows its owner and the donkey its master's crib; but Israel does not know, my people do not consider. Alas, sinful nation, a people

---

68   Deut. 31:24-9.
69   Kgs 1. 19:14.
70   Jer. 3:20.
71   Mark 7:6.
72   Isa. 1:13.
73   Isa. 29:13.

laden with iniquity, a brood of evildoers, children who are corrupters! They have forsaken the LORD.... You will revolt more and more. The whole head is sick, and the whole heart faints. From the sole of the foot even to the head, there is no soundness in it, but wounds and bruises and putrefying sores; they have not been closed or bound up, or soothed with ointment."[74]

In particular, Isaiah indicted Israel's religious leadership for the same kind of Talmudic hair-splitting that led the Pharisees eight centuries later to condemn the Lord Himself for supposedly violating God's Law.

But the word of the LORD was to them, "Precept upon precept, precept upon precept, line upon line, line upon line, here a little, there a little," that they might go and fall backward, and be broken and snared and caught. Therefore hear the word of the LORD, you scornful men, who rule this people who are in Jerusalem, because you have said, "We have made a covenant with death, and with Sheol we are in agreement. When the overflowing scourge passes through, it will not come to us, for we have made lies our refuge, and under falsehood we have hidden ourselves."[75]

Such men were concerned only with remaining atop the social hierarchy and suppressing any rival, even the Messiah Himself, on any possible pretense. They were men who refused to see the forest for the trees, who bogged themselves down in

---

74   Isa. 1:2-6.
75   Isa. 28:13-15.

minutiae, and who "neglected the weightier matters of the law: justice and mercy and faith."[76]

Israel's disobedience is a constant theme throughout the Old Testament. The history of the Hebrews is the recurrent story of God's call to His beloved people, their forsaking His commands, God permitting disaster to befall them, a remnant repenting of their evil, and God restoring their fortunes.

> And they shrugged their shoulders, stiffened their necks, and would not hear. Yet for many years You had patience with them and testified against them by Your Spirit in Your prophets. Yet they would not listen; therefore, You gave them into the hand of the peoples of the lands.[77]

The coming of the Lord Jesus Christ was the culmination of the historical process identified by the Prophet Nehemiah in which God sent prophets to a "stiff-necked people," who rejected and killed them, such that He finally sent His only-begotten Son such "that everyone who sees the Son and believes in Him may have everlasting life.[78]" The Lord Jesus Himself explained this process by parable:

> There was a certain landowner who planted a vineyard and set a hedge around it, dug a winepress in it and built a tower. And he leased it to vinedressers and went into a far country. Now when vintage-time drew near, he sent his servants to the vinedressers, that they might receive

---

76   Matt. 23:23.

77   Neh. 9:29-30.

78   John 6:40. "Know then that even then it was Christ in God who led the people out of Egypt (See Jude 5), and it was Christ in God who was tempted by the people who tempted (See 1 Cor. 10:9, Exo. 17:2, 7), and it was Christ in God who saved all the righteous men by His lavish grace." (St. John Cassian, *The Seven Books of John Cassian on the Incarnation of the Lord, Against Nestorius*, Book V, Chapters VIII, IX, B#60, 586-7 as quoted in Manley, *The Bible and the Holy Fathers*, 587)

its fruit. And the vinedressers took his servants, beat one, killed one, and stoned another. Again he sent other servants, more than the first, and they did likewise to them. Then last of all he sent his son to them, saying, "They will respect my son." But when the vinedressers saw the son, they said among themselves, "This is the heir. Come, let us kill him and seize his inheritance." So they took him and cast him out of the vineyard and killed him. Therefore, when the owner of the vineyard comes, what will he do to those vinedressers?

They said to Him, "He will destroy those wicked men miserably, and lease his vineyard to other vinedressers who will render to him the fruits in their seasons."[79]

Ancient Israel was both the chosen nation of God's priests and prophets as well as of those who killed them; of Moses and the Ten Commandments and of Korah, Dathan, Abiram and the golden calf;[80] of the righteous King David and the wicked Ahab; of Jesus Christ and the Apostles as well as of Herod, the Sanhedrin, and the Pharisees, who defied the Lord and persecuted the early Church. It seems that the Israelites were given a special capacity by God for great good and great evil, to build the eternal Church of God as well as the "synagogue of Satan."[81]

---

79   Matt. 21:33-41. "Many things does He intimate by this parable: God's providence, which had been exercised towards them from the first; their murderous disposition from the beginning; that nothing had been omitted of whatever pertained to a heedful care of them; that even when prophets had been slain, He had not turned away from them, but had sent His very Son; that the God both of the New and of the Old Testament was one and the same; that His death should effect great blessings; that they were to endure extreme punishment for the crucifixion and their crime; the calling of the Gentiles, the casting out of the Jews." (St. John Chrysostom, *Homily LXVIII on Matthew XXI*, 1. B#54, 414 as quoted in Manley, *The Bible and the Holy Fathers*, 646-7)

80   Exod. 32:1-4.

81   Rev. 2:9, 3:9.

The Judaic Messiah

The coming of the Lord Jesus Christ in fulfillment of the Old Testament prophecies was the defining moment in world history and of the people of Israel. The crucial choice then and now is whether to accept Jesus as the Christ and the Church that He founded as the fulfillment of God's salvific promise to man, or not. Those Israelites who followed the Lord became the first Christians, who looked to a heavenly kingdom "not of this world," in which "God shall wipe away all tears from their eyes; and there shall be no more death, neither sorrow, nor crying, neither shall there be any more pain: for the former things are passed away,[82]" of which the Church is the earthly manifestation; those who rejected the Lord sought to restore the lost Kingdom of Israel as an unending kingdom of this world, exalted among the nations, in place of Christian salvation.

The choice of this world over the next, of a temporal kingdom over an eternal one, of a worldly savior rather than an otherworldly one, was dramatically played out in ancient Jerusalem on Great Friday, the day of the Lord's crucifixion. It was then that the city mob, incited by the temple priests, condemned their Messiah and God to die and in His place saved the life of the rebel and murderer, Barabbas.

> Now at the feast Pilate was accustomed to releasing one prisoner to them, whomever they requested. And there was one named Barabbas, who was chained with his fellow rebels; they had committed murder in the rebellion. Then the multitude, crying aloud, began to ask him to do just as he had always done for them. But Pilate answered them, saying, "Do you want me to release to you the King

---

82   Rev. 21:4.

of the Jews?" For he knew that the chief priests had handed Him over because of envy. But the chief priests stirred up the crowd, so that he should rather release Barabbas to them. Pilate answered and said to them again, "What then do you want me to do with Him whom you call the King of the Jews?" So they cried out again, "Crucify Him!" Then Pilate said to them, "Why, what evil has He done?" But they cried out all the more, "Crucify Him!" So Pilate, wanting to gratify the crowd, released Barabbas to them; and he delivered Jesus, after he had scourged Him, to be crucified.[83]

The choice to save the blood-stained Barabbas over the Prince of Peace reflects the same choice made over and over by revolutionaries of myriad stripes throughout history, who chose the path of rebellion and political action over salvation in the Church. It is the same choice that the globalists of our time, bent on ushering in a world empire that will know no end, persist in making today. The dichotomy is not always clear; as we have seen, history is full of self-proclaimed "Christian" rebels; yet the spirit they partake of in their political machinations is recognizably not that of the meek, long-suffering Savior they claim to follow.

It was the same men who had rejected their Messiah and God before Pilate who embarked on the first antichristian political movement of the Christian era, the Great Revolt of the year 66 AD. In the wake of their ancestors' cry, "We have no king but Caesar!"[84] which affirmed their preference for worldly power

---

83   Mark 15:6-15. "Let Him be crucified, was the shout of those who always had enjoyed your gifts. The release of a malefactor, in the place of their benefactor was the deed of those guilty of the deaths of all the righteous. But you kept silent, O Christ, enduring their insolence, in your desire to suffer and to save us as the Lover of Mankind." (Aposticha, Great Vespers—Tone 2)

84   John 19:15.

over heavenly authority, the rebels revolted against Caesar in order to rebuild the lost Kingdom of Israel. As the self-professed chosen people, the rebels that led the First Jewish-Roman War believed that God was on their side and thought themselves unconstrained by considerations such as the actual balance of forces between them and the Romans. Four years after it had begun, the ill-fated revolution collided with reality in the form of the armies of Emperor Titus. Titus crushed the rebels and obliterated the Jerusalem temple, the physical symbol of the Old Testament dispensation.

The Judaic leadership would try again in 115 and 132 to throw off Roman rule with similarly disastrous results. These later Second and Third Jewish-Roman Wars, far more than localized upheavals, involved the extensive diaspora throughout the Empire and threatened Roman hegemony over the eastern Mediterranean. The slaughter was truly enormous: the rebels, better organized and led than in 66, massacred non-Jews by the hundreds of thousands and received in kind from the Roman legions.[85] Emperor Hadrian, finally getting the upper hand in 135, banished Jews from Jerusalem and attempted to eradicate Judaism from the Empire. It was in this atmosphere of military defeat and political exile that the Judaic conception of the messiah developed.

> The Messiah became for the oppressed Jewish people "a mighty warrior" to destroy Israel's foes and "take captive the leader of the Romans and bring him in chains to Mount Zion, where he will put him to death" and "establish a kingdom which shall last to the end of the world." Deliverance from political oppression would occur in the only manner the Jewish people considered possible—through a mighty general who "would show himself invincible in war." As the conflict with Rome became bitterer,

---

85   Jones, *The Jewish Revolutionary Spirit*, 48.

"messianic fantasies became with many Jews an obsessive preoccupation."[86]

To this day, Judaic conceptions of the messiah retain decidedly political and military attributes.

> The mashiach [messiah] will be a great political leader descended from King David (Jer. 23:5). The mashiach is often referred to as "mashiach ben David" (mashiach, son of David). He will be well-versed in Jewish law, and observant of its commandments (Isa. 11:2-5). He will be a charismatic leader, inspiring others to follow his example. He will be a great military leader, who will win battles for Israel. He will be a great judge, who makes righteous decisions (Jer. 33:15). But above all, he will be a human being, not a god, demi-god or other supernatural being.... The mashiach will bring about the political and spiritual redemption of the Jewish people by bringing us back to Israel and restoring Jerusalem (Isa. 11:11-12; Jer. 23:8; 30:3; Hos. 3:4-5). He will establish a government in Israel that will be the center of all world government, both for Jews and gentiles (Isa. 2:2-4; 11:10; 42:1). He will rebuild the Temple and re-establish its worship (Jer. 33:18).[87]

> The Messianic Era [sic] will herald the onset of a single, universal political system, with the Messiah at its helm. There will no longer be localized concern over natural resources. The spirit of universal cooperation and brotherhood will reign supreme. There will no longer be the need to accumulate wealth.... There will no longer

---

86   Resnick, *The Mystery of Bar Kokhba*, 4 as quoted in Jones, *The Jewish Revolutionary Spirit*, 29.
87   "Mashiach: The Messiah," *Judaism 101*. http://www.jewfaq.org/mashiach. htm. Accessed September 17, 2019.

be diverse cultures and philosophies. Just as in the very
beginning of time, a single man was created, so, too, in
the end of days, all Mankind will unite as a single entity.
There will no longer be the need for war.[88]

From what has been revealed about Antichrist and his reign,
the true identity of this anticipated Judaic messiah could hardly
be clearer.[89]

Orthodox Christianity and Orthodox Judaism—far from
capable of being united into some kind of "Judeo-Christianity"—
amount to polar opposites of each other: while they substantially
agree on the course of history and of history's end, like Christ
and the Pharisees of two thousand years ago, they utterly disagree as to its ultimate meaning and to the nature of God's
covenant with man. It is only the Orthodox Church that possesses
true knowledge of the True Messiah, the Lord Jesus Christ, Who
will come again—not as an exalted political figure bestowing
worldly satisfactions—but as the Dread Judge of all mankind
and the vanquisher of the great fraud, Antichrist.[90]

---

88   Resnick, *The Mystery of Bar Kokhba*, 137-8 as quoted in Jones, *The Jewish
Revolutionary Spirit*, 51-2.

89   Fantasies about what such a Judeo-Christian messiah will do when he arrives
can run to the outright bizarre, and explicitly confirm elements of Antichrist's reign.
"When Jesus returns, He will actually kill a host of unrighteous, self-serving politicians,
dictators, and leaders throughout the earth. And not only will He cleanse the earth
of oppressive and self-serving leaders, but He will also replace them with those who
have proved themselves faithful and humble in the small things of their lives....
How many reading this would jump at the opportunity to be part of Jesus's official
kingdom architectural and engineering team, of His official Global garden-planning
committee? What primary architectural style will be used during this time? . . . This
may all sound a bit silly in its speculation, but I actually believe we should get lost in
such dreaming as we meditate upon the nature of the age to come.... This kind of
dreaming is very much the hope of the Gospel [sic]." (Joel Richardson, *When A Jew
Rules the World: What the Bible Really Says About Israel in the Plan of God*, [Washington,
WND, 2015], 82, 83-4)

90   "Do not be deceived, O Jews! Learn the sayings of the prophets and understand!
Truly, Christ is the almighty redeemer of the world." (Stichera of the Resurrection,
Tone 5)

THE RETURN OF THE JEWS

Significantly, however, Antichrist will prove a false messiah even by Judaic standards. First, as we have seen, he will be descended from the tribe of Dan, whereas "mashiach ben David" must be descended from the royal Davidic line (from the tribe of Judah in the manner of our Lord), and therefore will he have a false pedigree. Second, while the Lord Jesus Christ rightly receives worship as the God-Man, the Second Person of the Holy Trinity, when the man-god Antichrist at last receives worship of himself in the restored Jerusalem temple, he will violate the Judaic stipulation that the messiah be a mere human being who must not receive the worship due to God alone. It then seems at least possible that many Judaists will see Antichrist for the fraud that he is and renounce their allegiance to the imposter messiah. Those who will have no doctrinal guidance to save them will include those heterodox Christians who are anticipating an earthly reign of Jesus Christ and who will thus welcome the proclamation of Antichrist as both messiah and god.

Indeed, it is wrong to believe that Jews of today, however they may be defined, have no place in the divine economy. God does not abandon any of His peoples. As long as this world lasts, He calls out even to those who reject Him. In the words of the Israelite and ex-Pharisee, St. Paul:

> I say then, has God cast away His people? Certainly not! For I also am an Israelite, of the seed of Abraham, of the tribe of Benjamin. God has not cast away His people whom He foreknew.... I say then, have they stumbled that they should fall? Certainly not! But through their fall, to provoke them to jealousy, salvation has come to the Gentiles.

> Now if their fall is riches for the world, and their failure
> riches for the Gentiles, how much more their fullness![91]

As in the time of the Prophet Elijah, who protested to God
that he alone remained faithful, yet God had "reserved seven
thousand in Israel, all whose knees have not bowed to Baal,"[92]
so even now is there a remnant which the Lord will draw, and
is drawing, into His Church. Scripture and the Holy Fathers
testify that, in the last times, many Jews will be received into
Orthodoxy.

> For I do not desire, brethren, that you should be ignorant
> of this mystery, lest you should be wise in your own opinion,
> that blindness in part has happened to Israel until the
> fullness of the Gentiles has come in…. For as you were
> once disobedient to God, yet have now obtained mercy
> through their disobedience, even so these also have now
> been disobedient, that through the mercy shown you they
> also may obtain mercy. For God has committed them all
> to disobedience, that He might have mercy on all.[93]

> It is a familiar theme in the conversation and heart of
> the faithful that in the last days before the judgment the
> Jews shall believe in the true Christ, that is, our Christ,
> by means of this great and admirable prophet Elias who
> shall expound the law to them.[94]

---

91   Rom. 10:1-2, 11-13.
92   Kgs 1. 19:18.
93   Rom. 11 h 25, 29-32.
94   St. Augustine, *City of God*, XX, 29. http://www.newadvent.org/fathers/120120.
htm. Accessed September 17, 2019. St. Augustine here refers to the prophecy in
chapter 11 of the Book of Revelation describing the "two witnesses who will prophesy
one thousand two hundred and sixty days, clothed in sackcloth" (Rev. 11:3) against
Antichrist, who are generally understood to be the Prophets Enoch and Elijah, who
were physically translated to heaven and have not died natural deaths. Enoch shall

Of course, for Jews to find the Church, there must be Orthodox Christians willing to testify to the saving truth within her and to the lie of Judeo-Christianity.

The greatest tragedy among self-identified Jews of today is their continued rejection of Jesus of Nazareth as the Christ and their forsaking of the Orthodox Church, the Body of Christ, the Ark of Salvation. They are kept from their Savior by the canards of Judeo-Christian ideology that permeate contemporary society. Orthodox Christians must witness to this deception, out of love for the truth and for those who are perishing for want of it. To Jews throughout history, and to those of today, Christ's Holy Church cries out, "Behold your King!"[95]

---

testify to the gentiles and Elias to the Jews against Antichrist during his reign in Jerusalem. "When they finish their testimony, the beast that ascends out of the bottomless pit will make war against them, overcome them, and kill them. And their dead bodies will lie in the street of the great city, which spiritually is called Sodom and Egypt, where also our Lord was crucified." (Rev. 11:7-8) After a brief period, the two Prophets will be dramatically resurrected. "Now after the three-and-a-half days the breath of life from God entered them, and they stood on their feet, and great fear fell on those who saw them. And they heard a loud voice from heaven saying to them, 'Come up here.' And they ascended to heaven in a cloud, and their enemies saw them." (Rev. 11:11-12)

95   John 12:15; Zech. 9:9.

THE SHAPE OF THINGS TO COME

> When it is evening you say, "It will be fair weather, for the sky is red"; and in the morning, "It will be foul weather today, for the sky is red and threatening." Hypocrites! You know how to discern the face of the sky, but you cannot discern the signs of the times.
>
> Matthew 16:2-3

As long as this world lasts there will be speculation as to how it will end. Such speculation is fraught with peril and not only because of the risk of looking foolish if things turn out differently from one's predictions. Becoming wedded to scenarios of how the future will unfold is spiritually dangerous because, in the event that our pet ideas turn out incorrectly (and they undoubtedly will to some degree), we risk losing our bearings in the larger struggle for salvation. Having gone to lengths in this work to analyze the error of Gnosticism, we must be careful not to commit the error ourselves, to imagine that we are possessed of some special knowledge that makes us privy to the future course of history. If we begin to imagine that the end of history will come in one or another particular way—that nation A will conquer nation B; a great king will arise from nation C; Antichrist will appear by year such-and-such—we risk losing our faith should things turn out differently. It is quite possible then for us, in our study of the end of this world, to bring about exactly the thing it is intended to forestall, namely, our being deceived and losing our salvation. We must tread with care and "be sober"[1] and remember the nature of the enemy that we are fighting, that "we do not wrestle against flesh and blood, but against principalities, against powers, against the rulers of the darkness of this age, against spiritual hosts of wickedness in the heavenly places."[2]

> The evil one is well aware of all that the Bible has to say about him and, as he is far more subtle and clever than the mind of man can fathom; he will almost certainly fulfill scriptural prophecies in some unexpected way. Christians must guard against assigning interpretations based on fallen human reason, or confidently assuming that "Y" is impossible because "X" has not happened yet.[3]

In this work, we have endeavored to "take heed,"[4] to "discern the signs of the times,"[5] even while bearing in mind that we "know not when the time is."[6] This apparent paradox reflects the state of man in this world in which "we see through a glass, darkly."[7] We must bear in mind the words of St. John Chrysostom: "Do not seek clarity in prophecies, where there are shadows and riddles, just as in lightning you do not seek a constant light, but are satisfied that it flashes only momentarily."[8] While our vision is dim, yet we are not blind, for we have the light of Christ. The

---

1   1 Thes. 5:8.
2   Eph. 6:12.
3   Dennis E. Engleman, *Ultimate Things* (Ben Lomond, Conciliar, 2005), 44-5.
4   Mark 13:33.
5   Matt. 16:3.
6   Mark 13:33.
7   1 Cor. 12:13.
8   Taushev and Rose, *The Apocalypse,* 69.

study of history and of history's end cannot but spur ideas as to what the future may hold. Thus, bearing in mind all that we have said, we will proceed, cautiously, with our analysis into the future.

An Outline of History

An authoritative summary of the course of world history and the events leading to its end is offered by the Lord Himself in chapter twenty-four of the Gospel of St. Matthew (alternately Mark thirteen and Luke twenty-one). The Lord's purpose it seems is not primarily historical, in the sense of specifying in detail the course of future events, but hortatory, to encourage the faithful to persevere and to remain watchful in whatever historical circumstances they may find themselves. Even so, He does provide a synopsis of sorts with respect to major historical episodes and their significance for the life of the Church. The twenty-fourth chapter of Matthew begins:

> Then Jesus went out and departed from the temple, and His disciples came up to show Him the buildings of the temple. And Jesus said to them, "Do you not see all these things? Assuredly, I say to you, not one stone shall be left here upon another, that shall not be thrown down." Now as He sat on the Mount of Olives, the disciples came to Him privately, saying, "Tell us, when will these things be? And what will be the sign of Your coming, and of the end of the age?"[9]

In verses one and two, the Lord foretells the destruction of the Jerusalem temple by the Roman armies that would occur

---

9   Matt. 24:1-3.

during the first Jewish-Roman War in 70 AD. The disciples' questioning is twofold. First, they enquire with respect to the destruction of the temple; second, with respect to the Lord's Second Coming and the end of history. It is not by chance that the Holy Spirit guided St. Matthew to separate these events because indeed they would occur separately in history. The horrific events surrounding the destruction of the temple as recorded by Flavius Josephus[10] constituted the figurative end of one world—the provisional political dispensation to tribal Israel that was fulfilled by the Church—and a prefigurement of the literal end of the world at the Second Coming.

> And Jesus answered and said to them: "Take heed that no one deceives you."[11]

Significantly, the Lord's first words with regard to the "end times" are an admonition not to be misled; indeed, as we have seen, history is full of misleading and confusing speculation as to its end, much of which has proven enormously destructive.

> "For many will come in My name, saying, 'I am the Christ,' and will deceive many."[12]

Here the Lord prophesies the rise of antichrists through history—from Bar Kochba to Jim Jones to the globalizing demagogues of our time—who have led astray countless multitudes through various heresies.

> "And you will hear of wars and rumors of wars. See that you are not troubled; for all these things must come to

---

10   See Josephus' *Wars of the Jews*, bk. V. https://www.gutenberg.org/files/2850/2850-h/2850-h.htm#link2HCH0005. Accessed September 17, 2019.
11   Matt. 24:4.
12   Matt. 24:5.

pass, but the end is not yet. For nation will rise against nation, and kingdom against kingdom. And there will be famines, pestilences, and earthquakes in various places. All these are the beginning of sorrows."[13]

Warfare, political upheaval, and natural disasters all presage the end of history, but—and this is critical—"the end is not yet." In and of themselves, terrible and frightening events are not indicative of the "end," even while they remind us of the ephemeral nature of this world and that it will ultimately pass away.

"Then they will deliver you up to tribulation and kill you, and you will be hated by all nations for My name's sake. And then many will be offended, will betray one another, and will hate one another. Then many false prophets will rise up and deceive many. And because lawlessness will abound, the love of many will grow cold. But he who endures to the end shall be saved."[14]

Tribulation, infighting, persecution, and apostasy will accompany this "beginning of sorrows." Then—of great interest to our study—will come great deception, confusion, and "lawlessness" sown by "false prophets" and antichrists such that the distinguishing characteristic of true Christians—that they "love one another"[15]—will wane. Of all the times of trial that have visited God's Church on earth, this period above all will require patient endurance from the faithful.

---

13   Matt. 24:6-8.
14   Matt. 24:9-13.
15   John 13:34-5.

At this same time, however, amidst great and confusing events, the salvific message of the Gospel will reach the far corners of the earth.

> "And this gospel of the kingdom will be preached in all the world as a witness to all the nations, and then the end will come."[16]

While the Holy Apostles preached to the greater part of the known world in their time, it was not until the beginning of the modern age that a Christian message of any kind reached the New World and not until the late eighteenth century with the Russian mission from Valaam monastery, which included St. Herman of Alaska (+1837), that an organized Orthodox presence established itself on American soil. It has only been in our electronic age that the saving message of Orthodoxy is freely able to reach virtually anyone desirous of hearing it. Globalization, while setting the stage for the regime of Antichrist, is also facilitating the Lord's promise that the Gospel—in Orthodox form—will in time reach the entire world. Because history is the designated arena for mankind to work out its salvation, only when Christ's Church has completed her evangelical mission can the end of history finally come. When humanity at large will no longer seek salvation in the Church; when the great "falling away"[17] will have reached its final stages; when all of those who will be saved will have finished "working out" their "salvation"[18]—only then will the purpose of history finally be exhausted and then the end may come. "The Lord is not slack concerning His promise, as some count slackness, but is longsuffering toward us, not willing that any should perish but

---

16   Matt. 24:14.
17   2 Thess. 2:3.
18   Phil. 2:12.

that all should come to repentance."[19] God permits the fallen realm of profane history—the realm of sin, death, injustice, and suffering—to perdure so that all may have the opportunity to repent and find salvation. When all of humankind, save for a small remnant of the faithful, will have abandoned the Church, the Ark of Salvation, there will no longer be a reason for the all-loving God to permit further sin and suffering on earth and He will bring history to an end.

> In referring to the end of the world, Christ likens the destruction of Jerusalem to the destruction of the world and ends with the following assurance: "Verily I say unto you, this generation shall not pass, till all these things be fulfilled. Heaven and earth shall pass away, but my words shall not pass away."[20] The destruction of Jerusalem came about before the passing of the generation to which Christ spoke. And the final destruction will come about before the passing of the generation of Christians.[21]

Continuing in the Gospel of St. Matthew, the Lord proceeds to describe events surrounding both the destruction of the temple in 70 AD as well as the end times of Antichrist.

> "Therefore when you see the 'abomination of desolation,' spoken of by Daniel the prophet, standing in the holy place" (whoever reads, let him understand), "then let those who are in Judea flee to the mountains. Let him who is on the housetop not go down to take anything out of his house. And let him who is in the field not go back to get his clothes. But woe to those who are pregnant and

---

19   2 Pet. 3:9.
20   Matt. 24:34-5.
21   Mantzaridis, *Time and Man*, 56.

to those who are nursing babies in those days! And pray that your flight may not be in winter or on the Sabbath. For then there will be great tribulation, such as has not been since the beginning of the world until this time, no, nor ever shall be. And unless those days were shortened, no flesh would be saved; but for the elect's sake those days will be shortened."[22]

The Lord's mention of the "'abomination of desolation,' spoken of by Daniel the prophet, standing in the holy place," a reference to Antichrist's reign from the rebuilt Jerusalem temple, is immediately followed by St. Matthew's exhortation, "whoever reads, let him understand"; indeed, it is important for us to understand the significance of Antichrist's coming. What will befall the Church on earth during the reign of Antichrist is not possible to tell. Certainly the terrors of the Roman legions in the time of the early Church had nothing on the persecutions of later Islamic and Communist regimes. Indeed, the ubiquitous, systematic brutality experienced by Orthodox lands conquered by totalitarianism in the twentieth century fairly constituted "great tribulation, such as has not been since the beginning of the world."

The Lord proceeds to warn that, as the end of history approaches, antichrists and false prophets will multiply, which the faithful must not heed.

"Then if anyone says to you, 'Look, here is the Christ!' or 'There!' do not believe it. For false christs and false prophets will rise and show great signs and wonders to deceive, if possible, even the elect. See, I have told you beforehand. Therefore if they say to you, 'Look, He is in the desert!' do not go out; or 'Look, He is in the inner

---

22   Matt. 24:15-22.

rooms!' do not believe it. For as the lightning comes from the east and flashes to the west, so also will the coming of the Son of Man be. For wherever the carcass is, there the eagles will be gathered together."[23]

The Lord's return will not, as in His first advent, originate from within the ranks of human society, but will be in the miraculous manner of his Ascension into Heaven as related in the Book of Acts:

Now when He had spoken these things, while they watched, He was taken up, and a cloud received Him out of their sight. And while they looked steadfastly toward heaven as He went up, behold, two men stood by them in white apparel, who also said, "Men of Galilee, why do you stand gazing up into heaven? This same Jesus, who was taken up from you into heaven, will so come in like manner as you saw Him go into heaven."[24]

The true Christ, the Only-begotten Son of God, comes no more from the earth. If any come making false shows in the wilderness, go not forth; if they say, *Lo, here is the Christ, Lo, there,* believe it not. Look no longer downwards and to the earth; for the Lord descends from heaven; not alone as before, but with many, escorted by tens of thousands of Angels; nor secretly as the dew on the fleece; but shining forth openly as the lightning.[25]

---

23   Matt. 24:23-8.

24   Acts 1:9-11.

25   St. Cyril of Jerusalem, *Catechetical Lectures*, XV, 10. http://www.newadvent. org/fathers/310115.htm. Accessed September 17, 2019. "How then does the lightning shine? It does not need anyone to talk of it, it does not need a herald, but even to those who sit in houses, and to those in chambers, it shows itself in an instant of time through the whole world. So will that Coming be, showing itself everywhere by reason of the shining forth of His glory. But he also mentions another sign, 'where

St. Zosima of Solovki (+1478) warned his flock that should they live to hear that Christ has come again to earth they must know that it is Antichrist. It is imperative for Christians of the last times to be able to identify and reject Antichrist and the antichristian principles of "lawlessness" which are "already at work"[26] that threaten our salvation. As difficult as it may be to accept, many Christians will fail to recognize Antichrist and will worship him as Christ. It is the gravest error to expect Christ to come again from within the ranks of human society as He did in His first advent. Christ's Second Coming will be an awesome supernatural cataclysm that will overwhelm all human logic and reasoning. In short, if one has to ask the question, *Is this the Christ?* the answer is a definitive, *No.* "And He said: 'Take heed that you not be deceived. For many will come in My name, saying, "I am He," and, "The time has drawn near." Therefore do not go after them.' "[27]

The Lord continues in the Gospel of St. Matthew to describe the great tribulation that will befall the Church during the days before His Second Coming:

> "Immediately after the tribulation of those days the sun will be darkened, and the moon will not give its light; the stars will fall from heaven, and the powers of the heavens will be shaken. Then the sign of the Son of Man will appear in heaven, and then all the tribes of the earth will mourn, and they will see the Son of Man coming on the clouds of heaven with power and great glory. And He will send His angels with a great sound of a trumpet, and they will gather together His elect from the four winds, from

---

the carcass is, there also will the eagles be,' meaning the multitude of the angels, of the martyrs, of all the saints." (St. John Chrysostom, *Homily LXXVI on Matthew XXIV,* 2, 3 B#54, 458-9 as quoted in Manley, *The Bible and the Holy Fathers,* 298)

26   2 Thess. 2:7.

27   Luke 21:8.

one end of heaven to the other. Now learn this parable from the fig tree: When its branch has already become tender and puts forth leaves, you know that summer is near. So you also, when you see all these things, know that it is near—at the doors! Assuredly, I say to you, this generation will by no means pass away till all these things take place. Heaven and earth will pass away, but My words will by no means pass away."[28]

That "the powers of the heavens will be shaken" may refer to astronomical events and/or to the falling away of the Orthodox hierarchy. In the Apocalypse of St. John, "stars" are equated with the "angels of the seven churches"[29] to whom the Apocalypse (a letter) is addressed, who in turn are the bishops of those churches.[30] Thus, "the stars will fall from heaven" could imply the apostasy of the Orthodox hierarchy (or some part of it) or some other such "fall."

Events presaging the Second Coming of Christ and the end of the world are often depicted in spectacular and frightening terms. Here, however, even while the Lord admonishes us that "when you see all these things, know that [the end] is near, even at the doors,"[31] yet will there be a strange feeling of normalcy such that most will be caught unawares.

"But of that day and hour no one knows, not even the angels of heaven, but My Father only. But as the days of Noah were, so also will the coming of the Son of Man be. For as in the days before the flood, they were eating and drinking, marrying and giving in marriage, until the day that Noah entered the ark, and did not know until

28   Matt. 24:29-35.
29   Rev. 1:20.
30   See Taushev and Rose, *The Apocalypse*, 70.
31   Matt. 24:33.

the flood came and took them all away, so also will the coming of the Son of Man be. Then two men will be in the field: one will be taken and the other left. Two women will be grinding at the mill: one will be taken and the other left. Watch therefore, for you do not know what hour your Lord is coming. But know this, that if the master of the house had known what hour the thief would come, he would have watched and not allowed his house to be broken into. Therefore you also be ready, for the Son of Man is coming at an hour you do not expect."[32]

It seems that at the end of history, as at the time of the great flood when "the LORD was sorry that He had made man on the earth, and He was grieved in His heart,"[33] mankind will have become so spiritually corrupt, so destitute of genuine Christian love, that the signs sent by God to bring the earth to repentance will be heeded by only a few. As during the great flood, when only a very small number—eight persons—were saved from the deluge, so the remnant of true Christians that will be saved from the deception of Antichrist will be few. Having consolidated his world empire, it will appear to most that Antichrist will have brought humanity to its highest point in history, which will actually be its lowest. "For when they say, 'Peace and safety!' then sudden destruction comes upon them, as labor pains upon a pregnant woman. And they shall not escape."[34] As a matter of logic, the time of least anticipation of a coming event is when people believe that it has already occurred: when the world will have received Antichrist as the Lord come again, then it will be the least prepared to receive the True Master at His great and terrible Second Coming.

---

32   Matt. 24:36-44.
33   Gen. 6:6.
34   1 Thess. 5:3.

"Who then is a faithful and wise servant, whom his master made ruler over his household, to give them food in due season? Blessed is that servant whom his master, when he comes, will find so doing. Assuredly, I say to you that he will make him ruler over all his goods. But if that evil servant says in his heart, 'My master is delaying his coming,' and begins to beat his fellow servants, and to eat and drink with the drunkards, the master of that servant will come on a day when he is not looking for him and at an hour that he is not aware of, and will cut him in two and appoint him his portion with the hypocrites. There shall be weeping and gnashing of teeth."[35]

While the Lord provides an outline of history in the synoptic Gospels, some believe that there is also an outline of the historical life of the Church provided in the Apocalypse of St. John, written as a letter "to the seven churches which are in Asia."[36]

There is an opinion that the seven churches signify seven periods in the life of the whole Church of Christ from its foundation to the end of the world:
1) The church of Ephesus signifies the first period, the Apostolic Church which labored and did not faint while fighting with the first heretics, the Nicolaitans, but soon abandoned the good custom of doing good to others— the "communion of goods" ("thy first love").
2) The church of Smyrna signifies the second period, the period of [Roman] persecutions against the Church, of which there were ten in all.

---

35   Matt. 24:45-51.
36   Rev. 1:4.

3) The church of Pergamos signifies the third period, the epoch of the Ecumenical Councils and the battle with the heresies by the sword of the word of God.

4) The church of Thyatira is the fourth period, the period of the blossoming of Christianity among the new peoples of Europe.

5) The church of Sardis is the epoch of humanism and materialism of the 16th to 18th centuries.

6) The church of Philadelphia is the next-to-last period in the life of the Church of Christ, the epoch contemporary to us, when the Church will in fact have "little strength" in contemporary humanity and new persecutions will begin, when patience will be required.

7) The church of Laodicea is the last, most frightful epoch before the end of the world, characterized by indifference to the faith and outward prosperity.[37]

It seems at least possible that globalization is preparing the way for the seventh and final period of the Church's earthly life, in which Orthodoxy is both persecuted and jumbled together with the myriad variations of worldly "Christianity." While we do not know what the future will bring, we can be confident in the ultimate victory of our King, Who showed on the Cross that His Kingdom is imminently at its most triumphant just when it seems the most vanquished.

---

37   Taushev and Rose, *The Apocalypse*, 101-2.

"THE FUTURE OF RUSSIA AND THE END OF THE WORLD"[38]

In the course of this book, we have had occasion to mention the plight of Russia in the ongoing saga of history and, in particular, her role as a counterweight to Western-dominated globalization. Here we will mention her possible future role in the life of the Church worldwide. Significantly, as the long shadow of Communism descended on the Russian Empire and cut her off from the world as a Christian nation in the early twentieth century, numerous holy men and women prophesied that Russia would one day be resurrected as an Orthodox country and would have a seminal role to play in a flowering of Orthodoxy before the days of Antichrist and the end of the world.

Elder Barnabas of the Gethsemane Skete spoke before the Revolution [of 1917] of the disaster coming upon Russia and the cruel persecutions against the Orthodox Faith. He said: "Persecutions against the faith will constantly increase. There will be unheard-of grief and darkness, and almost all the churches will be closed. But when it will seem to people that it is impossible to endure any longer, then deliverance will come. There will be a flowering. Churches will even begin to be built. But this will be a flowering before the end."

Schema-monk Aristocleus, not long before his death in August 1918, said that "now we are undergoing the times before Antichrist, but Russia will yet be delivered. The-

---

38   Blessed Hieromonk Seraphim Rose, *Lecture Given at the Youth Conference of the Russian Orthodox Church Outside of Russia*, San Francisco, August 3, 1981. Accessed September 17, 2019. http://www.orthodoxphotos.com/readings/seraphim/russia/.

re will be much suffering, much torture. The whole of Russia will become a prison, and one must greatly entreat the Lord for forgiveness. One must repent of one's sins and fear to do even the least sin, but strive to do good, even the smallest. For even the wing of a fly has weight, but God's scales are exact. And when even the smallest of good in the cup overweighs, then will God reveal His mercy upon Russia."[39]

Archbishop Theophan of Poltava summed up in the 1930s the prophecies which he had received from such elders as these: "You ask me about the near future and about the last times. I do not speak on my own, but give the revelation of the Elders: The coming of Antichrist draws nigh and is very near. The time separating us from him should be counted a matter of years and at most a matter of some decades. But before the coming of Antichrist Russia must yet be restored—to be sure, for a short time. And in Russia there must be a Tsar forechosen by the Lord Himself. He will be a man of burning faith, great mind and iron will. This much has been revealed about him. We shall await the fulfillment of what has been revealed. Judging by many signs it is drawing nigh, unless because of our sins the Lord God shall revoke, shall alter what has been promised. According to the witness of the word of God, this also happens."[40]

The martyrdom of the Russian Imperial family at the hands of the Bolsheviks in 1918 figured large in the understanding of Russia's suffering under the Communist yoke. For many, it was the seminal crime that brought down upon Russia the scourge

---

39   Ibid.
40   Ibid.

of Communist tyranny, while its subsequent atonement would give rise to Russia's redemption. Priest-Confessor Gleb Yakunin went so far as to affirm that,

"The tragedy of the Royal Family has lain like a curse on the Russian land, having become the symbolic prologue of Russia's long path of the Cross—the death of tens of millions of her sons and daughters. The canonization of the Imperial Martyrs will be for Russia the lifting from her of the sin of regicide; this will finally deliver her from the evil charms." It is too simple, of course, to say that the glorification of the New Martyrs, including the Royal Family, will bring about the restoration of Holy Russia. But if the Orthodox people, both in Russia and in the Diaspora, would receive this act with all their hearts, and use it as an opportunity to repent deeply of their sins, there is no calculating the impact it might have on Russia.[41]

The Imperial family were canonized as saints of the Orthodox Church by the Russian Orthodox Church Outside Russia on November 1, 1981, and by the Moscow Patriarchate on August 20, 2000.[42] "As Father Dimitry Dudko and others have said, it cannot be that the blood of Russia's innumerable martyrs will be in vain; undoubtedly it is the seed of the last great flowering of true Christianity."[43]

Indeed, it seems that now Russia is experiencing the sort of spiritual renaissance that many of her holy people had foreseen.

---

41   Ibid.

42   Furthermore, the "Act of Canonical Communion of the Russian Orthodox Church Outside Russia with the Russian Orthodox Church Moscow Patriarchate" reunited the Moscow Patriarchate with ROCOR, the Russian Orthodox Church Outside Russia, and restored full communion, on May 17, 2007.

43   Rose, *Lecture Given at the Youth Conference of the Russian Orthodox Church Outside of Russia,* San Francisco, August 3, 1981. http://www.orthodoxphotos.com/readings/seraphim/russia/. Accessed September 17, 2019.

The long nightmare of atheist Communism is over as are the years of Western-dominated chaos and destitution that followed in the 1990s. While the Western nations continue to suffer the erosion of what remains of their Christian culture, the examples of which grow ever stranger and more virulent by the day, Orthodoxy in Russia is expanding both quantitatively and qualitatively.

> "Over the last six years [since 2010] our Church increased by 5,000 churches and 10,000 clergymen, which means that people need the Church's mission. There could not be such growth in the Church if there were no demand. That is why we feel so special when we place the foundations of new churches," the [Russian] patriarch said at the ceremony of laying the first stone in the foundation of the Assumption Cathedral of the Sarov Hermitage, where St. Seraphim of Sarov lived.
>
> According to Patriarch Kirill, this is a testimony to "the faith of our people, their spiritual power, to the vector of spiritual and even social development that connects material prosperity with spiritual growth."
>
> The patriarch has recently said that churches in Russia are built because people have the need, and not by command from the hierarchy.
>
> "This is not because someone ordered to build [a church], but because of enormous strength of the faith of our people, who support the authorities' wish," the Church primate said on July 28 after consecrating the restored Church of Smolensk icon of the Mother of God in Oryol.[44]

---

44   "The Russian Orthodox Church Increased by 5,000 Churches and 10,000 Clerics Over the Last Six Years," *Orthodox Christianity.* http://orthochristian. com/95868.html. Accessed September 17, 2019.

Patriarch Kirill has noted the improvement in both Russia's spiritual and material condition. Indeed, Russian per capita GDP (PPP) had more than doubled from its nadir of $12,000 in 1998 to a high of $29,267 in 2018, and her overall economic output has reached $4.3 trillion (PPP).[45] While she remains a relatively small military and economic power compared with her cohorts in the West and with China, she nonetheless enjoys a relatively light debt burden and energy and food self-sufficiency.[46] Despite punitive sanctions leveled by the United States and the EU over her 2014 reunification with Crimea, as well as a widespread Western media and policy campaign that seeks to denigrate and villainize her ("a gas station masquerading as a country"[47]), Russia has shown an ability to defend her national and cultural interests that mark her as the last remaining Orthodox great power. With some 100 million Orthodox Christians, she is far and away the largest Orthodox country on earth and holds the potential to emerge as the leader of Orthodoxy worldwide.

Nearly thirty years after the collapse of the failed Western import of irrationalist, atheist Marxism into Russia, it is already clear that the Russian Orthodox Church, renewed

---

45   "List of Countries by GDP (PPP) Per Capita," *Wikipedia*. https://en.wikipedia. org/wiki/List_of_countries_by_GDP_(PPP)_per_capita. Accessed September 17, 2019. "List of Countries by GDP (PPP), *Wikipedia*. https://en.wikipedia.org/ wiki/List_of_countries_by_GDP_(PPP). Accessed September 17, 2019.

46   "Percentage of Public Debt to GDP Around the World 2018," *Global Finance*. https://www.gfmag.com/global-data/economic-data/public-debt-percentage-gdp. Accessed September 17, 2019. "Is Your Country Food Independent?" *National Geographic*. https://www.nationalgeographic.com/people-and-culture/onward/2014/04/13/is-your-country-food-independent/. Accessed September 17, 2019.

47   The words of the late US Senator John McCain, who thus showed himself ignorant of a thousand years of Christian history in Russia, among other things. "John McCain: Russia is a 'gas station masquerading as a country.' " *The Week*. https://theweek.com/speedreads/456437/john-mccain-russia-gas-station-masquerading-country. Accessed September 17, 2019.

by the greatest persecution in world history, is the leader of World Orthodoxy.[48]

As long as a strong, independent, Orthodox Russia remains on the world stage, the Western program of antichristian globalization will have a robust challenger. Still, Russia's role as a resurgent Orthodox power should not be taken for granted. As Archbishop Theophan of Poltava has warned above, "because of our sins the Lord God [may] revoke, [may] alter what has been promised." Russia presents a challenge to Western globalization and, indeed, a target. As the end of history approaches, it may be that the forces that would oppose globalization will gravitate ever more strongly toward Russia as a center of resistance, while Russia herself comes under ever greater attack precisely for not giving in to globalization's mounting pressures. On the one hand, an ascendant Russia could serve as the natural leader of Orthodoxy worldwide; on the other, Russia's geopolitical adversaries may interpret her connection to Orthodox Christians abroad as a nefarious projection of "soft power" and, dispensing with the bromide of "freedom of religion," persecute the Orthodox on their own territories, such as is now happening in Ukraine.[49]

---

48   "A Vision for the Post-2020 World," *Orthodox England.* http://www.events. orthodoxengland.org.uk/a-vision-for-the-post-2020-world/. Accessed September 18, 2019.

49   A developing corollary to the current round of Western antipathy to Orthodoxy is the encouragement of schismatic groups as a means to weaken the Mother Churches, especially the Russian. ("How Schismatics Are Being Used Against the Orthodox Church," Orthodox Christianity. https://orthochristian.com/123911.html. Accessed September 21, 2019.) "We all know about the geopolitical projects of Westerners and the Pope to weaken Orthodoxy, especially such strongholds as Greece and Russia, with the help of the explicit intervention of American citizens and diplomats, who put pressure on primates and bishops, forcing them to follow Patriarch Bartholomew into a new great split, as well as to the loss of the First See of the Greek Patriarch in the synodal system of the Orthodox Church." ("Greek Priest Reminds Phanar of the Document on 'Ukrainian Issue,'" Union of Orthodox Journalists. https://spzh.

Time alone will tell.[50]

THE END OF HISTORY

Christians throughout history have been convinced that the end is around the corner, and they have been right. We are, indeed, living in the last times. There will be no "new age" of history; no *novus ordo saeclorum*; we are in the final age, *now*, the age of the Church militant, which began with the birth of the Church at Pentecost and will conclude with Christ's Second Coming. The end may come soon or not for many generations — "no man knows the day nor hour"—but as individuals we may be called to account at any moment. Are we ready, *now*, to face the Dread Judgment that will assign us our place among the saints or the condemned? As Blessed Elder Ephraim (+2019) of St. Anthony's Monastery in Florence, Arizona, put it, we are private soldiers in a giant battle whose plan of campaign is not known to us—and the telegram from HQ may come at any

news/en/news/65322-grecheskij-svyashhennik-napomnil-fanaru-o-dokumente-po-ukrainskomu-voprosu. Accessed October 2, 2019.)

50   In the opinion of Father Andrew Phillips, the global Orthodox Church will, in the future, "... be cared for by the infrastructure and influence of the Russian Orthodox Church, with its two Exarchates in Eurasia and its Church Outside Russia (ROCOR) in the Atlanto-Pacific.... The Church Outside Russia (ROCOR) may yet see its best years. . . Having shorn itself of its secular side which compromised it for so long, that is, the old racist nationalism, Cold War politics and narrow and sectarian bigotry, it has yet to assume its full destiny. This could be to care for all those of the authentic Orthodox Tradition of all nations and languages in the Atlanto-Pacific, the AP. Its future may then be to become ever more missionary, multilingual and multi-Metropolia-ed, to be tri-Continental, covering both the Americas and Oceania, the Atlantic and Pacific Continents and Islands. The billion people of the Americas and the Caribbean, those of Oceania and the Pacific Islands, large and small, as well as the Atlantic Islands with Great Britain and Ireland await missionary leadership. The challenge is immense, but all is still possible. May Thy will be done, O Lord." ("A Vision for the Post-2020 World," *Orthodox England*. http://www.events.orthodoxengland.org.uk/a-vision-for-the-post-2020-world/. Accessed September 18, 2019.)

time calling us to explain our soldierly—or unsoldierly—conduct. Will it be decorations for valor—or the brig? This is the daily, existential question for the Christian whether Orthodox monarchs sit upon their thrones or Antichrist in the temple of his blasphemy. If we do not "take up our cross daily,"[51] if we are not today "working out our salvation with fear and trembling,"[52] speculating on the end of the world is only a distraction from our necessary cooperative labor of salvation. The way to fight the spirit of antichrist, which has been in the world since the primordial sin, is not through idle speculation on the end of the world but through cultivation of Christian virtue as shown to us by the examples of the Lord and His saints throughout history. The struggle is the same, then and now. World history marches on to its twisted end, but God's Church remains, which "the gates of Hades shall not prevail against,"[53] and "Jesus Christ is the same yesterday, today, and forever."[54]

History will end when the mission of the Church is fulfilled, when all of the souls that will be saved will have completed their journey and "run with endurance the race that is set before" them.[55] God forbears toward this fallen world so that individual souls may work out their salvation. When the process of salvation stops, when the Church on earth is too grievously compromised through the slackness of her members and the hostility of the world, only then will the long-suffering and merciful God bring this world to its end; it will no longer have a reason to continue.

We who are trying to acquire basic Christian knowledge and understanding must do so by means of trials; we must be tested and thereby become sober and discerning.

---

51   Luke 9:23.
52   Phil. 2:12.
53   Matt. 16:18.
54   Heb. 13:8.
55   Heb. 12:1.

At the same time, in the midst of this, seeing all kinds of tragedies around us, we must be joyful, knowing that the end of the contest is the end of this whole corruptible world. If we prepare ourselves with the knowledge born of spiritual struggle, we will be able to recognise Christ when He comes. But if we do not recognize the signs of the times and the Antichrist, and if we do not have Christ dwelling in our hearts, then when Christ comes we will be with those nations which will be lamenting because they are with Antichrist. They will see Christ coming, and all their Christianity will have been proved false. This is a tragic thing. Such deception is allowed, as St. Paul says, because there is a lie in the heart of man, and this lie wishes not the real thing, not the true Christianity.[56]

While the Christian struggle today is qualitatively the same as it always has been, in one respect the degree of difficulty appears to have markedly increased. It is harder and harder "to keep oneself unspotted from the world,"[57] to be *in* the world without becoming *of* it. The danger now—at least for the time being—is not the instruments of death and torture of the Roman legions, Islamic warlords, or Communist secret police, but the pressures, pleasures, and seductions of the new world order that poison the soul.

The world prepared for Antichrist is one deprived of any sure standing, where nothing is as it seems, where, in the words of Lactantius, "all things shall be confounded and mixed together against right, and against the laws of nature." The wars, revolutions, and upheavals of the modern era served not merely to weaken Christian society (both Orthodox society and the remaining genuinely Christian elements of the West) but also

---

56   Damascene, *Father Seraphim Rose*, 1054.
57   Jas. 1:27.

adulterated its remaining supports with base and contrary elements. In our age of confusion, evil is everywhere commingled
with the good, the ugly with the beautiful, the profane with the
sacred, the false with the true, the base with the noble, the pure
with the impure. St. Paul's exhortation to discern and cling to
the good, the pure, and the true as naturally supportive of the
Church's mission is increasingly difficult to carry out:

> Finally, brethren, whatever things are true, whatever
> things are noble, whatever things are just, whatever things
> are pure, whatever things are lovely, whatever things are
> of good report, if there is any virtue and if there is
> anything praiseworthy—meditate on these things.[58]

Thus does St. Paul summarize what is properly the cultural
content of any Christian society as well as the thought life of
a Christian individual. But where are such things to be found
in our time? The antichristian culture of today exalts all that is
dishonest, base, vile, ignoble, and inane. That which remains
of the honest, just, pure, lovely, and of good report is systematically defamed, defiled, or destroyed. When Antichrist at last
arrives, he will appear to a world that has lost its bearings and
will be unable to see him for who he is. Indeed, he may seem
to return the world to the good, the pure, and the true, perhaps
in the form of some great "Christian revival." Tragically, save
for a miracle of God, most of the world will be too bewildered
to see the fraud for what it is.

Antichrist will appear as Christ to the mass of the world
because of its spiritual blindness and because he will fulfill everything that it thinks Christ should be. Antichrist will be a messiah
that the world can accept; not a messiah of the Cross, but one
of worldly gratifications. His kingdom will be decidedly of *this*

---

58   Phil. 4:8.

world. He will seem to give the world everything it wants: peace, safety, prosperity, an end to strife and division, an ersatz—and ephemeral—earthly paradise. Antichrist will satisfy the world's great pride and impatience for salvation *now*, in this life, without the need for patient struggle in the way of the Cross.

> In an age of almost universal darkness and deception, when for most "Christians" *Christ* has become precisely what Orthodox teaching means by *antichrist*, the Orthodox Church of Christ alone possesses and communicates the grace of God. This is a priceless treasure the very existence of which is not so much as suspected even by the "Christian" world. The "Christian" world, indeed, joins hands with the forces of darkness in order to seduce the faithful of the Church of Christ, blindly trusting that the "name of Jesus" will save them even in their apostasy and blasphemy, mindless of the fearful warning of the Lord: *Many will say to me in that day, Lord, Lord, have we not prophesied in Thy name? and in Thy name have cast out devils? and in Thy name done many wonderful works? And then will I profess unto them, I never knew you: depart from Me, ye that work iniquity* (Matt. 7:22-23).[59]

Because God is personal, we run the risk of giving our hearts and minds to the wrong person, the wrong god, even while the name of the true God is on our lips. In marriage, one owes love and loyalty to one's spouse; to marry another, even with the same name, call her wife, and treat her with love and loyalty is to commit adultery. The world will commit spiritual adultery with Antichrist, a sincere love for a false god. Like ancient Israel on so many occasions, the world has gone "whoring after other

---

59   Rose, *Orthodoxy and the Religion of the Future*, 186.

gods."[60] The followers of Antichrist may well call themselves Christians, believing that they have found Christ and God, but they will be mistaken and will "believe a lie."[61]

Last Words

Discussion of the end of this world is meant as a warning to "watch and pray," which is the duty of Orthodox Christians "in season and out of season."[62] Whether Antichrist appears tomorrow, or whether Almighty God, in His merciful forbearance, will permit the sinful earth another thousand years, the Orthodox must cling with all their strength to God's True Church—praying, fasting, and giving alms, struggling, striving, loving and forgiving, as their Lord has commanded them from the beginning. Amidst "distress of nations, with perplexity; the sea and the waves roaring,"[63] we must, above all, not lose our heads. We must not be taken in by the seductions of the Gnostic ideologies of our time that promise salvation without the Cross; we must avoid the contagion of "millennial fever" in any of the progressive, utopian, or doomsday variants so rampant in our times among the heterodox, which must contribute to exactly the thing they are supposedly trying to forestall, namely, the giving over to the lies of the enemy and in time to Antichrist himself. Merely *knowing* that Antichrist will come, and that his spirit is already in the world, will not be sufficient to save us: "one who merely *knows* these truths in the mind will be helpless to resist the temptations of those times, and many who recognize the Antichrist when he comes will nonetheless worship him—only the power of Christ given to the heart will have strength to

---

60   Judg. 2:17.
61   2 Thess. 2:11.
62   2 Tim. 4:2.
63   Luke 21:25.

resist him."[64] Having examined the heresy of Gnosticism that permeates the course of Western history, we must not commit a Gnostic error ourselves. It is indeed a delusion to believe that the true Christian life is about *knowing* or the mere rational acceptance of propositions. "You believe that there is one God. You do well. Even the demons believe—and tremble!"[65] Very, very deep down, mankind, which, even at the end of time, will still bear the image of its Creator, will *know* that it is living a lie—even as it now knows—yet it will nonetheless love the lie. It will be this inexpungible knowledge, the imprint of our true, God-given nature, that will rise up to condemn us at the last day.

While many endeavor to be vigilant to the coming of Antichrist, they may not appreciate that his "spirit is already in the world" and hard at work preparing his coming. The appearance into history of the person of Antichrist will be the fulfillment of centuries of labor, of the movement and growth of the spirit of antichristianity through the entire course of human history. If today we are seduced by and partake of the spirit of antichrist that pervades contemporary culture, no matter how aware we try to be in discerning the signs of the times, we will certainly not be able to withstand Antichrist (should he appear in our lifetime) or the pressures already at work in the world that precede his coming. Devoid of labors that transform the heart, we may lose our salvation without even knowing it. By being so vigilant and looking all around us for signs of the end we risk forgetting that the "Kingdom of Heaven is within" us[66] and that to reach it requires the transformation of the heart into—back into—the image of God through Christian labor as demonstrated by Christ and His saints through the ages.

---

64   Damascene, *Father Seraphim Rose*, 688.
65   Jas. 2:19.
66   Luke 17:21.

The question for us all, now as it has always been, is whether we succumb or stand fast. Whom do we love? The eternal, suffering, and loving God, or the things of this world and the lies of the great murderer of mankind? There is no third way. To remain uncommitted, to endeavor to straddle the fence between the two, is to be "vomit [ted] out of [the] mouth" of the Lord as "lukewarm."[67]

In closing, let us recall the words of the Apostle Peter:

> But the day of the Lord will come as a thief in the night, in which the heavens will pass away with a great noise, and the elements will melt with fervent heat; both the earth and the works that are in it will be burned up... Nevertheless we, according to His promise, look for new heavens and a new earth in which righteousness dwells. Therefore, beloved, looking forward to these things, be diligent to be found by Him in peace, without spot and blameless; and consider that the longsuffering of our Lord is salvation... You therefore, beloved, since you know this beforehand, beware lest you also fall from your own steadfastness, being led away with the error of the wicked; but grow in the grace and knowledge of our Lord and Savior Jesus Christ. To Him be the glory both now and forever. Amen.[68]

And those of the *Didache: The Lord's Teaching Through the Twelve Apostles to the Nations*:

> Watch for your life's sake... be ready, for you know not the hour in which our Lord will come... for the whole time of your faith will not profit you, if you are not made

---

67   See Rev. 3:16.
68   2 Pet. 3:10, 13–18.

perfect in the last time. For in the last days false prophets and corrupters shall be multiplied, and the sheep shall be turned into wolves, and love shall be turned into hate; for when lawlessness increases, they shall hate and persecute and betray one another, and then shall appear the world-deceiver as Son of God, and shall do signs and wonders, and the earth shall be delivered into his hands, and he shall do iniquitous things which have never yet come to pass since the beginning. Then shall the creation of men come into the fire of trial, and many shall be made to stumble and shall perish; but those who endure in their faith shall be saved from under the curse itself.... Then shall the world see the Lord coming upon the clouds of heaven.[69]

Amen. Come, Lord Jesus. The grace of our Lord Jesus Christ be with you all. Amen.[70]

---

69   *Didache* (~80 AD), ch. 16. http://www.newadvent.org/fathers/0714.htm. Accessed September 17, 2019.

70   Rev. 22:20.

EPILOGUE

BY JAMES GEORGE JATRAS

Watch, stand fast in the faith, be brave, be strong. Let all that you do be done with love.

1 Corinthians 16:13-14

It's later than you think.

Hieromonk Seraphim Rose

For almost two thousand years the Church has been living in the last days. The earliest Christians' expectation that the Lord's Second Coming would occur in their lifetime in due course gave way to the realization that He would not return until the fullness of the nations would be brought in. It cannot be said too often: our measure of time is not God's. However delayed His return may seem to us in our fleeting and transitory lives, we know that His sudden appearing will be as a thief in the night. It could occur at any time: "Watch therefore: for you do not know what hour your Lord is coming."[1]

That said, it is difficult to look back on the events of the *annus horribilis* of 2020—and to anticipate worse to come—without a foreboding that the world is nearing some sort of crescendo. The Gnostic tendency described by Voegelin, fitfully growing year by year, decade by decade, century by century, seems to have

---

1   Matt. 24:42

achieved an unprecedented and decisive degree of domination in a few short months. Against the accelerating workings of the mystery of iniquity, it is increasingly difficult to see any signpost of restraint, much less of restoration.

Perhaps this crescendo will be similar to earlier ones, each with its "many antichrists": collapse of the Western Roman Empire, the Islamic conquest of the Eastern Empire, the East-West Great Schism and the Crusades, the neopagan humanism of the Renaissance, the religious strife of the Reformation, the misnamed Enlightenment with its malign offspring Revolution and "Progress," the world wars and totalitarianisms of the modern era. Yet with each seeming turn of the wheel, with each ebb and flow between disorder and partial restabilization, the net linear advance of antichristian Gnosticism towards its foreordained conclusion is undeniable. How soon before the "thousand years"[2] finally are ended and Satan is loosed out of his prison for a little season?

Even a cursory search of the internet yields multiple references to the congealing omnipresence of powerful actors in every sphere of life to implement a program called the "Great Reset." Released in May 2020 by Prince Charles of the United Kingdom and Klaus Schwab, founder and executive chairman of the World Economic Forum (commonly known as Davos, after its meeting place in Switzerland), the Great Reset takes its cue from the "Covid-19 crisis, and the political, economic and social disruptions it has caused"[3] as—no, not as a misfortune, not a calamity—but as "a unique window of opportunity to shape the recovery,"[4] informed by the insights of "global stakeholders" in "determining the future state of global relations, the direction of national economies, the priorities of societies, the nature of

---

2   Rev. 2:3
3   https://www.weforum.org/great-reset/
4   https://www.weforum.org/great-reset/

business models and the management of a global commons"[5] in order to "build a new social contract that honors the dignity of every human being,"[6] summed up in the ubiquitous slogan "Build Back Better." The initiative's list of Partners ("global stakeholders") reads like a *Who's Who* of the most powerful international corporations and other members of the vanguard of the 21st Century Open Conspiracy.

While the provenance, natural or artificial, of the viral disease that served as the justification—or pretext—for this "unique opportunity" may remain forever in the shadows (except perhaps to the small group of *cognoscenti* who feel they are guiding the process) the primary manifestation of the crisis is all too public: a relentless incitement of paralyzing and irrational fear—of a malady that has an almost universal survival rate for anyone not in a handful of comorbidity categories. The very success of this terror campaign is a testament to the extent to which post-modern and (mostly) post-Christian society has reached the point of deeming physical death, though inevitable, as the worst possible fate, to be avoided at all costs. Imposed via *diktat* by the very government and corporate entities force-feeding the scare propaganda, the costs—in the form of lockdowns (heretofore a term relevant exclusively to prisons), travel bans, compulsory masking, denial of opportunity to earn a living, "distance learning" in place of education, "virtual" social inter-actions, mass transfer of assets from the middle class and small enterprises to a *rentier* elite, and the prospect of an unavoidable, and perhaps a mandatory, biometric "passport" as proof of vaccination—continue to rise.

In sum, these measures and their justifications (which, though constantly changing and often contradictory, are all the more obligatory) taken together have all the appearance of a controlled

5   https://www.weforum.org/great-reset/
6   https://www.weforum.org/great-reset/

demolition of all established human interactions in anticipation of their replacement by something we are assured by our betters will be an improvement. The contours of the "new normal" hurtling in our direction have already become so familiar as to need little elaboration:

•   Creating a proletarianized middle class eager to exchange freedom for security and minimal support in the form of "relief"—no, not relief from governments' destruction of their livelihoods, but from the fearsome virus, leading to "universal basic income" (i.e., the dole in place of self-support), profligate production of fiat money (which unavoidably means inflation and destruction of whatever assets the disdained middle class might have left), and moves toward a cashless society: in a word, serfdom;

•   We have elevated levels of substance abuse, mental and emotional illness, social alienation and isolation, domestic abuse, suicide, immune deficiency, and other morbidities caused not by the illness but by measures imposed supposedly to save lives but probably taking a higher toll than the disease itself;

•   Immunization (with repetition *ad infinitum* required in light of "mutations" and the expected future appearances of new plagues), if not legally required at least will be so universally demanded by ostensibly private business (notwithstanding real concerns about the vaccines' safety, efficacy, and long-term effects, including infertility and problems associated with "gene therapy") that it amounts to a license for basic living—we offer a pinch of incense before the genius of "science," a false savior, like Caesar required in order to be allowed to buy or sell, work, go to school, etc. As a seamless, global regime of "vaccine apartheid" becomes inescapable, with every human being, whether small or great, rich or poor, bond or free, threatened with pariah status for refusing the injection of a substance of unknown safety (numbers of those suffering serious adverse consequences are suppressed), effectiveness (as new "variants" arise even many who have gotten jabbed get sick), and morality (how attenuated exactly are the aborted fetal cell lines used in development?), the enforcement mechanisms are becoming clearer as well: mandatory carrying of a scannable "health status" record on smart phones' QR app facilitating the precise location and activities of every human being on the planet every second of their lives. It's hard to avoid the suspicion that that was a goal of the entire pandemic response in the first place;

• Society's further blurring of the lines between Big Government, Big Finance, Big Pharma, Big Data, etc., amounting to corporate state capture ("Faucism");

• Travel limits are expected on law-abiding people (but not for illegal migrants), not for the purpose of restoring sovereign state boundaries (which would be deplorably nationalist) but for what amounts to herd control and monitoring;

• Not directly based on anti-virus measures but closely tracking with them, we suffer under joint government and corporate promulgation of socially destructive, historically counterfeit "Woke" ideologies (LGBTQ+, feminism, multiculturalism, "critical race theory," suppression of "populism" in the name of "democracy") with principal targeting of children subject to sexualization and predation by those expressing what were once quaintly known as abnormal appetites and identities, in turn accelerating longstanding trends towards infertility and demographic collapse (decline in marriage, family formation, and childbearing) pointing to population reduction and replacement via transhumanism and bio-engineering; and Replacement of "real" reality based on physical proximity with other people with virtual or augmented (i.e., fake) reality, combined with universal surveillance via artificial intelligence, 5G and blockchain technology, facial recognition, and biological tagging, backed up by omnipresent social credit, cancel culture, and digital censorship penalties.

In short, what could not be implemented over decades solely by fear of climate change and rising oceans is now being swiftly achieved via fear of a submicroscopic infectious agent. (Actually, according to one world-famous, white-clad religious leader, the latter may be nature's "revenge" for mankind's failure to take sufficient action on the former.)[7] No one should doubt that the old, pre-2020 world is forever gone.

Whether we are seeing yet another of the various transitory types of the coming kingdom of Antichrist or a harbinger of the final arrival of the *antitype*, the new normal transcends merely political or economic categories (the kingdom of Caesar) and lays claim to the spiritual as well (the kingdom of God). Sadly, it is in perhaps the spiritual realm that the failure of those with a duty to discern, and where needs be, to defy, has been most notable. Religious leaders—shamefully, not excluding Orthodox Christian hierarchs, with some praiseworthy exceptions—have fallen into line in their rush to follow Caesar's "therapeutic" edicts, and in some cases to exceed them. Indeed, even some prominent Orthodox hierarchs have denounced believers for declining to be vaccinated, accusing them committing a grave sin that imperils their eternal destiny! Worship services have been disadvantaged as compared to other social gatherings, with churches closed in some places while more "vital" needs such as liquor and cannabis vendors, abortion clinics, and big box stores remained opened. Where churches kept holding live

---

7   "Pope says coronavirus pandemic could be nature's response to climate crisis," CNN, April 9, 2020; https://www.cnn.com/2020/04/08/europe/pope-francis-coronavirus-nature-response-intl/index.html

services they often were subject to humiliating and (seemingly deliberately) irrational mandates regarding face coverings, social distancing, venue capacities, and bans on group singing. In some places even the mode of serving the Eucharist has been modified, with Orthodox Christians who object being accused of idolatry. Not even the very icon of Christ on the face of each one of us has been spared desecration.

Much of what is described above centers on the United States. To note that is not to be unduly parochial or "political" any more than would have been noting Russia's centrality to an earlier Gnostic outbreak a century ago. Given America's global dominance in virtually every field of human endeavor—politics, military, finance, economy, science, medicine, media, popular culture, etc.—in the wake of the collapse of the earlier communist eruption (and before that, national socialism), it is to be expected that a global crisis would begin, and perhaps will end, in the United States. There is a remarkable congruence, though not an exact identity, between the divisions in American society pitting those who accept the therapeutic narrative on the virus and supposed countermeasures against those who reject them, and between those who accept and reject the violent "social justice" campaign championed by groups like Black Lives Matter and Antifa (themselves sponsored by the government and corporate establishment), culminating in a contested presidential election that fully half the electorate believes was the result of fraud. The conclusion that the US Constitution and the rule of law, which have been declining for many years, may have in fact reached a terminal point is reluctantly dawning on tens of millions of ordinary, decent Americans. Not only are we more divided than at any time since 1861–1865, we are even more aliens, indeed enemies, to one another than were Northerners and Southerners back then in terms of fundamental questions of who we are, what man is, Who God is, and how we should order our lives and our country. The term "cold" civil war, a war that might possibly turn "hot," has become a commonplace in American discourse. That should not come as a surprise when we remember how the Red Gnostic seizure of power in Russia, to which many draw parallels to America today, didn't triumph without bloodily overcoming ferocious popular resistance. The rising tide of Rainbow Gnosticism in America, whether it succeeds or fails, may turn out to be just as destructive.

Finally, "wars and rumors of war" may not be confined to the United States. As the dysgenic impacts of the virus scare affect other countries to a greater or lesser degree, so America's growing instability must have its international reverberations. Suggestions have been made that internal crises may force the United States, willy-nilly, to withdraw from the program of global hegemony launched after the demise of the USSR, with a multipolar world finally emerging. That could happen, but it's not likely. Realism is a scarce commodity among Washington's *nomenklatura*, where the penalties for strategic failure are few but rewards for aggression are great. While American "humanitarian intervention," "democracy promotion," and "regime change" have been to little advantage but much harm to the supposed beneficiaries (Serbia, Iraq, Libya, Ukraine, Syria, Yemen, etc.) the benefits are clearly visible in the form of the "McMansions" around the Washington Beltway, which continue to sprout like mushrooms after heavy rains. As America continues down the road of confrontation with Russia, and increasingly with China, the prospect of the first major global conflict since the Long War of 1914–1945 grows. A self-interested, arrogant, ignorant, and spiritually stunted leadership class caught in a Thucydides Trap (a declining power confronted by a rising opponent or opponents) may well be tempted to launch a war to eliminate the "threat" if it feels victory may be in reach today but might not be tomorrow. To call such a prospect apocalyptic is not hyperbole.

In the end, the impact any one of us can expect to have in the face of world-historic trends before which the fates of nations and empires fly like leaves in the autumn winds is vanishingly small. Even our ability to discern the signs of the times in an era of pervasive Gnostic deceit abetted by technologies unimaginable just a few years ago is limited. Nevertheless we have three tasks that none can afford to shirk. First, we must be vigilant against deception, in a day when assuredly "evil men and impostors will grow worse and worse, deceiving, and being deceived."[8] Second, as stewards of every worldly charge placed on us by God and by other people—as fathers and mothers, as husbands and wives, as sons and daughters, as neighbors, as workers, as citizens, as patriots—we must prudently care for those to whom we have a duty within the limited power and wisdom allotted to us, without deluding ourselves that the "big picture" is under our control. Third, we must "pray without ceasing,"[9] firm in faith that, through whatever hardships may lie ahead, even the "very hairs of" our "head are all numbered,"[10] and the final triumph of Truth is never in doubt.

---

8   2 Tim. 3:13
9   1 Thes. 5:17
10   Matt. 10:30

Coda

A Prayer Against
the Antichrist

"O Lord Jesus Christ, Son of God, deliver us from the seductions of the coming Antichrist, abhorred by God and crafty in evil, and from all his snares. Protect us, and all of our Christian neighbors, from his devious nets—keeping us in the hidden refuge of Thy salvation. Grant, Lord, that our fear of the devil may not be greater than the fear of Thee, and that we not fall away from Thee and Thy Holy Church. But instead, grant us, O Lord, to suffer and die for Thy holy Name and for the Orthodox Faith, and never to deny Thee, nor to receive the marks of the cursed Antichrist, nor to worship him. Grant us, O Lord, day and night, tears and lamentation for our sins. And on the day of Thy dread Judgment, O Lord, grant us pardon. Amen."

St. Anatoly the Younger of Optina

UNCUT MOUNTAIN PRESS TITLES

Books by Archpriest Peter Heers

Fr. Peter Heers, *The Ecclesiological Renovation of Vatican II: An Orthodox Examination of Rome's Ecumenical Theology Regarding Baptism and the Church*, 2015

Fr. Peter Heers, *The Missionary Origins of Modern Ecumenism: Milestones Leading up to 1920*, 2007

The Works of our Father Among the Saints, Nikodemos the Hagiorite

Vol. 1: *Exomologetarion: A Manual of Confession*

Vol. 2: *Concerning Frequent Communion of the Immaculate Mysteries of Christ*

Vol. 3: *Confession of Faith*

Other Available Titles

Elder Cleopa of Romania, *The Truth of our Faith, Vol. I: Discourses from Holy Scripture on the Tenants of Christian Orthodoxy.*

Elder Cleopa of Romania, *The Truth of our Faith, Vol. II: Discourses from Holy Scripture on the Holy Mysteries*

Fr. John Romanides, *Patristic Theology: The University Lectures of Fr. John Romanides*

Archimandrite Ephraim Triandaphillopoulos, *Noetic Prayer as the Basis of Mission and the Struggle Against Heresy*

Robert Spencer, *The Church and the Pope*

Select Forthcoming Titles

St. Gregory Palamas, *Apodictic Treatise on the Procession of the Holy Spirit*

The Lives and Witness of 20th Century Athonite Fathers

Protopresbyter Anastasios Gotsopoulos, *On Common Prayer with the Heterodox, According to the Canons of the Church*

St. Hilarion Troitsky, *An Overview of the History of the Dogma Concerning the Church*

Elder George of Grigoriou, *Catholicism*

Let No One Fear Death - Collection of essays from Orthodox leaders reflecting on Covidism

Nicholas Baldimtsis, *Life and Witness of St. Iakovos of Evia*

Georgio Kassir, *Errors of the Latins*

This 1st Edition of

ANTICHRIST:

THE FULFILLMENT OF GLOBALIZATION
The Ancient Church and the End of History

written by G. M. Davis, PhD, with an epilogue by Jim Jatras, and cover design by Michael Jackson, typeset in Baskerville MT Std, and printed through HolyOrthodox Books.com in this two thousandth and twenty second year of our Lord's Holy Incarnation, is one of the many fine titles available from Uncut Mountain Press, translators and publishers of Orthodox Christian theological and spiritual literature. Find the book you are looking for at

www.uncutmountainpress.com

GLORY BE TO GOD
FOR ALL THINGS

AMEN.

www.ingramcontent.com/pod-product-compliance
Lightning Source LLC
Chambersburg PA
CBHW051242020426
42333CB00025B/3020